AN ALBUM OF SCOTTISH FAMILIES

1694-96

AN ALBUM OF SCOTTISH FAMILIES

1694-96

Being the first instalment of
George Home's Diary,
supplemented by much
further research into the
Edinburgh and Border
families forming his extensive
social network

HELEN and KEITH KELSALL

ABERDEEN UNIVERSITY PRESS
1990

First published 1990
Aberdeen University Press
A member of the Pergamon Group

Production and page make-up by SCVO Publications,
18/19 Claremont Crescent, Edinburgh EH7 4QD

British Library Cataloguing in Publication Data
Home, George *b.1660*
 An album of Scottish families, 1694-96 : being the first
 instalment of George Home's diary, supplemented by much
 further research into the Edinburgh and border families
 forming his extensive social network.
 1. Scotland. Social life, 1603-1714
 I. Title II. Kelsall, Helen M. III. Kelsall, R. K.
 (Roger Keith) *1910-*
 941.106

ISBN   0 08 040930 X

PRINTED IN GREAT BRITAIN
THE UNIVERSITY PRESS
ABERDEEN

Contents

returned in the afternoon and stayd at me till night he borrowed from me Flow upon thought falows for to morrow Marg. Turner brought me ane account of what money was given out when I was at Ed: this winter for the houses use and ane account of the Rain fouls she hes got in and how they were dy posed of.

I wrote on Munday to Mr Al: Home anent Freershaws affair this morning I received one from Mr Al: wherin he writes that Freer shaw would delay till Lammas and desired his interest now but he having so he wints write to me and not having done it Mr Al: thinks he may delay till martimes as I desire I wrote likewise to Gideon Elliot to get me some slips of sage jersy from Mr Southerland and some dryd if he have any and he returns me answer he shall try for them agst next occasion.

And Wutherel hes brought me a sugar loaf but no bread I went to Belshele and counted wt my tenants und. ther several accounts. I went along the March betwixt Kettleshele and me wher ther is some difference and wher my tenants all sage he hes cast turfs upon my ground wch I caused stop James Redpeth tells me that Robert Winter and Robert who were present when Rowistone and Sr Ro: St clair partied the Ground common to Herdlaw Rawburn and Weelfitt betwixt them wt this clause that thir parting the sd common betwixt them should not wrong Weelfit nor hinder Argueing thro both partys whe those two men heard Sr Ro: Sinclair say but Weelfit having been now of a long time keept fro the possession by Robert Tom Jogos simplicity and those two men being now dead it will be hard for me to prove my possession she tell me ther is one Waddell in who knows something of it. I went by the peet mosse and

PREFACE

George Home's diary proved invaluable when in the mid-1980s we embarked on a study of life in the Scottish Borders 300 years ago, and it was then that we resolved to try and make this unique and remarkable storehouse of information available to a much wider audience than those able to visit the Scottish Record Office in Edinburgh where it is now housed. Ailsa and Stuart Maxwell felt equally strongly about this, and most generously undertook the tremendous task of transcribing this first part of the diary, as well as making maps and an index; but for their dedication and skill the venture would never have got off the ground. We ourselves set to work to provide the introduction and explanatory notes without which a proper understanding of the complex relationships in the diarist's social network would have been difficult if not impossible.

It is our earnest hope that enough interest will be aroused by the publication of this first instalment to ensure that arrangements for making the remainder of the diary available will be made without adding materially to the three-century delay that has already taken place.

Helen Kelsall

Keith Kelsall

April 1990

ACKNOWLEDGEMENTS

The Scottish Record Office
Lord Polwarth
A. Rosemary Bigwood
Ian Maxwell and Geraldine Foulds
Scottish Council for Voluntary Organisations
Edinburgh Make-up Services

INTRODUCTION

This is the first instalment of a remarkable diary kept by a 17th-century Scotsman. Leaving aside its enormous scale, the diary is remarkable in many ways. First, as it was written solely for the benefit of its author and his only son, it has not been used as a vehicle for trying to convert others to the diarist's religious or political views; and there are few if any Scottish diaries of the period of which that can be said. Secondly, the range of subjects on which material is recorded is quite astonishing. It is an absolute storehouse of information on matters of interest to specialists in a very wide variety of fields. Whether you are interested in botany, agriculture, or medicine, in industrial, social, legal or political history, or in genealogy, there is enough here to form the basis of innumerable studies.

A third remarkable feature of the diary is that the new knowledge it provides, complements and dovetails into that previously available in printed sources of similar date relating to the same general area. And by so doing, the value of these existing printed sources is very greatly enhanced. Take, for example, Crossrig's *Domestic Details,* which has been available for scholars to study since it was published in 1843. By integrating the material in Crossrig with that in George Home's diary a much more satisfactory picture of what was happening can be provided than it has ever been possible to obtain before. Exactly the same is true of *Foulis of Ravelston's Account Book 1671-1707,* of which not nearly enough use has been made by historians since it was first published by the Scottish History Society in 1894. And of course there is *Lady Grisell Baillie's Household Book 1692-1733,* the first volume in the Scottish History Society's second series, 1911. As a further example, the *Extracts from the Records of the Burgh of Edinburgh, 1689-1701,* only available in printed form since 1962, link up closely with much that appears in the diary, to the very great benefit of both. Again, although it has been invaluable to have in print since 1951 the poll tax records for two Edinburgh parishes, the diary's new information about very many of the people in that printed source often adds an exciting new dimension to what is recorded there.

Why then, if the diary is as valuable as this, has it been almost entirely neglected for nearly 300 years? One possible line of explanation suggests itself. In the early years after the diarist and then his son died, when his moveables were being dispersed, someone might, had circumstances been different, have felt that to have a grandfather who had produced four or five volumes of a closely-written diary would cast some reflected glory on the present generation, and so it might have become a treasured family possession. But with no direct descendants, and his brother and sisters having none either, the diary seems instead to have come into the category of the worthless scribblings of an obscure cousin whose life and work had never matched up to those of more illustrious family predecessors (such as Sir Patrick Home, 1st Earl of Marchmont). And the one occasion when someone seems to have bothered to *read* the diary, instead of leading to recognition of its outstanding qualities, had precisely the opposite effect. For a substantial block of pages in one volume, from 7 April 1696 to 19 September 1697, has been cut out with a sharp knife and subsequently destroyed or lost. As we do not know the content of the missing pages any attempt to establish a motive for doing this can only be speculative. As, however, the Earldom of Marchmont (created in 1697) became dormant in 1794, and as in 1804 the dignity was claimed by Alexander Home R.N., followed by protracted consideration of the claim, it seems at least possible that genealogical information in this part of the diary was felt by someone with access to it to have an important bearing on the case one way or the other.

From this unfortunate episode until late in the 19th century we do not know what happened to the diary, which must have been somewhere in Marchmont House. Then in 1883 A.C. Swinton published the study of his own family *The Swintons of that ilk and their Cadets* and quoted a few sentences from George Home's diary ' a curious record...preserved in the Marchmont repositories' (p 78). Eleven years later it began to look as though recognition of its value might be on the way. For Margaret Warrender, in *Marchmont and the Humes of Polwarth* said (p 165) she had made copious use of the diary in writing her study; but only a few very short extracts were included in her book. In the same year (1894) the 14th Report of the Historical Manuscripts Commission contained (appendix, part III, p 98) a very brief, and slightly discouraging reference to its existence. 'The diary contains many notices of current public events and private affairs. It has never been published.'

Nothing more seems to have happened until, on 22nd May 1907, John M. Howden of 8 York Place, Edinburgh had a talk at his request with D. Hay Fleming, Secretary of the Scottish History Society. He wanted suggestions as to how he might track down missing volumes of the diary and also ' a vellum bound notebook ' of George Home's. In the event, he apparently found none of this missing material. But a related development took place at roughly the same time: William Campbell Lord Skerrington, one of the Senators of the College of Justice, became a tenant of Marchmont House and lived there with his family for several years. Lady Skerrington made an important discovery there. ' I found three of the volumes of the diary hidden under a heap of rubbish in a space at the back of the bookcases in the library, where someone had apparently thrown them. ' She makes no mention of the fourth volume, which she must have found at this time.

So this priceless record was evidently still not regarded as a family heirloom to be treasured. However, Lady Skerrington was so impressed with it that in 1909 she made a typescript of the entire text (SRO GD1/649). This was a mammoth task, and because of its difficulty, a *perfect* transcript of the original could not be expected. However, our gratitude to Lady Skerrington for what she did to preserve the text is greatly heightened by the fact that one volume of the surviving manuscript went missing some time after Sir Alexander Purves-Hume-Campbell came back to live in Marchmont House, and has not since turned up. As a result, her typescript is all we have for the period 13 April 1702 to September 1705. Over the centuries, this was not the first time that part of the diary had disappeared. For we know from the opening sentences in the present instalment that there had been a previous volume, which will certainly have covered 1693 and may even have been started in 1692. That original first volume most probably disappeared before the 1880's, as the quotations from the diary in Swinton and Warrender all come from the text now surviving. And now that both the manuscript and the typescript of what is left are in the safe keeping of the Scottish Record Office (SRO GD1/891 and GD1/649) we can at last be sure that no further disappearances of parts of this unique record will occur. It was certainly found to be of enormous help in the research on which Kelsall, *Scottish Lifestyle 300 Years Ago* (1986) was based.

We can follow this attempt to piece together what has happened to the *diary* in the three centuries since it was started, by trying to establish what happened to the *diarist* in the part of his life coming before he began to write it (since the rest of his life story is told in the diary itself). George Home's approach to adult life was certainly traumatic. For only a few months after his 17th birthday he got caught up in a bizarre sequence of events which were to affect his life for very many years to come. It all happened because when the laird of Ayton, a very important Home estate in Berwickshire, died, the heiress, Jean Home, a little girl not yet twelve years old, was put by the Privy Council in the care of her grandmother Jean, Countess Dowager of Home (widow of the 3rd Earl), and Charles, younger brother of the 5th Earl. Another relative, John Home of Prendergast, applied with some others to the Privy Council, on 6 December 1677 for the sequestration of the pupil from the influence of these two, and it was accordingly ordered that they and Jean Home should appear before the Council forthwith to answer or object to this petition.

Instead of doing so, Charles, and a group of five lairds, all but one of whom represented different branches of the Homes, decided immediately to take the young heiress and her future quite literally into their own hands. In the Council's words, they ' did ride away the said night and seiz upon the persone of the said Jean and caried her away to the English bordours'. Having done this, the lairds involved - Alexander Home of Linthill, Sir Patrick Home of Polwarth, John Home of Ninewells, Robert Home of Kimmerghame and Joseph Johnstone of Hilton - after considering what it would be most advantageous to do next, sent Ninewells to Edinburgh to ' take a poor young boy, George Home...out of his bed' and bring him to England to be married to the heiress by ' ane English minister'. How the Countess Dowager, her son Charles and the five lairds could possibly have expected to avoid disaster in such a project almost passes belief. And in no time at all the provisions of the Act for punishing all concerned in 'clandestine and disorderly marriages by persons not authorised by the Kirk ' were put into force. Three months in Edinburgh Castle and heavy fines for George and his bride, as well as the loss of any rights they might have had by their marriage was the sentence. Similar fines were imposed on some of the others involved, with imprisonment in the Tolbooth until the fines were paid. In a few cases - the Countess, Polwarth and Linthill - the matter was not pursued. The only individual to gain anything from the episode was John Home of Prendergast, to whom some of the fine money was paid.

No-one reading the diary can be in any doubt how devastating the long-term results of this ill-conceived attempt to boost the fortunes of the families concerned turned out to be. Instead of any financial benefit, young George Home found himself with a burden of debt from which he could not escape, and the prospect of never-ending expensive legal wrangles over everything connected with Ayton. And though the heiress was so young, he did not even have the benefit of her company for more that five years or so, when she died. His father, upset by the Ayton heiress fiasco, had already died in 1678. And in May 1684 George, in company with the young laird of Blackadder, set forth on what proved to be a lengthy trip to France.

There are only two glimpses showing what his life was like in the six years between finishing his prison sentence and going to France. The first is that he and others - Borthwick and Eccles are mentioned - went to the battle of Bothwell Bridge in June 1679. The only reason we know this is because they had to borrow 1000 marks to go there, and in his diary entry for 25 July 1694 he is still having to take account of this debt. The second glimpse arises from the contents of a surviving notebook which seems to date from around 1684 (SRO GD158/674). One of the most interesting pages in that notebook contains 26 titles or first lines of musical items, and a very full treatment of these can be found in ' Music Making in the Scottish Borders in the 1680's' *Lore and Language* January 1988. On other pages in the notebook can be found lists of some of the books in his library, Thomas Flatman's 'On the death of the Earl of Rochester', and a list of sizes and colours of hangings, and of covers for furniture, to be bought for his house (on which he is going to take advice from Lady Lintone and from Ann Home, Alexander Home's wife). Amongst the things he reminds himself he must try and obtain (apart from household items) are a hood for his hawk, and 'to try among my tenants wifes daughters servants or others whether any of them have a good head hair and will part with it'.

Journeying to France, he probably followed the same procedure as Crossrig had done some years previously - he rode to Newcastle, thence by sea to London, rode to Dover and then embarked for Calais. George Home wrote a letter to

Polwarth from Newcastle dated 23 May 1684. ' I would not let slip the occasion of my uncles returne [Crossrig must have gone with him as far as Newcastle] to write to you knowing your concerne to hear how I am and take with my journey.' He seems to be all right, and encloses a receipt for the 1000 marks he got from Mr. Alexander Home - presumably a loan from Polwarth to help towards the expenses of the trip - and ends up 'giving my Service and best wishes to your Lady and children and begging I may hear frequently how you all are' (SRO GD158/1012/2).   Sadly, we know nothing of his adventures in France, and but for Crossrig would even be unaware of when he got back again: 'against the mind of all his friends, Kimmerghame came to Scotland in January 1687' (p 42).   For the next four years or so we again have no information about his life, except that his brother David was staying with him for most of the time.   And then something happened which nearly always gets recorded - on 26 May 1691 he married for a second time. The bride was Margaret, daughter of Sir James Primrose of Barnbougle (seven miles west of Edinburgh).   She went to stay with her mother when their first child was on the way, and Robie was born on 2 March 1692.   She herself died there a few weeks later, however, and was taken to Berwickshire for burial on 2 April. Foulis, though his accounts never mention having any contact with George (or, for that matter, with his father), travelled south on this occasion and stayed with the Polwarths, whom he knew.   The reason for this was that *his* first wife, Margaret, who had died only two years previously, was from the same branch of the Primrose family.

So when the surviving part of his diary begins, in May 1694, George Home is 34 years old, has been twice widowed, and has a two-year-old son to look after. His younger brother David has now left Kimmerghame and is living not far away, in Duns.   The elder of his two sisters, Isobel, with whom relations, as we soon learn from the diary, tend to be somewhat strained, has made Edinburgh her home; while Julian has stayed in Berwickshire.   Five years later David, who never married, went with the fleet to Darien and died of a fever.   Julian remained single until a year before then, when she married Dr. Trotter.   She had at least two children, who were not alive in 1738.   Isobel, very much later on, married James Morison of Maison Dieu co. Roxburgh; so far as is known they had no children.

The Kimmerghame house was a comparatively modest one with 7 hearths, the three other lairds in the vicinity with whom he was on particularly friendly terms - Sir John Home of Blackadder, John Carre of Cavers and West Nisbet and Lord Polwarth - all having establishments with more than twice that number of chimneys.   And the contrast is even more striking when we look at the size of the domestic staff; 3 in his case, as against 9, 17 and 17, though of course with only himself and a little boy to be looked after, his need for servants is less than that of the much larger families of his neighbours.

Every laird had a factor, or someone who kept the accounts, paid for what had to be done on the estate, received the rents paid by the tenants, and periodically submitted his statement showing the final balance either way.   In George Home's case David Robisone was supposed to be fulfilling this role, but from 13 June 1694 onwards the diary entries show how badly, in the laird's view, he did this. It certainly sounds as though his accounts were kept in a form so disorderly that it was virtually impossible to check them or make sense of them. He was one of the tenants on the estate, 'possessing the Heugh and Kimmerghame Mains' as we learn from the list provided on 3 October 1695. Some years later, George Home managed to recruit (perhaps on a part-time basis) John Dickson of Antonshill to perform these duties. He was a highly skilled account-keeper who afterwards became factor for Polwarth. The accounts he regularly presented to the Earl of Marchmont appeared to be models of their kind, but by mid- 18th century it was being claimed that he had for many years been falsifying them to his own advantage on a substantial scale. So perhaps, despite the hours the diarist had to spend on David Robisone's crude efforts in 1694-96, it was better than being lulled into a sense of false security by beautifully-presented financial statements.

So far, then, we have looked at the reasons why this diary is so important; at its survival and treatment over the centuries; and at the key points in its author's life before he started to write it. So we can now turn to the most difficult task of all, an attempt to decide what manner of man he was. In one sense there is no need to do this, as everyone who reads the diary will make his or her own personal assessment of the diarist. There are, nevertheless, a few points worth making, particularly as later instalments of the diary, to which most readers of this first volume have not as yet had access, throw further light on the issue. First of all, attention must be drawn to one very unfortunate gap in our knowledge - no portraits, or reproductions of portraits, of George Home have survived. And coupled with the fact that descriptions of, or comments about him by his contemporaries are almost completely lacking, this means that we cannot say whether he was short or tall, fat or thin, thought by most to be a nice person to know or the reverse. He certainly had his enemies, and Isobel, at least, obviously thought that as the brother holding the family purse-strings he left much to be desired, but we only know of all this to the extent and in the way that George himself tells us, not at first hand.

Even a casual reading of this first volume makes one characteristic of the diarist clear - he is someone who never looks back. For despite having lost two wives, and serving a prison sentence instead of a honeymoon, there is not a mention of any of these events. When his or his son's birthday comes round, hopes are expressed that they will behave better, or fare better, in the future than in the past, but only in the most general terms, almost in a standard form of words. A virtual absence of self-pity, or regret about what has happened (except in financial matters), may be no bad thing, but to keep it up for a decade or more is quite an achievement. And on the rare occasion when he breaks his rule it is such a minor infringement as hardly to be noticed. In a later volume, for instance, he encounters Carstares unexpectedly, and suddenly remembers the last time they saw each other. 'Tis now 20 years since I was prisoner with him in the Castle' (4 March 1698); that's quite enough about the past, so he immediately gets back to the present.

No-one can fail to be struck by a second characteristic of the diarist, for it surfaces on virtually every page, and that is his obsession with money problems. Life seems to have been a perpetual balancing act, trying to extract money from one's debtors to keep creditors at bay. Given the debts he had inherited from his father, and those resulting from the Ayton heiress fiasco, it was perhaps inevitable that this should be so. He certainly does not give the impression of being recklessly extravagant, and though apparently ill-served by his factor David Robisone, did his best to live within his means. For instance, when he realises how much he has been spending on books, he resolves, however half-heartedly, not to overspend in that way in future.

Closely related to his pre-occupation with financial matters is his constant resort to legal remedies. Here he seems to have been merely a man of his time, social position and country. For it is clear that, though he may sometimes seem to have been carrying this tendency too far, most of his friends were doing much the same. Instituting legal proceedings against a neighbour or kinsman apparently in no way precluded continuing friendly social intercourse. And on the evidence of the diary, and what can be gleaned from other sources, Crossrig, Polwarth, the Earl of Home and many others also seem to have regarded the law as a first rather than a last resort.

Two other matters are mentioned with similar frequency, the weather and his state of health, and these two sometimes have a close relationship in his mind. If he was not feeling well, and the weather was bad, it was better not to venture abroad. But he put on record what the weather was like in any case. And we have no means of knowing whether his concern for his health was excessive, or greater than that of his contemporaries.

The three things he was really proud of were Robie, his garden and his library. In his situation it was natural that his only son should be the apple of his eye. There is plenty of evidence to show how concerned he was when the boy was ill, and we know of his efforts to obtain suitable toys for him. At this stage Robie was not old enough for his father to play an active part in his education, but later in the diary we find him doing so to a marked degree. His experiments with ways of treating different varieties of fruit trees to obtain the best results, his orders for new stock from London and from Edinburgh, and his pleasure in discussing matters with well-informed people, all show what a keen interest he had in his garden. And the frequency of his borrowing, lending and buying books, together with the list of what was in the library in the 1684 notebook, are ample proof of his being a scholarly man who was also a keen and knowledgeable student of home and foreign affairs.

His sociability is also beyond question - how else could one account for the time he spent in visiting friends and entertaining them at home or in hostelries in Edinburgh and elsewhere. It also looks as though for him the benefits of church-going (and he was a regular attender) lay mainly in the opportunity to exchange news and views, though he often also reported who was taking the service. An academic approach, in this case as in much else, had a very strong appeal to him, and it will be noticed how fully he reports the explanations he was given in the course of lengthy conversations with a biblical scholar.

Some of the examples needed to show the various facets of his character can only be found in later volumes of the diary (a good many of these are discussed in Kelsall pp. 31-8), but the overall impression is of a man it would have been a pleasure to meet and to get to know. Perhaps at times - on money matters, legal arrangements and his state of health - he would have been rather a bore, and one might occasionally have wished (as with Crossrig and Foulis) for a missing element of humour, but by and large there is nothing to dislike about him. And as a source of accurate, reliable and often new information on a whole range of important subjects he is clearly quite unrivalled.

EXPLANATORY NOTES

The main reason why such a substantial quantity of explanatory notes has been provided for the present volume lies in the fact that George Home's diary was written for himself alone, so that he did not feel it necessary to explain anything. All that was needed was to put on record what he would otherwise inevitably forget. The task of filling in the background has proved a formidable one, so in the case of some difficulties that arise on almost every page of the diary the reader has been left to furnish himself with the necessary aids to understanding. Sources are readily available for interpreting obsolete legal terminology, for explaining coins in use and their relative values, and for giving some account of the national and foreign politics of that time. Only where the diarist himself is personally involved in some event specific to the period, or where on one particular occasion the meaning and significance of a phrase he uses cannot be understood without additional information, has it been felt necessary to provide a brief explanation in Section III on Topics.

The number of *people* mentioned even in the short period covered by the present instalment of the diary runs into so many hundreds that it would be quite unrealistic to attempt to say something about each of them. Instead, the cases chosen for comment and explanation are limited to those where it was felt that, without the provision of some background information about them, understanding the diary entries where they were mentioned would become difficult. In very many instances, however, there has been no need for this, as it is sufficiently clear from the context who the people are. Thus at one end of the social scale, when he is talking of his servants or his tenants (and he provides a full list of the latter on 3 October 1695) it is clear who they are from the nature of the dealings he has with them. And the same is true of keepers of shops, hostelries and lodging-houses, where he is generally quite specific about the service they are providing. At higher social levels, the leading politicians and landed magnates whom he mentions but does not normally have any dealings with, have all figured in writings about this period of Scottish history to an extent making it unnecessary to provide background information about them.

In between these two extremes, however, there are several types of case where some explanation is needed. Foremost among these is the one where a territorial designation is employed instead of a family name. In common with his contemporaries, the diarist nearly always does this when referring to a laird or to a laird's immediate family, so it has been necessary to provide a key to the territorial designations used in this part of the diary; where in this key several lairds, or families, are given for one such designation it is either because some change took place or, in a very few cases, because there is uncertainty as to which of two possible people the diarist was talking about [I 3)]. With the aid of this key, the territorial designation can be translated into a family name, and information

[16]

about the person concerned can then be looked for in the appropriate one of several lists provided [II 1)-11)].

Another type of case is that of certain categories of professional people. 'Mr. Borthwick Minister of Greenlaw' presents no difficulties, and when the diarist goes to church he usually says who is taking the Service. But with people providing legal or medical services it is often important to give rather more information than can be gleaned from the diary itself as to who they are and what kind of work they do. Finally, the extent not merely of social intercourse but of intermarrying among members of a wide range of families to whom the diarist refers, makes it desirable to say something about them, making use for this purpose of the many contemporary sources of information available, both in manuscript and printed form.

The order of treatment of all the *people* about whom information to supplement what is in the diary is provided, is as follows. After the Homes/Humes [II 1) a)-g)], then in alphabetical order some of the main family names in the Borders are dealt with - the Carres/Kers, Cockburns, Douglasses, Eliots/Elliots, Johnstones, Pringles,Rutherfords, Trotters and Waddells [II 2)-10)]. Those not coming into any of the previous groups are then divided into two sections, each arranged alphabetically - one comprising those described in the diary as Earls or Lords [II 11) a)], and the other those not so described [II 11) b)], the latter being listed according to family name and not territory. The comparatively small number of *topics* where it has been thought desirable to provide a brief explanatory note are given in Section III in the order of the date where the matter was first mentioned in the diary, each with a heading indicating the event or the unusual phrase concerned.

I KEYS

1) KEY TO ABBREVIATIONS USED IN THE INTRODUCTION AND EXPLANATORY NOTES

Creswell = C.H. Creswell, *The Royal College of Surgeons in Edinburgh* Edinburgh 1926

Crossrig = Sir David Hume, Lord Crossrig, *Domestic Details* Edinburgh 1843

DNB = *Dictionary of National Biography*

Edinburgh Burgh Records = *Extracts from the Records of the Burgh of Edinburgh 1689 - 1701* Edinburgh 1962

Foulis = *Foulis of Ravelston's Account Book 1671 - 1707* (Scottish History Society) Edinburgh 1894

GEC = G.E. Cokayne, *Complete Baronetage* London 1904

Grisell Baillie = *Lady Grisell Baillie's Household Book 1692 - 1733* (Scottish History Society) Edinburgh 1911

Kelsall = Helen and Keith Kelsall, *Scottish Lifestyle 300 Years Ago* Edinburgh 1986

NLS = National Library of Scotland, Edinburgh

SHR = *Scottish Historical Review*

SRO = Scottish Record Office, Edinburgh

Veitch = 'Description of Berwickshire or the Mers' *Macfarlane's Geographical Collections III* (Scottish History Society) Edinburgh 1908; the author was the Rev. John Veitch, minister of Westruther, who died in 1702.

Wood = Marguerite Wood, *Poll Tax Returns for the Edinburgh Parishes of Tolbooth and Old Kirk 1694* (Scottish Record Society) Edinburgh 1951

GEORGE HOME'S CLOSE RELATIONS ON HIS FATHER'S SIDE

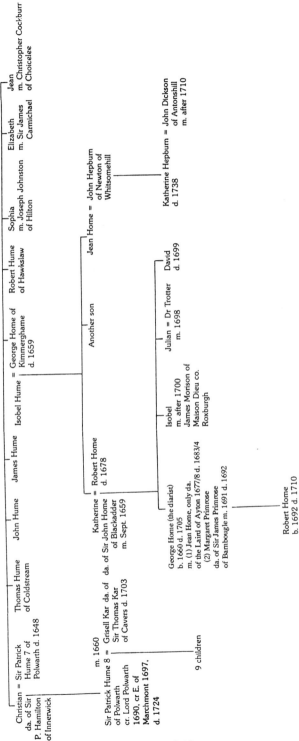

2) KEY TO SOME BASIC RELATIONSHIPS IN THE DIARY IN THE FORM OF THREE CHARTS

Three Charts have been provided to show certain relationships in diagrammatic form. One is for the diarist's relatives on the paternal side, one for those on the maternal side, and the third attempts to clarify the position in the Home of Ninewells and Home of Whitfield branches.

GEORGE HOME'S CLOSE RELATIONS
ON HIS MOTHER'S SIDE

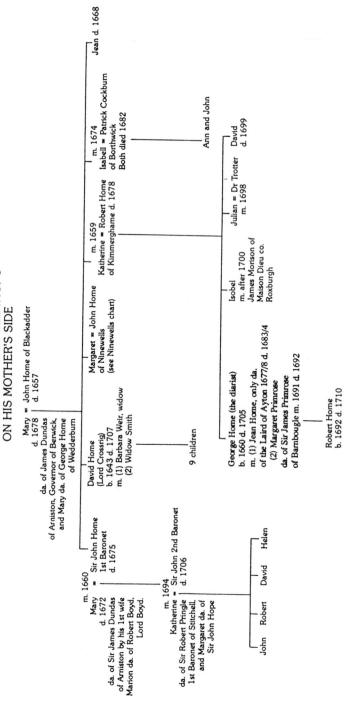

Mary = John Home of Blackadder
d. 1678   d. 1657
da. of James Dundas
of Arniston, Governor of Berwick,
and Mary da. of George Home
of Wedderburn

Mary = Sir John Home
m. 1660   1st Baronet
d. 1672   d. 1675
da. of Sir James Dundas
of Arniston by his 1st wife
Marion da. of Robert Boyd.
Lord Boyd.

David Home
(Lord Crossrig)
b. 1643 d. 1707
m. (1) Barbara Weir, widow
(2) Widow Smith

9 children

Margaret = John Home
of Ninewells
(see Ninewells chart)

Katherine = Robert Home
m. 1659   of Kimmerghame d. 1678

Isabell = Patrick Cockburn
m. 1674   of Borthwick
Both died 1682

Jean d. 1668

Ann and John

Katherine = Sir John 2nd Baronet
m. 1694   d. 1706
da. of Sir Robert Pringle
1st Baronet of Stitchell.
and Margaret da. of
Sir John Hope

George Home (the diarist)
b. 1660 d. 1705
m. (1) Jean Home, only da.
of the Laird of Ayton 1677/8 d. 1683/4
(2) Margaret Primrose
da. of Sir James Primrose
of Barnbougle m. 1691 d. 1692

Isobel
m. after 1700
James Morison of
Maison Dieu co.
Roxburgh

Julian = Dr Trotter
m. 1698

David
d. 1699

John   Robert   David   Helen

Robert Home
b. 1692 d. 1710

[20]

HOME OF NINEWELLS
and
HOME OF WHITFIELD

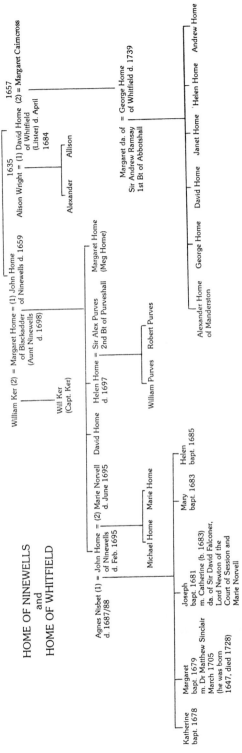

3) KEY TO TERRITORIAL DESIGNATIONS IN VOLUME 1 OF THE DIARY (EXCLUDING LORDS OF SESSION)

ABBEY ST. BATHANS	Alexander Home
ABERCORN	Sir Walter Seatone
AIMOUTH	Had been a Nisbet seat, but in the list of pollable persons George Winraham is 'of Eyemouth'.
ALLANBANK	Sir Robert Stewart
ANTONSHILL	John Dickson
ARDOCH	Two possibilities, both of which satisfy the ' and his Lady and sone' diary entry of 2 August 1695. (1) If co. Dunbarton, Nicol Bontein, 11th of Ardoch. (2) If co. Ayr, John Hamilton, 8th of Ardoch.
BALBIGNY	Middleton
BALGARE	James Galbraith
BELL	John Home
BEMERSYDE	Anthony Haig
BLACKADER	Sir John Home
BLACKBURN	Broun
BLACKWOOD	Three estates, all in the West of Scotland, have this name. The laird of one was Sir George Weir, 1st Baronet of Blackwood. The Blackwood with whom the diarist so often made, or tried to make, contact in Edinburgh over one particular legal matter may have been a relative of Sir George's; not a younger brother, who would not be old enough, but possibly an uncle.
BLEBO	John Bethune
BOGHALL	Michael Norvell
BONHILL	James Smollett
BORTHICK	Patrick Cockburn (d. 1682)
BOWHILL	Henry Scrimgeour
BRIMBLETON	Thomas Aikman
BROOMHOUSE	John Home
BUGHTRIG	John Frank
CARUBBER	Hay
CASTLELAW	John Fish
CASTLE HUME (Ireland)	Sir John Home
CAVERS and W. NISBET	John Carre
CESNOCK (co. Ayr)	Sir George Campbell
CHARTER HALL	Alexander Trotter

CLIFTONE	Andrew Pringle
COLDENKNOWES	James Daes
COLSTONE	Sir George Broun
CONDEE	An Oliphant seat in Perthshire
CROSRIG	Robert Hume (pre-1696)
CUNNINGHAMHEAD	Sir William Cunningham
DALMENY	Archibald Primrose
DEBURNIN	Binny
DEUCHER	Two possible seats, in co. Selkirk and co.Forfar
DRUM	Alexander Irvine
DUNGLAS	Sir John Hall/Sir William Ruthven
EARNSLAW	James Douglas. He probably spent most of his time in Edinburgh, for Mr. Alexander Paterson of Earnslaw was assessed for 4 hearths.
ECCLES	Home
EDGERSTONE	Andrew Rutherford
EDROM	John Brymer
FALSYDE	James Hume of Falsyde was assessed for 7 hearths. Veitch says 'a Gentleman's dwelling of the name of Mowet'.
FINGALTONE	Sir James Oswald
FLAS	Harry Fletcher
FREERSHAW	Henry Douglas
GLENKINDIE	William Strachan
GOSFORD	Peter Wedderburn
GRADEN	George Home, died at Bothwell Bridge 1679. Veitch speaks of it in the mid-1680's as ' a Gentleman's House of the name of Hume'. There is also Graden in co. Roxburgh.
GRANGE	Sir John Kirkaldy
GRUBBET	Sir William Bennet
GREENHEAD	Sir William Ker
GREENKNOW	James Pringle
GREENLAW CASTLE	William Hume
GREENLAWDEAN	James Home (d.1677)
HADDEN (co. Roxburgh)	Murray
HALYBURTONE	Home/Halyburton
HERVISTONE	Robert Dundas, died long before 1694
HEUGHEAD	Alexander Home
HILTONE	Joseph Johnstone (died 1695)
	Robert Johnstone
HOPTONE	John Hope (died 1682)
	Charles Hope (born 1681)

JERVISWOOD (Lanarkshire) and MELLERSTAIN	George Baillie
KETTLESHILE	Alexander Trotter
KETTLESTON	- Stuart (died pre-1689)
	John Stuart (died 16 February 1696)
KIMMERGHAME	George Home
LADYKIRK	Nisbet
LANTONE (LANGTON)	Sir Archibald Cockburn
LINTHILL	William Home
LINTONE	Andrew Ker
LONGFORMACUS	Sir John Sinclair
LUMSDEN	Sir Patrick Home
LYES (LEYS)	Sir Thomas Burnet
MANGERTONE (MANDERSTON)	'Shury' Home
MURRAYS	Al Home
NEWHOUSE	Walter Ridle
NEWMAINS	Thomas Halyburton
NEWTONE in FIFE or EDROM	John Brymer
NEWTONE	Sir Richard Newtone
NEWTOONE & WHITSOME	Alexander Home
NINEWELLS	John Home (died 1695): Joseph Home
NORTH BERWICK	Sir John Home (sometime)
OCHILTREE	Sir John Cochrane
PENICOOK	Sir John Clerk
PILMUIR	Harry Borthwick
PITTADRO	James Henderson
PITTFIRRIN	Sir Charles Halket
PLANDERGAIST	John Home (died long before 1694)
PURVESHALL	Sir Alexander Purves
RAVELLAW	John Johnstone
RAVILSTONE	Sir John Foulis
RENTON	Sir Alexander Home
RIDDLE	Sir John Riddle
ROWISTON	James Home
RYSLAW	Sir James Cockburn
ST. EBBS	Will Home
SALTONE	Fletcher
SCLATEHOUSE	Alexander Home

[24]

SORNBEG	Sir Robert Dicksone
SOUTHSYDE	Elliss
SPOT	Murray
STICHILL	Sir John Pringle
STOBS	Sir William Eliott (d. 1694)
	Sir Gilbert Eliott
STUARTONE	John Craik
SWINSIDE	Elliot
SWINTONE	Sir John Swintone
TARSAPPIE	Possibly a seat in Perthshire
THORNIDIKES	Alexander Broun
TODRIG	William Henderson
TOLQUHON	
WEDDERBURN	Home/Wedderburn
WESTERHALL	Johnstone
WEST NISBET	John Carre
WHITSLAID	Don
WHITSOME	Adam Waddell
WHYTEBANK	Alexander Pringle (d.1695)
	John Pringle
WHYTEFEILD	George Home

II PEOPLE FOR WHOM EXPLANATIONS ARE NEEDED

1) THE HOMES AND HUMES

It will be noticed that, despite the known preference for the spelling 'Hume' in certain branches of the family at this date and afterwards, the diarist almost always uses 'Home' throughout. In the explanatory notes that follow, the spelling Home will normally be employed, so as to link up more satisfactorily with George Home's text.

Veitch, when bringing his 'Description of Berwickshire or the Mers' to an end, says: 'The considerablest Names are 1. the Humes of which besides the Earle there will be above 30 families with Estates. 2. The Cockburns....' It will be noticed from what follows that the number of Home estates mentioned in the diarist's first volume falls not far short of this.

a) The diarist's grandparents, aunts and uncles

The first Home or Hume of Kimmerghame was the diarist's paternal grandfather George, a younger brother of Sir Patrick Hume, 7th of Polwarth. That George married Isobel Hume, and before he died in 1659 they had had three children who lived to become adults. The elder of the two boys, Robert, was the diarist's father; the other two children, a boy and a girl, are mentioned only once in the diary, when on 4 June 1694 George tells us that his father had had a brother and a sister. We know nothing more about this uncle, but from other sources it has been possible to discover that this aunt was Jean Hume who married John Hepburn of Newtoun of Whitsomehill in the parish of Whitsome in Berwickshire. This estate (now a farm) had ceased to belong to the Hepburns by the 1690's, when Thomas Roughead of 'Whittsimhill' was assessed for 12 hearths. The diarist's aunt Jean and her husband had at least one child, the Katherine Hepburn who was clearly a great friend of Isobel (4 June 1694). Much later on she was to marry John Dickson of Antonshill who became for a time George Home's, and then Marchmont's factor.

The diarist's mother was Katherine, sister of Sir John Home 1st Baronet of Blackadder. Sir John was therefore the diarist's uncle (he died in 1675), as was Katherine's other brother David Home, afterwards Lord Crossrig, who outlived the diarist and is very frequently mentioned. Katherine also had a number of sisters, who were George Home's aunts. There was Margaret, who married John Home of Ninewells (so he calls her Aunt Ninewells), forming the start of a long and complicated story which, after the death in Edinburgh of their son (14

February 1695), needs a great deal of elucidation. Then there was Isabell, who married Patrick Cockburn of Borthwick. Isabell and her husband both died in 1682, and Crossrig then looked after their two children. But for two years before she died, from 1680 to 1682, Isabell (whom the diarist calls Aunt Borthwick) looked after George Home's two sisters Isobel and Julian - as he reminds himself on 4 June 1694, after a quarrel with his sister Isobel. The diarist's mother had yet another sister, Jean, who died of a fever in 1668 according to her brother Crossrig, but who in some records is said to have married a Hepburn of Blackerstone.

There is also mention in the diary of a grand aunt and a grand uncle. The grand aunt he calls Sophia Lady Hilton, is a sister of his *paternal* grandfather. She married Joseph Johnstone of Hilton. Reference to her in the diary occurs when he attended the burial of Sophia Cockburn in Edinburgh on 5 February 1695. The grand uncle is James Home of Greenlawdean, brother of George Home's *maternal* grandfather, and uncle of Crossrig. He died in 1677. Here the diary mention is on 23 September 1695, but a much longer version of the financial matters involved can be found in Crossrig, pp 20-22.

The only one of his aunts and uncles who seems to need fuller treatment at this point is Crossrig. Aunt Ninewells will be discussed further when that branch of the Homes is dealt with, as will the person he calls, in some pre-diary manuscript sheets of accounts (SRO GD158/673) ' my aunt the Lady Lintone', to be identified when we examine the Carre/Ker group of families. David Home Lord Crossrig (1643-1707) has left a remarkable record of what he recollected of his life story in *Domestic Details*. In one respect at least it bears a marked resemblance to George Home's diary, in the author's continual preoccupation with his financial situation. Crossrig is the only contemporary we know of who was aware that his nephew kept a diary, for on one issue where he cannot clearly remember the details himself, he says (p 86) ' I cannot find a bond of relief...with many other papers relating to Kimmerghame, but no doubt it will be found in his diary of the said date...' George Home, as can be seen from many diary entries, did not always see eye-to-eye with his uncle, but he very much valued his advice, particularly in the early days. Thus under the heading 'Memoranda of my business, Kimmerghame Wednesday November 7 1683' he records in a notebook (SRO GD158/674) ' It. to give Mr. David my uncle ane account of the present posture of my affairs'.

The story of Crossrig's student days, of how he took responsibility for so many young people in the different families relying on him to look after their interests, his trip abroad to study in Paris, his being given recognition as an advocate in Edinburgh without having done the normal study there, and his final (and to him totally unexpected) nomination in 1689 as a Lord of Session and then a Commissioner of Justiciary, all this is told in the most delightful way in his own words in *Domestic Details*. He also tells us of his two marriages; when the Edinburgh pollable persons list was produced, nine of his *own* children were mentioned - James, David, Francis, William, Alexander, Margaret, Marion, Katherine and Jean (Wood, p49). Like Lord Polwarth he was for George Home, both a close relative, someone of his father's generation who had known all about the family's problems for a very long time, and also someone in a key position to give help and advice on legal, financial and related matters, and perhaps to use his undoubted influence (within the limits of what was permissible) on the diarist's behalf. The assistance he was able or willing to give may not always, as we can see from the diary, have been up to George's expectations or hopes, but at least one could, and did, go on trying to secure it. Thus on 29 May 1695 'I writt to my Lo: Crosrig wishing him joy of his knighthood and if he could conveniently to let me have some money'.

b) Polwarths

This family played a very important part in the day-to-day life of George Home. Sir Patrick Hume 2nd Baronet of Polwarth (born 1641) son of Sir Patrick 1st Baronet and Christian, daughter of Sir Alexander Hamilton of Innerwick, was a kinsman of the diarist. In 1660 he married Grisell (born 1642) daughter of Sir Thomas Kar of Cavers and Grisell Halkett. Of their marriage there were seven surviving children, Patrick aged 30 in 1694, Grisell 29, Julian 21, Alexander (known as Sandy) 19, Andrew 18, Anne 17 and Jean 11. As well as the blood tie and the fact that Kimmerghame was only a few miles from Polwarth House, the home of this branch of the Humes, there were other reasons why George found it expedient to keep in close touch with his relative, as will be seen later.

Sir Patrick held strong religious and political views which resulted in his imprisonment, and eventual exile in Holland for the whole family. They were staunch supporters of William of Orange, returning to England with him in 1688, and once William was enthroned Sir Patrick was duly rewarded for his loyalty. The Polwarth estates which had been forfeit were restored, and in 1690 Sir Patrick was created Lord Polwarth. A further expression of royal gratitude was the patent which assigned him the right to include an orange and an imperial crown in his coat of arms. At the same time he was made Sheriff of Berwickshire. In the future, and after this section of the diary finishes, further honours were to come to Lord Polwarth. On 1 May 1696 he was made Lord Chancellor of Scotland, and subsequently in 1697 created Earl of Marchmont. These last honours surprised most people and were really moves of political expediency on the part of King William. He felt he could rely on this faithful ally to keep a low profile and carry out the policies laid down in London for the troublesome northern kingdom of Scotland.

In this section of the diary although Lord Polwarth was a Privy Councillor and, since the early 1690's had changed sides and become a valued supporter of the administration, there was no hint that from May 1696 onwards he was to become a very important political figure. Even at the pre-May 1696 level, however, George Home found his kinsman a very useful source of information as to what was going on in the power struggle both in Edinburgh and in London, and he enjoyed the reflected glory from a relative with a certain amount of influence both locally and nationally. So a close watch was kept on Lord Polwarth's movements, as to whether he would be in Edinburgh or at Polwarth House, so that he could be visited.

The only one of the children who was married at this time was the eldest daughter Grisell. In 1691 she had married George Baillie of Jerviswood, son of Robert Baillie who had been executed for high treason in 1684. From his father, George Baillie inherited the estates of Jerviswood in Lanarkshire and Mellerstain in Berwickshire. In the early years of their marriage the Baillies lived in Edinburgh, but later made Mellerstain their main residence. There were two daughters and one son of the marriage, Grisell, born 1692, Robert, born 1694 and Rachel born 1696.

On 29 May 1695 George Home tells us that 'My Ldy Pol: came home yesterday and writt to me this morning for a cradle for Ro: Baylie who she has brought out with her'. Unfortunately the only son died on 28 February 1696. In later years the Baillie family travelled a good deal, to London and often abroad. Grisell Baillie is the only one of Lord Polwarth's children who is remembered today. She was a cultured woman who wrote songs and poetry, but is best remembered for her household account book which she kept meticulously, and which provides an interesting picture of the lifestyle of a laird's family at that time. In 1911 The Scottish History Society published *Lady Grisell Baillie's Household Book 1692-1733* which ever since then has had a wide readership.

Patrick, the eldest son, is frequently referred to in the diary as the Mr. of Polwarth, e.g. on 23 December 1695 ' I sat wt the Mr. of Polwarth sometime in his chamber...' It should be remembered, incidentally, that when the diarist talks about ' Mr Al. Home' or ' Sandy Home' he is sometimes referring to Lord Polwarth's son Alexander, and not to Commissary Home. Careful examination of the context will usually make it clear when Lord Polwarth's son is meant.

c) Blackadders

The laird, Sir John Home 2nd Baronet of Blackadder, had been looked after (except when he was at college) by Crossrig when his father, Crossrig's elder brother, died in 1675. In May 1684 he and the diarist went to France where, in 1685 or 86 'a wofull accident befell Sir John at Angiers, having in a scufle receeved a wound in his head from a Frenchman that had well nigh cost him his life' (Crossrig p.42). Though George Home returned to Scotland in January 1687, Sir John delayed doing so for a year or two. Nevertheless, the time they had spent together abroad undoubtedly helped to establish the firm friendship between them that is evidenced throughout the diary. In 1694 Sir John married Katherine, daughter of Sir Robert Pringle 1st Baronet of Stitchill and Margaret daughter of Sir John Hope, a Senator of the College of Justice. Katherine was one of their 19 children of whom 13 grew up. So when the surviving part of George Home's diary begins, his great friend Sir John had only just got married, whereas George himself had been married twice and lost both his wives, the last of them two years before. What happened to the family at Blackadder, therefore - births, illnesses and deaths, but naturally no marriages - including their day-to-day activities, is all reported in great detail throughout the whole of the diary. And when sleeping space was inadequate at Kimmerghame or supplies of wine ran short, it was to Blackadder that one turned.

Right at the outset we hear about them. On 8 May 1694 'Sr John Home & his Lady and his sister Helen and my sister Isbell came here a foot'. Then on 23 June 'Sir Jo: Home & his Lady and her sister Bethia and Cusen Lilias came this way going to Stichill'. Bethia Pringle, Katherine's sister, later married Deans of Woodhouselee and had children. On 8 February 1695 when 'Sr John Home of Bl: and his sisters and mine' turned up in Edinburgh, it seems unlikely that more than one Blackadder sister was involved, the use of the plural arising from one or more of George Home's sisters being there as well. For on 31 October only one Blackadder sister - Mrs. Helen - is again mentioned as being with George's sister. A few days later, on 5 November, 'Nelly Home and my sister Tibby' came from Blackadder, which means Helen and Isobel, even if the names used this time are a little unexpected.

Sir John also had a younger brother called James, who is specifically referred to as his brother in the diary entry for 2 November 1695. The Captain Home who appears in the same area two days later is probably the same person, as also are possibly the James Home who was with his Lady on 12 June, and the James Home who went with the diarist to Nisbet on 5 September 1695. The Blackadder's son who was born that night, and christened David some days after, lived for only seven years, his death being noted on 5 November 1702.

d) Ninewells

It is when we come to this branch of the Home kinship network that any attempt to understand who was who sometimes meets almost insuperable obstacles. The broad outline is, however, clear enough. The diarist's Aunt Ninewells (his mother's sister) had already, to all appearances, been a widow for some 36 years when her son John Home the laird of Ninewells became seriously ill in Edinburgh and died in February 1695. We learn from the diary that young Lady Ninewells arrived in Edinburgh at the time of his death and then returned to a mysterious place the diarist calls English Mauldy (or Mauldry) where she was living with her two young children. She dies there four months or so later, and the problem of who is going to, or who should, look after these children becomes a matter of constant discussion and argument.

Two of the difficulties can be resolved relatively easily. English Mauldy turns out to be Inglismaldie in Laurencekirk parish co. Kincardine. And young Lady Ninewells is Marie Norvell, daughter of George Norvell of Boghall an Edinburgh advocate (who died in 1672) and Margaret, daughter of Michael Elphinstone of Quarrell. Marie Norvell is only described as 'young' to distinguish her from Aunt Ninewells. For she had in fact already been married in 1678 (as his second wife) to Sir David Falconer of Newton, Lord Newton of the Court of Session; and four children, the oldest of whom was now 15, had resulted from that previous marriage. As John Home was dying we learn on 14 February 1695 'that his son Joseph came to toune yesternight'. This Joseph is clearly not one of the two very young children of John Home and Marie Norvell, whose names are known to have been Michael and Marie. So John Home also must have had a previous marriage. And as Crossrig remarks on another occasion (p.51), 'after many jars, woes and froes' it was found that this first wife was Agnes Nisbet, probably one of the Nisbets of Eyemouth or Ladykirk, and that they had five (or possibly six) children, of whom Joseph, baptised in 1681, was the third child but eldest, or only, son.

Of the remaining people mentioned at the time of John Home's funeral three (Sir John Home, Mr. Al. Home and Polwarth) are already well known to us. 'Da. Home of Ninewells brother to Ninewells' seems at this stage to need no elaboration either. 'Boghall' must be a brother of Marie Norvell, John Home's widow. And 'Balgaire' is James Galbraith who, along with Boghall, is brought into subsequent discussions on matters arising from John Home's death. There is, however, one person who is very frequently mentioned at this time, and who is obviously very concerned about the two young children Michael and Marie. Usually she appears just as 'Meg Home', but sometimes as 'Mrs. Margaret Home'. To try and explain exactly who she is, and how she fits into the picture, we have to go back to Aunt Ninewells and her husband John Home of Ninewells, mother and father of the John Home of Ninewells who died in February 1695.

We know (as with so much else, not from the diary itself but from other sources) that they had four children, two boys and two girls, and that their names were John, David, Helen (who married Sir Alexander Purves, 2nd Baronet of Purveshall, perhaps in the late 1670's), and Margaret. John and Helen we now know enough about. David, as the diarist mentions, came to his brother John's funeral, but was he married, and if so to whom? And most important of all, is the Margaret who was John Home's sister the same as the Meg Home/Mrs. Margaret Home in the diary? The wording there often speaks of Meg Home as being the daughter of Aunt Ninewells and the sister of John Home; but it also credits her with having a brother Will and a brother Captain Car/Ker, which cannot be reconciled with the other known facts. Reconciliation only becomes possible when we discover that Aunt Ninewells had not in fact remained a widow for the 36 years since her husband John Ninewells died in 1659. For in a document written at

Huesdon in Holland on 9 January 1690 a certain William Ker, son of the deceased William Ker (who was uncle to Sir William Ker of Greenhead), made provision for some of his relatives to be responsible for his affairs when he was out of the country. And he referred to Margaret Home Lady Nynwells as his mother and to David Home as his lawful brother.

So Aunt Ninewells had married a second husband, William Ker, who died some time before 1690; and had a son also called William, who was clearly abroad a good deal, probably in the army. This William Ker the younger was therefore half brother to David, Helen and Margaret, Aunt Ninewells' surviving children from her *first* marriage. So the Will, and the Captain Car/Ker mentioned in the diary as being brothers of Meg Home are almost certainly one and the same person, and that person is Aunt Ninewells' son by her second marriage. The only doubts remaining are as to whether either David Home or Meg Home ever married.

e) Earl of Home

At the very beginning of this first surviving part of the diary, 7 May 1694, George Home is talking about raising an adjudication against the Earl of Home's estate, and from then on hardly a week goes by without some reference to financial problems between him, the Earl, Ninewells and others for which legal redress is being sought on all sides. On 18 July that year the diarist speaks of a contract between him and the Earl dated, he thinks, February, and articles of agreement dated 14 December 1683. Obviously the problems are long-standing ones, partly tied up with things not having gone at all according to plan when George Home married the Ayton heiress, partly arising from the transaction when he, Ninewells, Borthwick and Eccles borrowed 1000 mks to go to Bothwell Bridge in 1679. Given this situation it may seem surprising that the diarist quite often took the opportunity to pay a visit to the Hirsel, though he tells us that he and the Earl, if he happened to be there, did not talk business. On 19 June 1694 he saw Jean, the Countess Dowager, widow of the 3rd Earl, whose death at 72 he reports a few days later and whose funeral he attended. He also spent an hour or so with Lady Anne, who had married Charles Home the 6th Earl in 1680 (and whose mother Dame Marjory Fleeming Lady Purveshall was still living in the 12-hearth house in Eccles parish). And as an added bonus he saw the heir, 'Lord Dunglasse', though his description - a very pretty boy - may seem strange to us when applied to a lad in his early teens.

f) Other Homes by territorial designation

Abbey St. Bathans

Alexander Home, in a 7-hearth house (7 miles N.W. of Duns), is the laird whose son told Thomas Pringle the story of a Johnstone having in the past bought the Hilton estate too cheaply from one of his relatives, so that later generations of Johnstones were being punished in consequence. See 22 January 1695.

Bell

It sounds as though John Home of Bell, mentioned on 2 March 1695, was a very young laird in George Home's father's time, so he is probably still laird in 1694-96.

Eccles

Veitch speaks of 'the Town of Eccles, where the laird dwells of the name of Hume'. That laird was probably the Eccles who, along with the diarist and others, borrowed 1,000 marks when they were going to Bothwell Bridge in 1679 (diary entry 25 June 1694).

Broomhouse

The laird of this estate a few miles N.E. of Duns does not figure significantly in the diary. He was John Home, 6th of Broomhouse, who succeeded his father (also John) in 1691. When the diarist was at Blackadder on 5 April 1695 he merely dined with the Vicar of Berwick and his father-in-law Broomhouse.

Falsyde

Veitch speaks of 'Fasyde, a Gentleman's Dwelling of the name of Mowet' in the parish of Gordon. By the 1690's it must have changed hands, for the hearth tax rolls show James Home of Falsyde in Gordon parish being charged for 7 hearths. And the diarist confirms this, for on 10 January 1695 ' Sir John Home came here this morning going Fulside to the buriall of one of the Lady Fulsydes daughtress wt Bellita called Margaret Home'. (Bellita was of course going *with* Sir John to the burial; it was not an alternative name to Margaret). Later, on 22 August of that year, we learn that Falsyde is an Ensign in Sir William Douglas' Regiment. Like so many of the other estates, Fallsidehill is now a farm.

Flas

The diarist tells us (4 December 1695) that the laird, James Home, was Sheriff Depute. Then and on an earlier occasion (27 November) the talk was, however, about money. Flas was in Westruther parish, and there is still a farm with that name in the parish.

Greenlaw Castle

Most of the diarist's dealings with the laird, William Home, related to payment of interest on a loan dating from his father's time, and George Home's failure to pay on time is evident - there are entries on 14 January, 8 and 13 April and 29 July 1695. We know from the manuscript list of pollable persons that his spouse was Isobel Ancrum, and that they had four children (three of them girls) and five servants (three of them men) living with them (SRO GD86/770A).

Halyburtone

Veitch tells us, in 1682 -85, that this is a Hume estate and the diarist remarks on 15 May 1694 that 'Halyburtone gets 12 Ms for the acre of his land which is not so good as mine in Betshile'. A farm in the parish of Greenlaw now has this name.

Heughead

On 19 October 1695 the diarist reports that 'Heughead was at Wedderburn this day'. The laird would be Alexander Home. A farm in the parish of Coldingham is called Heugh Head today.

Linthill

When Linthill is mentioned on 28 February 1695 it is as Trustee for the Earl of Dunfermline's Estate. But on 6 June in the same year the diarist went from Eyemouth to Linthill ' and saw him and his Lady'. On that occasion at least there can be no doubt that the two people concerned were William Hume and his wife, living in the 10-hearth house there with his Lady's mother (paying a third part of her deceased husband's poll tax), a child, and his brother John Home (of age, and polled as a gentleman), together with James and Janet, his under-age brother and sister (SRO GD86/770A). The editor of Foulis also gives Linthill as a Home estate. The editor of Crossrig, however, says that the person being referred to there is 'Thomas Kincaid of Auchinreoch, Surgeon-Apothecary in Edinburgh. He was proprietor, among others, of the lands of Linthill in Berwickshire' (p.xxvii); he did not, however, know of the relevant manuscript list of pollable persons.

Lumsden (and Renton)

Sir Patrick Home the laird is said on 30 March 1695 to be planning to buy Ayton, and on 26 October of the same year George Home is visited by the laird's son in company with others. Sir Patrick (an advocate) and his elder brother Sir Alexander, 1st Baronet of Renton, had many disagreements with each other, but as most of these took place before or after this section of the diary was written, they are not mentioned. Sir Alexander, G.E.C. tells us, was nearly ruined by his younger brother Sir Patrick, 'who (wrongfully) held from him the estate of Renton, and whom, in 1685, he accused of forgery'. And when Sir Alexander died on 28 May 1698 a ludicrous confrontation took place after the funeral between the widow and the heir on one side and Sir Patrick and his Lady on the other, which George Home talks about in a later section of the diary; an account of it can be found in Kelsall, pp. 94-5.

Mangertone (Manderston)

The Homes of Manderston (a mile or so east of Duns) were an important branch for a long time. But the current laird and his lady, who visited the diarist in company with others on 8 August 1695, soon suffered major misfortunes. Because she was Lady Hilton's daughter, these events are dealt with as part of the Johnstone story, in a later explanatory note.

North Berwick

A lady came to see the diarist in Edinburgh on 5 July 1695 about a matter which, though slightly complicated, does not itself seem to need any further explanation, as the position is set out quite clearly in the diary entry. However, the background to the Homes involved can be briefly sketched in. Sir John, son of George Home of North Berwick, was the 2nd Baronet, and was now of Castle Hume in Ireland, the North Berwick estate having been sold in 1633. He died on Midsummer Eve 1695, only weeks before his sister came to Edinburgh and called on George Home. The new laird and 3rd Baronet was to be Sir Gustavus Home, Sir John's 3rd but only surviving son, who was about 25 and unmarried at that time. Sir John had been married to Sidney, younger daughter of James Hamilton of Manor Hamilton, co. Leitrim; they had had ten children and she died in January 1685. In later volumes of the diary intermarrying between this Irish and the Scottish branches of the Homes is talked about.

Plandergaist

By 1694 the only representative of the Homes of Plandergaist, in Ayton parish in Berwickshire, was the widow of John Home, who had been the complainer when the diarist, his bride and others were brought before the Privy Council for the abduction of the Ayton heiress and her irregular marriage. In the list of pollable persons in 1695, 'Lady Planderguest' is paying a third part of her deceased husband's poll (which was on the same level as George Home, Sir John Home and others). and has two servants, a man and a woman.

Rowiston

The first reference, on 30 May 1694, is to the previous laird, now dead. Then we are told on 29 April 1695 that the present laird is James Home. And the wording of the entry on 10 March 1696 makes it unclear whether the diarist is talking about the place or the person.

St. Ebbes (sometimes St. Abbs)

Will Home, laird of this estate in Coldinhame parish, turns up a great deal in the diary. He often called to see the diarist when on his way to or from the Hirsel, but was also quite frequently seen in Edinburgh. The final mention is on 2 April 1696, about his wife's burial 'at Aitone' At fist reading it might seem as though both he and his wife had died, but this is merely because *two* burials are being talked about, the second being that of Mr. George Wilson.

Sclatehouse

From the list of pollable persions we learn that this was 'Alexr Houme of Sklaitthouse heritor'; that for himself, son and two daughters he was assessed at £10-4-0 (about half the laird's usual rate - his yearly valued rent was £200-£500), and that a Mr. Alexander Home his friend was in the house with him but got no wages (SRO GD86/770A). John Home is also included in the list, but in a separate Sclatehouse dwelling.

Of the diary references the most interesting are those for 20 May and 6 June 1695. From the first of these we learn that 'Jo: Home Sclatehouses brother' is getting a house absurdly cheaply. In the second, it emerges that he has now come to the Sclatehouse and sells wine. Except for these two, the diary references mostly relate to financial matters affecting the diarist.

Wedderburn

Normally when the diarist talks of 'Wedderburn', 'old Wedderburn' or ' young Wedderburn' it is a territorial designation for the branch of the Home family living there. This is also true of the Wedderburn references in Crossrig's *Domestic Details*. As there was a Wedderburn family in the area as well, however, the context has to be used as a guide in dealing with doubtful cases. The laird, George

Home of Wedderburn (born 1641), married Isobel, daughter of Sir Francis Liddell, and died about 1716. However, his first son and heir, also George Home, was apparently put in charge of the family estate in 1695, long before the laird's death. *His* Lady was Margaret, daughter of Sir Patrick Home of Lumsden. So Sir Patrick Home's son was *young* Wedderburn's brother-in-law, which makes it possible to interpret correctly the opening sentences of the diary entry for 26 October 1695. When Frank Home, Wedderburn's son, is talked of on 27 November and 1 December 1695, the Wedderburn reference is presumably to the laird, *old* Wedderburn, who had a second son Francis (called after his maternal grandfather).

Whytefeild (in Coldinghame parish)

The Homes of Whitfield (the more usual spelling) were a cadet branch of the Homes of Ninewells. The John Home of Ninewells whom the diarist's Aunt Ninewells had married, had a younger brother David Home of Whitfield. He was a litster, who seems to have become a burgess of Edinburgh through marrying Alison Wright, daughter of John Wright, maltman; their children were Alexander and Alison. After his wife's death, David Home married Margaret Cairncross in Edinburgh in November 1657. She was the only sister of the Alexander Cairncross who, after also starting as a litster (his father had been one), acquired the necessary educational qualifications to embark on a career in the Church. In the course of this career Alexander Cairncross became Archbishop of Glasgow, was removed from that office in 1687, and then after an interval of six years was made Bishop of Raphoe in Ireland; the essential features of this story are recounted in the diary entry for 20 June 1695. David Home and Margaret Cairncross had a son, George Home (called simply Whytefeild by the diarist) whom we find our George Home meeting quite often. David Home was Collector of Supply for Berwickshire and at his death in April 1684 had many creditors; his son George seems to have held the same post from 1686 to 1704. Crossrig was one of a group (including the diarist's father) who had borrowed 3000 merks from David Home at the time of the Ayton heiress fiasco; he reports (p.26) repaying some of it to '-- Cairncross' (David's widow and George's mother) in 1687 or 1688.

Whytefeild often seems to have acted as a go-between in the diarist's continuing difficulties with the Earl of Home. He married Margaret, daughter of Sir Andrew Ramsay, 1st Baronet of Abbotshall co. Fife and Anne Montgomerie (daughter of the Earl of Eglinton). In later years he had very mixed fortunes. Being served heir to his uncle the Bishop, who died unmarried in May 1701, he acquired the Manderston estates. But when he became implicated in the 1715 uprising, he was for a time imprisoned in the Tower of London, forfeiting his property rights. He died in 1739; his eldest son Alexander apparently fell heir to the Manderston lands, those of Whitfield going to a relative, Patrick Home of Billie.

There were, of course, other estates in Berwickshire where the laird was a Home - for example, George Home of Bassendean, George Hume of Kaims- which do not happen to be mentioned in this section of the diary.

g) Other Homes by name

Home, Mr. Al

Alexander Home, second son of John Home of Manderston, was some 14 years older than the diarist. His first wife, whom he married in 1676, was Polwarth's sister Anne. She died in September 1690 and three years later he married Euphan, daughter of Thomas Young of Leny. We hear of a son, perhaps of the previous marriage, whom he is going to see ' in Gallasheils' on 5 May 1695. He was the first person of the name of Home to become a Writer to the Signet. This was remarked upon much later in the diary, when Dr. Pitcairne was running through the names of Homes who had distinguished themselves in different fields. And he was Commissary of Lauder from 1690 until his death in May 1702; so it is rather surprising that George Home, who was usually meticulous in giving people their appropriate designations, does not until the late 1690's, begin to speak of him as Commissary Home instead of just Mr. Al.

Within a few days of the opening of this section of the diary the first mention of him occurs - on 8 May 1694. He was the person to whom George Home most frequently turned on legal and financial problems, and references to him are very numerous.   Some of these, of course, relate to social occasions rather than business matters, and he is also often to be found, as a companion on such occasions, in Foulis.

For a long time it looked as though the Sandy Home, who also lived in Edinburgh and seemed to have had some legal training, was a different person from Mr. Al Home, largely because he was often asked to perform relatively unskilled tasks such as buying plants and seeds and arranging for their transport to Kimmerghame.   One sentence in the diary, however, makes it absolutely certain that they are one and the same person. When Harry Borthwick is referred to as Sandy Home's son-in-law it is only Alexander Home, Writer to the Signet, who can (through his second marriage) fulfil this condition (see 11) b) below).

Home, Bailie

This is George Home of Kello, who first became Bailie in 1689 and was to become Lord Provost of Edinburgh in October 1698. His first mention in the diary, on 27 June 1695, tells us that yesterday Bailis Home, whose daughter was to be married on the 28th, had issued an invitation to dine with him on the 29th.

This is all duly reported, and it emerges that the bridegroom is William Elliot, a brother of Stobs and a merchant in Edinburgh. Some months later the three of them called at Kimmerghame.

Home, James

James Home is mentioned on three occasions. Once, on 2 November 1695, we are told he is Sir John Home's brother, and two days later Captain Home is referred to, the context strongly suggesting that this is the same person. The two previous occasions in the same year, on 12 June (with his Lady) and 5 September, do not provide any clue to his identity.

Home, Sandy

Once the Edinburgh-based Sandy Home was found to be the same person as Mr. Al Home, there remained the problem of the London-based Sandy Home - the context always makes it clear when the diarist is talking about the latter. He is sometimes referred to as ' Mr. Home', occasionally as ' Sandy Home writer' and sometimes just as 'Sandy Home'. On very many occasion he is asked to obtain fruit trees and seeds in London and arrange for their transport by ship; and where this is convenient, things wanted by Lord Polwarth are sent at the same time. On the evidence provided in the diary it is not possible to say of which branch of the Homes he is a member, but he could well be a relative of the diarist.

Home, Will

He sometimes appears as 'blind Will Home'. He clearly has a financial interest in one or more linen/paper mills, and wants to raise money for projects in those fields. From the diary entries for 27 March and 30 March 1695 it becomes clear that he and Will Home of St. Ebbs are one and the same person. For on the earlier date blind Will Home and Whytefeild are on their way to the Hirsel, while three days later, Will House of St. Ebbs comes *back* from the Hirsel with e note from Whytefeild.

2) THE CARRES AND KERS

In most branches of this group of families the name is spelt Kar or Ker, but in the one with which George Home was most closely in touch the spelling Carre had been adopted after the present laird's father had married Jean, daughter of the Carres of Crailing. The present laird was John Carre of Cavers (co. Roxburgh) and West Nisbet (Berwickshire), but his family lived in the second of these two. Veitch speaks of 'the Palace [place] of West Nisbet..... an estate with large Planting and fruitful Orchards'. Like the Polwarth, Blackadder and Johnstone establishments it had fifteen hearths, and John and Margaret his Lady (daughter of Sir Andrew Ker or Cavers) lived there with four sons (Robert, John, James and Thomas) and three daughters (Jean, Margaret and Anna) and a fairly large staff, eleven men and eight women plus Mr. William Knox, described as ' pettigougie' (there were certainly enough children to warrant having him). The pollable persons record (SRO GD/86/77OA) also mentions two other relatives living there. One of these can be easily identified: she was Jane, sister of the deceased Sir Andrew Ker of Cavers. and therefore an aunt of the present laird's wife. ' Mrs. Christian Ker, given no description, could either have been another such aunt, or else Cavers' sister (for no one is given the spelling Carre in the list of pollable persons in this establishment). Her positioning in the list may make it slightly more likely that she is the laird's sister, but her frequent need for Dr. Abernethy's help (e.g. 27 March 1695, when she is still troubled with fits of her ague, and on 5 April 1696 when she is given a vomit) would lend support to the other possibility. When on 11 June 1694 he reports that Dr. Abernethy had been sent for to go to Nisbet ' to Mrs. Margaret who was ill' it could be either the laird's wife or daughter who was meant, but the former seems much the more likely. To see Robie on 22 June 1694 it was the two youngest boys, James and Thomas, who came.

Apart from the Cavers family, the easiest of the Carre/Ker group to identify is Sir William Ker 3rd Baronet of Greenhead, married to Jean Cockburn, said to be ' not improbably a daughter of Sir James Cockburn of Ryslaw by his second wife Jean, daughter of Andrew Ker of Lintoun ' (GEC). On 10 July 1694 he, his brother Gilbert and five others came to Kimmerghame on their way to meet the Countess of Roxburgh and the Earl her son who were going to Scarborough Wells. On 30 April 1695 the diarist met Sir William and a group of Teviotdale people again going to meet the Earl of Roxburgh. Both encounters were clearly brief.

However, there was rather more to it than this. For at the end of the entry for 10 July 1694 there is what seems at first a rather odd sentence. 'He desired me to tell Julian his Lady Desired her to goe to her till he came home' To explain this, we have to identify the three people to whom the diarist merely attaches the territorial designation 'Lintoun'. 'Old Lintoun' must have been Andrew Ker and 'young Lintoun' his son Henry. The two of them sold the Lintoun estate in co. Roxburgh to Andrew Pringle of Clifton in 1699, but at the time this section of George Home's diary was written this was a Ker estate and not a Pringle one. The third person whom we have to identify does not appear in the diary because she had died (in March 1686). Variously referred to in earlier manuscript material relating to George Home, and in Crossrig, as 'old Lady Lintoun' or 'Aunt Lintoun', she was the widow of the Andrew Ker of Lintoun who predeceased her in the 1680's. If the GEC attribution quoted earlier is correct, she was the mother of Sir William Ker of Greenhead's Lady. And as we know from Crossrig (p.41) that George Home's two sisters had stayed with old Lady Lintoun for most of the time the diarist was in France (May 1684 to January 1687), they must have been in the same house that was home to Lady Greenhead before her marriage. What more natural, therefore, than to ask Julian, one of George Home's two sisters, to go and stay with a friend in whose mother's home she had lived for two years ten years before? All that still needs explanation is the link between the Homes of Blackadder and 'old Lady Lintoun'. She was, as we have said, the widow of Andrew Ker of Lintoun who predeceased her in the 1680's; she had in fact been born a Home, and was a daughter of the Sir John Home of Blackadder who married a Haldane of Gleneagles. So she was, as a result, Crossrig's aunt and George Home's great aunt.

The Earl of Roxburgh whom the Teviotdale people were on their way to join was the 4th Earl, Robert Ker, who would only be about 17 years old then. His father had been drowned on 6 May 1682 in the wreck off Yarmouth of the *Gloucester* carrying the Duke of York and others to Leith. His widowed mother Countess Margaret was about 37 at this time. The Earl only lived until 13 July 1696, dying unmarried and in his 19th year at Brussels. His tutor, who accompanied him on his visits to the Continent, was Patrick Cockburn. One other link between the Ker and the Home groups with whom the diary is concerned has already been explained in dealing with the Homes of Ninewells. As we saw there, the diarist's Aunt Ninewells married a second husband after the death of her first one in 1659. This second husband was William Ker, uncle to Sir William Ker of Greenhead whom, as we said a paragraph or two above, the diarist encountered on 10 July 1694 and on 30 April 1695, when groups of Teviotdale people were on their way to meet the Earl of Roxburgh.

3) THE COCKBURNS

As we have already seen, Veitch states that in Berwickshire or the Mers ' the considerablest Names ' are the Humes and the Cockburns. He is particularly eloquent about the Langtoun seat. 'On this water [Langtoun Water] stands the Dwelling of Sir Archibald Cockburn of Langtoun, build by the present Laird, a stately House commodiously contriv'd with all Office houses, large stables and stable - Court, large Avenues, Orchard, Bowling Green, Garden, Woods, Planting and variety of Parks, whereby the Ground is wonderfully improven' (p.180). Its magnificence is reflected when Sir Archibald is assessed for no fewer than 23 hearths for that house. In the case of Borthwick House nearby, another Cockburn seat, rated for 11 hearths, both Patrick and his wife Isobel Cockburn had died in 1682; before that George Home's sister Isobel had stayed there with her Aunt Borthwick, and afterwards Crossrig looked after the two Borthwick children, who were his nephew and niece.

Sir Archibald, who had built Langtoun, was the 4th Baronet, succeeding his elder brother in 1657 or so, and was MP for Berwickshire in 1678, 1685-86, 1689 and 1702, dying in 1705. His first wife was Marion, daughter of John Sinclair the younger of Stevenson; and his second was Anna, daughter of Sir Thomas Stewart of Coltness. The diary entry of 9 September 1695 refers to his son, Captain Cockburn, who lived in Duns, having had his cellar broken into; other references include fox and hare hunting with greyhounds. This son did not become laird, as the Sir Archibald who succeeded to the baronetcy in 1705 was an earlier laird's grandson. The other Cockburns mentioned in this section of the diary cannot easily be allocated to particular branches of the family. Patrick and Alexander, Edinburgh based, seem to have been writers. Sam Cockburn, with whom, along with two other friends, the diarist dined in Rosses in Edinburgh on 4 July 1695, is also difficult to identify. One last Cockburn is the Sophia whose burial the diarist attended on 15 February 1695. Because of her apparent connection with the Annandales, she is grouped in these explanatory notes with the Johnstones.

It may seem odd that George Home appears to have had no dealings in this section of the diary with two other major Berwickshire branches of this family - the Cockburns of that ilk, whose seat was Duns Castle, an 18-hearth mansion, and the Cockburns of Ryslaw. Later volumes of the diary, however, show more contact between George Home and these Cockburns. Thus Lady Ryslaw's death on 8 November 1701 is reported.

4) THE DOUGLASSES

They were, and had been for a long time, an important group of families in Edinburgh and the Borders. The one most frequently mentioned in this section of the diary is Henry Douglas of Freershaw (co. Roxburgh), but nearly always it is to report efforts on his part to get payment from the diarist and others, or to record efforts on their part to postpone or avoid such payment. The debt does not seem to have been of very long standing, for there is no mention of Henry Douglas in the lists George Home made in the 1680's of those to whom he owed money. One of Henry's sons, George Douglas, who was born in 1673 and lived to the age of 80, was an advocate in Edinburgh; and the Freershaw estate was still owned by a Henry Douglas around 1770.

Another Douglas with whom the diarist had contact (e.g. on 17 July 1694) was James Douglas of Earnslaw in Berwickshire, Writer to His Majesty's Privy Seal, who had married Grace Graden in Edinburgh in January 1668. He died in July 1699 intestate, his wife having died earlier. The diarist remarks, when attending the burial of Sir John Kirkaldy of Grange on 14 January 1696, that 'he was Earnslaw Cusen German'.

There is a fleeting reference to the Marquess of Douglas (on 20 July 1694), whom we know to have had such difficulty in managing his affairs that shortly before he died in 1699 a commission was appointed to look after them. George Home quite often saw Mr. Daniel Douglas, clearly a biblical scholar and also a good story teller - on 18 January 1695 ' he spoke by way of Rapsodie but very pleasantly'. He was sometimes found at Blackadder (formerly Douglas territory) and sometimes at Hutton Hall; perhaps he was related to Marie Douglass Lady Hiltone. Mr Douglas, Chamberlain to the Earl of Roxburgh, was one of the party calling at Kimmerghame on 10 July 1694 on the way to a meeting with the Earl and his mother on a trip to Scarborough Wells. Sir William Douglas, who comes into the diary because of correspondence Polwarth had with him (3 September 1695) was in command of a regiment disbanded some years later. Mr Archibald Douglas, one of several people with whom the diarist dined in Arnotts when in Edinburgh on 6 February 1695, was probably the minister at Saltoun. And the Marie Douglass who had married Joseph Johnstone will be discussed with the Johnstones, along with her Douglass sister Lady Kettlestone..

Finally, we learn from the diarist that Helen Douglas was Whytefeild's niece, so that either he or his wife Margaret Ramsay must have had a sister who married a Douglas, though of which branch of that family is uncertain.

5) THE ELIOTTS AND ELLIOTS

Surprisingly few members of this important family are mentioned in this section of the diary. Two of the four people concerned are from the Stobs branch. When in Edinburgh in June 1695 the diarist is told about, and invited to a wedding. Baillie Home's daughter is marrying 'Will. Elliot a brother of Stobs ane merchant in this toune' (28 June 1695). Identification of the bridegroom is, however, unexpectedly difficult. For 'Stobs' could on the face of it mean the 1st Baronet Sir Gilbert, or his eldest son by his first marriage, the 2nd Baronet Sir William who succeeded him in the 1680's, or *his* son Sir Gilbert the 3rd Baronet (who succeeded his father in 1694). The third possibility is unlikely, for it would make the bridegroom too young; the first would make him far too old; so we have to fall back on his being a *son* of Sir Gilbert the 1st Baronet by his second wife Magdalen Nicolson. She kept an account book from 1671 to 1693, the manuscript of which has survived (NLS MS2987); see Kelsall pp. 158-62. There is a related identification problem with the Sir William Elliot who was 'sadly tormented wt a gravill' on 13 October 1695. For though it would be natural to suppose he must have been the 2nd Baronet of Stobs, he had already died (if we accept the GEC date) in 1694.

Fortunately no such difficulties arise with the fourth member of this group mentioned, Dr Gideon Elliot of North Sinton, who comes from a different branch, the Elliots of Bewlie. Thomas, the laird who died in 1696, was, a resourceful farmer, and he and his wife Margaret (daughter of William Scott of Chamberlain Newton) had three sons and two daughters. Gideon was the third son, was apprenticed to a surgeon in October 1681 and ten years later married an heiress,

Margaret Cunningham of North Sinton. He was highly successful in his chosen field of work, and we find mention of him almost everywhere. Foulis refers several times to Gideon Elliot's forthcoming marriage to Jean Lock in 1705, his second venture into matrimony. The Edinburgh Burgh Records report his being Deacon of the Craft of Surgeons in September 1693 and thereafter annually into the 1700s, except for 1697 when he was fined for declining office. He also became one of the Commissioners to the Convention of Royal Burghs, as Convenor of Trades. In July 1701 'Gideon Elliot chirurgeon apothecarie and present deacon conveener' had approved his account of £949-6s Scots ' for performing of cures and furnishing of droges and medicaments be him to the souldiers of the Touns guard at the late rable and dreadfull fyre and other occasions' (p.284). References in the diary start on 8 June 1694, when George Home writes asking him to 'get me some slips of Jerry sage from Mr. Southerland'. This was the 'maister of the Physick garden'; see Section III on that topic under that date. Gideon Elliot appears in the diary again on 9 April 1695, when we learn that he must have attended John Home of Ninewells before he died. Finally in this section of the diary, on 19 February 1696 'I caused Gideon Elliot to put in ane issue in my left Shoulder whi has been out some time'.

6) THE JOHNSTONES

George Home, in common with all his friends and relatives in Berwickshire, was always closely involved with the Johnstones of Hilton. Joseph, the laird whose grandfather, after marrying one of the Homes of Polwarth, had in 1633 purchased the estate of Hilton, had apparently been killed following a game of cards at the Hirsel in December 1683. More tragedy was to follow some eleven years later. For the new laird, another Joseph, died unexpectedly when still comparatively young. George Home reports on 20 January 1695 that he was dead and buried; 'he was at the Colledge at Edr'. His death prompts Sir John Home of Blackadder to recount the story the diarist tells two days later, in which the young laird's failure to live longer is made out to be part of God's punishment of the Johnstone family for having paid far too little to the Home who sold them Hilton more than sixty years before. 'Young Abbey, now Minister of Aitone' who told this tale to Thomas Pringle, was a younger brother of Alexander Home, laird of Abbey St. Bathans.

On 2 May 1695 preliminary moves to serve the next in line, Robert Johnstone, heir to his brother and father are mentioned. Marie Douglass (Lady Hiltone in the diary) had another son, John, and also three daughters, Katherine, Rachel and Susannah (Shusy). The first of the daughters married a Home of Manderston ('Shury Mangerstone') and apparently at some point they went to live at Langhame. On 13 January 1695 we learn that she had, about a month ago, been brought to bed of a daughter (it was in fact a son). Things did not go smoothly here either, for later in the diary we hear that Shury fell ill, went to England where he was fed on ass's milk, and died there. And their only child did not reach adult life, dying in April 1699.

There were other misfortunes in the family. For Marie Douglass's sister Elizabeth had married the laird of Kettlestone, and he became mentally deranged. This had happened before the diary begins, but we learn of it from letters that have survived both from Marie herself (SRO GD 158/1015) and from Grisel Kar, Polwarth's wife, who tried to raise money and support for her. By the time of the diary Elizabeth lost her son, when he was only ten years old, which George Home reports on 17 February 1696: 'yesterday died John Stuart the Lady Kettlestons son a boy of about 10 years of age'. A few months earlier, in the list of pollable persons in the parish of Hutton dated 12 November 1695 (SRO GD 158/679), 'Elizabeth Douglass her sister', is shown as living with Marie Douglass at Hutton Hall (a house of comparable size to those of Polwarth, Blackadder and Cavers, but with rather fewer living-in servants).

Marie herself seemed, as we see from the diary, to be always going around visiting friends, usually accompanied on these trips (which had to be on horseback, as she had no coach) by several of her children. She was also often in Edinburgh, where her brother-in-law Patrick Johnstone (the murdered Joseph's brother) had since 1677 established himself as a major figure. George Home, on 1 January 1696, says ' I went at night and visit Pa: Johnstone (now Bailiff) and his wife'; he does not mention that he was one of the Hilton Johnstones. A fuller account of this remarkable lady will be found in Kelsall, pp.49-52.

The other Johnstone whom the diarist frequently mentions is William 4th Earl (and afterwards 1st Marquess) of Annandale. Notorious for changing sides and double dealing in the political arena, his behaviour in more mundane matters was, if we take the diary record as reliable, little better. Two of these episodes require some elucidation.

1) *5 February 1695*, when there was a debate in Committee among the Earl of Home's creditors (of whom Annandale was one), he 'made a discourse and told he had been at a great losse by the family of Home and that he was very ill requited for that the family of Coldenknows would never have succeeded in the Earldome of Home without his assistance'. As the events he is referring to took place in 1633 (when James Home, a distant cousin of the 2nd Earl, and heir of the Homes of Coldenknows, was served heir male in general to him) and 1636 (when he obtained a new charter ratifying all the honours enjoyed by his predecessors to him and his heirs male), Annandale, who was not born then, can hardly have claimed that ' his assistance ' played any part in the outcome. What he probably meant was that John Murray, the 1st Earl of Annandale (a great favourite of James IV and I, of whom it has been unkindly said that ' he was by no means nice as to whom he sold his influence, or from whom he took money'), had been helpful to the

Coldenknows family at that time. Yet how the Annandale who was George Home's contemporary could claim any credit for this is very strange, for he was a Johnstone and not a Murray, his father James Johnstone having merely received a grant of the Earldom of Annandale in 1661, the *Murray* Annandale peerage having become extinct in 1658. From what George Home says of the affair, it seems clear that Annandale's outburst gained little support.

2) *15 February 1695* ' At 4 I went to Sophia Cockburn's buriall'. George's interest in the affair is that he thinks Sophia Cockburn's mother was a daughter of his grandaunt Sophia Home (who had become Lady Hilton by marrying Joseph Johnstone, 1st of Hilton). If this is so, however, it must have been by his grandaunt's *second* marriage, if such a marriage took place. The *Annandale* connection with Sophia Cockburn is, he says, that she was a niece of Annandale's Lady's Mother. Annandale's Lady's Mother was in fact Sophia, daughter of one of the Hilton Johnstones, who married John, one of the Fairholmes of Craigiehall. The diarist was critical of the Annandales for treating Sophia Cockburn (who had lived with them until her death) as a servant rather than either a relative or a friend, and for making her pay for her board when she had little money. Whether she was related in the way he suggests both to them and to him cannot be clearly established from the evidence he provides.

The remaining Johnstones mentioned in the diary can be identified as the diarist's tenants or servants except for Captain Johnstone of Westerhall where it was simply a matter of the best price being discussed when a horse was being sold.

7) THE PRINGLES

Most of the Pringles mentioned in this section of the diary are from one seat, Stichell. Veitch, writing in 1682-85 talks of ' the parish of Stitchell in Teviotdale, belonging to Sir Robert Pringle, where there is a considerable House, Avenues, Parks and Planting stately seated on a rising ground' (p.177). Manuscript tax records tell us it had 21 hearths in February 1694, which puts it on an equal footing with the Floors house. Sir Robert, the first Baronet, (who died in 1692) married in 1660 Margaret, daughter of the late Sir John Hope, a Senator of the College of Justice, and they had nineteen children, of whom thirteen reached adult life. George mentions six of these. Sir John, who became laird and 2nd Baronet on the death of his father, was born in 1662 and died in 1721. In 1685 he had married Magdalen only daughter of the late Sir Gilbert Eliott of Stobs. The second son, Walter, had become an advocate in 1688 and later, as Sir Walter, became Lord Newhall, dying in 1736. The third son Robert had, after studying at the University of Leyden, taken service under William of Orange, laid down his commission, was admitted as an advocate in Edinburgh in 1691, and was made Under-Secretary in the 1696 administration, which meant attending King William in his campaigns. With the fourth son, Thomas, a Writer to the Signet, George Home more frequently had dealings.

Of Robert the 1st Baronet's daughters, Katherine had married George Home's close friend and relative Sir John Home of Blackadder only a year or two before, so there are naturally numerous references to her in the diary. For another daughter, Anne, the entry for 17 February 1696 tells of her having 'been long under a Rheumatisme which turned in end to a decay' and consequent death unmarried.

By comparison with the Stitchell group, there is relatively little that can be said about the other Pringles mentioned in the diary. Greenknow, 4 miles S.W. of Greenlaw in Berwickshire, was a 12-hearth seat, where James Pringle and his family were living, while his widowed mother (Janet Pringle, one of the Torwoodlee branch) lived nearby in her house in Rumeltoun with half that number of hearths. His father had been Walter, and it is not quite clear where the *George* of Greenknow mentioned in the diary entry of 8 March 1695 fits in. Clifton in co. Roxburgh, was another Pringle seat, where Robert was succeeded by his brother Andrew, the laird at the time of the diary entry of 10 July 1694, when 'Young Clifton' and others called on George Home. This is the laird's son Robert, who had in 1687 married his cousin Janet, only daughter of his late uncle Robert, by which marriage, it appears, all the family estates were united. Apart from the notary in Kelso, Thomas Pringle, whom the diarist consulted, no other Pringle appears to be mentioned in this two-year section of the diary.

8) THE RUTHERFORDS

Of this very old-established Border family, with many estates (particularly in co. Roxburgh) the only large proprietors mentioned in this section of the diary are Andrew, laird of Edgerstone and his brother, who was living at Whytbank but later became Rutherford of Bowland (and so an ancestor of Sir Walter Scott). Edgerstone's house was a modest 7-hearth one compared with 14 hearths in the case of Rutherford of that ilk. George Home's main interest in Andrew and Robert seems to be that they were willing to lend money, on proper security, to him and his brother David (11 and 12 February 1696). The other Rutherfords featuring in this part of the diary are Thomas and his son, both tenants of George Home, where the main problems are local complaints (21 May and 16 June 1694) or securing payment of overdue rent (28 and 30 July); though an element of compassion for the father creeps in on 30 March 1695, as he is now very old being past 77 and his sight is beginning to fail him.

9) THE TROTTERS

In 19th century editions of Burke's Landed Gentry the opening sentence relating to the lineage of this family is invariably this. 'The surname of Trotter is of considerable antiquity in Scotland, the estates of the family of this name being chiefly in Berwickshire'. Although Mortonhall in Midlothian was a very important Trotter seat, Alexander Trotter, the first of this family mentioned in the diary about whom we can be definite, was the new laird of Kettlesheil in Berwickshire, who succeeded his father in 1693 and lived in Charterhall, which with office houses was assessed for nine hearths. Veitch's description of it is short - 'a Dwelling belonging to a gentleman of the name of Trotter'. Some years after George Home died, this Alexander married a daughter of Sir Robert Steuart, 1st Baronet of Allanbank. Another member of this branch of the family who appears quite frequently in later volumes of the diary is Dr.Trotter, who was to marry George Home's sister Julian in 1698.

The other people of this name in the present section of the diary cannot be quite so positively identified. The Mr. Trotter mentioned on 16 November 1695 is clearly a writer, and can probably be taken to be Robert Trotter, an Edinburgh writer at this time. William Trotter, whose daughter was married to his factor John or James Denholme, seems likely to have been a laird with a Berwickshire estate. George paid him interest twice a year on a loan. This may have been a long-standing debt originally contracted by the diarist or his father (along with a Johnstone of Hilton and a Hume of Polwarth) when they borrowed from Alexander Trotter, perhaps the father of the William Trotter to whom the interest is still being paid. There are frequent references to Elshy Trotter, about whom all we know is that he had a wife and a daughter Jane and seems to have lived in Kelso. Neither he nor William, unfortunately, can be identified with any of the small number of Trotters to be found in the surviving poll and hearth tax records of the relevant date and area.

Finally, the diarist tells us something about one more person of this name. On 25 March 1696 he mentions John Trotter *in* (not *of*) Ayton's burial. This can be identified as the John Trotter ' fewar and gentilman' in the manuscript list of pollable persons (SRO GD 86/77OA) living there just before this with his wife Ann; his poll tax assessment was only £3-12-0 as against the £24-6-0 of people who were lairds.

10) THE WADDELLS

This group is significantly different from any of those discussed so far. For though Waddells clearly formed an important part of George Home's social network, the range of contexts in which they appear in his diary is much narrower than it is with the other family groups. When he needed medical or legal help he does not seem to have turned to anyone of this name. On his visits to Edinburgh, Waddells do not figure amongst those joining him on either social or business occasions, and the name does not occur in Foulis nor in the Edinburgh Burgh Records. More surprisingly still, Veitch does not give them a single mention. And despite the constant inter-marrying amongst Border families, this name seems to occur relatively rarely in the pedigree of the other groups.

So who were the Waddells on roughly the same social level as the diarist? In terms of the frequency with which he turns up, Mr. Adam, minister at Whitsome, comes to the top of the list. He lived at Whitsome with his mother and had at least two brothers, Mr. George and Mr. Andrew; his sister was Mrs. Comry. He was a constant visitor to Kimmerghame, sometimes staying three days - clearly a very close friend indeed, with a major common interest in exchanging books (and presumably views about them). Adam's brother Andrew must have been the Mr. Andrew Waddell who is described in the manuscript list of pollable persons in November 1695 (SRO GD 158/679) as being on the staff of Marie Douglas Lady Hiltone as 'governour of Hiltone' (Robert Johnstone, her son), whose wage was sixty pounds a year. His other brother George may have served the Earl of Home in a similar capacity, perhaps only occasionally, depending on how we interpret the account of George Home's visit to the Hirsel on 19 June 1694. ' I see my Lord Dunglasse who is a very pretty boy. I went and took a turn in the garden wt Mr. Geo:Waddell who waits on him.' Was he merely waiting to see him, or was he rather more involved? It may or may not be significant that on 17 January 1695 George Home reports ' Mr. Adam Waddell sent to me for a french Dictionary for his Brother George'.

Finally, Dr.Waddell appears in the diary in a context not of a specifically medical character. For on 7 June 1694 a group of people turn up at Kimmerghame on their way to Wintone. The group consists of Dr. Waddell and his wife and Mr. Adam and Dr.Comry, and they are going there ' the Earl having made him [Dr. Waddell] Chamberlaine to his Estate'. The 4th Earl of Winton, George Seton, who had fought under Monmouth at Bothwell Bridge in 1679, and with the Duke of York survived the wreck of the *Gloucester* on 6 May 1682, went to Germany in June 1689 on grounds of ill-health. He was now coming home after a very long absence, and Dr. Waddell's appointment as Chamberlain may well have been part of the process of getting his estates back to a more satisfactory condition. Being with Mr. Adam Waddell suggests that Dr. Waddell was a member of that family circle, possibly another brother. It may or may not be significant that a document dated 1739 (SRO GD 158/160) speaks of 'the deceased Mr. Andrew Waddell surgeon in Dunse' whose only son was Mr. David Waddell.

11) OTHERS

a) Described as Earls or Lords

ANNANDALE, E. William Johnstone, 4th Earl and afterwards 1st Marquess. See II 6).

ANSTRUTHER, Lo. Sir William Anstruther of Anstruther, sometime a Lord of Justiciary, married to Helen, daughter of John Hamilton, 4th Earl of Haddington. He was one of five brothers, all of whom were knighted; he died in 1711.

ARNISTONE, Lo. Robert Dundas, an eminent lawyer appointed Judge of the Court of Session in 1689 who filled that office for 37 years. He was married to Margaret, daughter of Sir Robert Sinclair of Stevenson, so it was natural that the diarist should report that he had 'gone to Stevensone wt his Lady' on 23 August 1695.

CARDROSSE, Lo. David Erskine, 4th Lord Cardross, born 1672, succeeded to the title 1693.

CASTLEHILL, Lo. Sir John Lockhart, Lord Castlehill of the Court of Session. Foulis attended his burial on 27 July 1696.

CRAWFORD Lo. William Lindsay, 18th Earl of Crawford and Earl of Lindsay. Born 1644. He was a principal leader in the Presbyterian party, and President of the Council 1689-93. He married Henrietta, daughter of the 2nd Earl of Dunfermline. He and George Home discussed gardening when they met in George Mosman's bookshop; Lindsay was a keen and knowledgeable gardener. Died in 1698.

CROSRIG, Lo. Sir David Home, made Lord of Session in 1689. See II 1) a).

EDMISTONE, Lo. John Wauchope of Edmonstone, Lord Edmonstone, Senator of the College of Justice.

FESDO, Lo. Sir John Falconer of Phesdo was made a Lord of Session in 1689.

FOUNTAINHALL, Lo. Sir John Lauder appointed a Lord of Session 1689, then a Lord of Justiciary in 1690 (but resigned the latter on health grounds 1693). Mainly known as a Chronicler - his diary was printed in full by the Bannatyne Club in 1840. He was MP for co. Haddington 1685-1707.

GOSFORD, Lo. Sir Peter Wedderburn, Lord of Session.

HADDINGTON, E. Thomas Hamilton, 6th Earl of Haddington. Born 1680, married Helen Hope, daughter of Lady Margaret Leslie. Died 1735.

HALCRAIG, Lo. Sir John Hamilton, son of Sir John Hamilton of Halcraig and Jean daughter of William Mure of Glanderstone. He took his seat as Lord of Session in 1689. Father and son were both imprisoned after Bothwell Bridge.

HARCASSE, Lo. Sir Roger Hog of Harcarse in the parish of Fogo, Berwickshire. The house was described by Anon. as 'Harkeis a considerable dwelling', and was a 14-hearth establishment. Sir Roger Hog was born c. 1635, was appointed a Lord of Session and knighted in November 1677; in the following year he became a Lord of Justiciary.   He married Jean, daughter of Sir Alexander Don, 1st Baronet of Newton in 1685. In 1688 Lord Harcarse fell under a cloud over his decision in matters dealing with the young Marquis of Montrose, and was removed from the bench by James II. The latter part of his life was spent in retirement, and he died in 1700.

HATTON, Lo. The context suggests that the diarist probably meant to write 'Halton', in which case this is John Maitland, sometime Lauder, an advocate made a Lord of Session in 1689, first styled Lord Ravelrig and then Lord Halton.   His elder brother Richard Maitland, 4th Earl of Lauderdale went to France with James II in 1689, was outlawed, and died childless in Paris in 1695. John then succeeded his brother, becoming 5th Earl. He was MP for Midlothian 1685-86 and 1689-96. Alternatively, if the diarist meant Hatton (in the Parish of Ratho, Midlothian), the hearth tax rolls refer to ' The Lord Hatton's lands' there. But in Peerage volumes the only possible person mentioned is Christopher Hatton, Viscount Hatton of Gretton in Northamptonshire.

JEDBURGH, Lo. William Kerr, born c.1661 who succeeded to the title on the death of his cousin Robert Kerr.

MERSINGTON, Lo. Alexander Swinton, a Lord of Session appointed to the bench, June 1682. Uncle of the diarist's great friend Sir John Swinton. When at his seat in Berwickshire he lived in an 11-hearth house.

NEWBAITH, Lo. Must be John Baird of Newbyth, advocate, made Senator of the College of Justice in 1689. The diarist's spelling is the same as that in an undated Description of East Lothian 'Newbaith was a Fort'.

OXFORD, Lo. Had a very fine property in Cranstone, which had 33 hearths. Foulis reports 'Lady Oxford's buriall' on 6 November 1696.

PITTMEDDEN, Lo. Sir Alexander Seton of Pittmedden, Lord of Session, living in Edinburgh with his father-in-law Mr. William Lauder, their wives, 8 children and 5 servants (2 men and 3 women) (Wood p.61). The Mr. William Lauder whose death the diarist reports on 1 December 1695 is Lord Pittmedden's father-in-law, not his father.

POLWARTH, Lo. Sir Patrick Hume. See II 1) b).

PRESMENNEN, Lo. Robert Hamilton of Presmennon born 1622. He was appointed a Lord of Session in 1689 and, as the diarist tells us, died in November 1695 aged 73. Lord Presmennon's second son, James, was Town Clerk in Edinburgh 1683, and became Lord Pencaitland.

RAITH, Lo. Alexander Melville, styled Lord Raith. He was the eldest son of George, Earl of Melville. He married Barbara, daughter of Walter Dundas of that ilk. From 1689 to 98 he held the post of Treasurer Depute.

RANKILLAR, Lo. Archibald Hope was the second son of Sir John Hope, Lord Craighall, a Scottish judge. He was appointed a Lord of Session in 1689 and Lord of Justiciary in 1690, taking the title of Lord Rankeillor. It was he who bought the estate from Sir David Sibbald, 2nd Baronet of Rankeillor.

WINTONE, E. George Seton, 4th Earl of Winton. He was born in 1650 and succeeded to his grandfather's estates in 1653 and 55. He fought at Bothwell Bridge under Monmouth: He attended some of the Bank meetings in Edinburgh. He was married several times. He died in 1703.

WHYTELAW, Lo. Sir William Hamilton, Lord Whytelaw of the Court of Session.

b) Others, not so described, classified by name and not by territory.

ABERNETHY Dr. When medical help was required George Home and his fellow lairds would send for Dr. Abernethy. He lived in Kelso, so a servant would be despatched on horseback with a letter for the doctor. It was fortunate if he was at home; if he was out visiting a patient the letter had to be left for his return, and there might well be a delay of several days before he could attend to the message. The distances involved in the doctor's travels often meant that he stayed one night at one patient's home, then proceeded to the next. Dr. Abernethy was more than the family doctor as far as George Home was concerned, he was a personal friend with common interests in reading and other matters. On 15 October 1695 we are told he 'went to Newcastle being to goe ther to the fair and see Mr. Strauchan his brother in law and his sister'.

AIKMAN, Mr. Tho. This is Thomas Aikman of Brimbleton, a Writer to the Signet. He was 2nd son of John Aikman of Cairnie. His second marriage, in 1687, was to Margaret, daughter of James Winram of Liberton.

ARESKINE, Mr. Wm. This is William Erskine, brother of Lord Cardross. He sold wine in Leith.

BAILLIE, See II 1) b) for this family.

BAYLIE, Ro. This is the baby son of George and Grisell Baillie. See II 1)b).

BELSHESSE, Sandy. 'Alexander Belches Esq., Advocate', wrote the preface to one of Crossrig's books. Foulis had dinner with Cairnie and ' alexr belshes' on 27 July 1698, and was with him on 15 March 1705.

BENNET, Sir William, 1st Baronet of Grubet (co. Roxburgh).

BETHUN, Mr. John. An Advocate, William Bethune (2nd son of Robert Bethune), married a daughter of Andrew Bethune of Blebo, and died in 1699. Mr. John may have been a member of one of these families.

BLACKWOOD, Mr. Robert. This is the Edinburgh merchant who also played a very active part in establishing the Company of Scotland Trading to Africa and the Indies (one of its two real founders).

BORTHWICK, Hary of Pilmer. This is the laird of Pilmuir, *de jure* 13th Lord Borthwick. Difficulty only arises from the diarist's remark (20 May

1695) that he was Sandy Home's son-in-law; for we know that in fact he married Mary, daughter of Sir Robert Pringle. It seems at first sight impossible to reconcile this diary entry with the known facts. Reconciliation is, however, possible by taking account of Harry's father, William Borthwick the Edinburgh surgeon, having married a 3rd time after Harry's mother died. For this 3rd wife was Euphame Young, whom he married in 1682; and, some years after his death in 1689, she, in 1693, married Alexander Home WS as his second wife. So Harry Borthwick was in fact the step-son of Sandy Home's second wife, which (at this time) justifies the diarist's description of him as Sandy Home's son-in-law. Three years after George Home himself died, Captain Harry Borthwick was mortally wounded at Ramillies.

BROUN, Sir George. This is the 2nd Baronet of Colstone co. Haddington, who succeeded his father Sir Patrick Broun in 1688.

BROUN, the laird of Blackburn in Berwickshire.

BROUN, Heugh. 'Clerk to the Committy for the Old Pole'.

BRYMER, of Newtone in Fife or Edrom. This is John Brymer, the laird living in the 9-hearth Edrom House with his Lady, David and William their sons, Rachel, Mary, Isobell and Katherine their daughters, and three men and five women as servants (SRO GD86/770A).

BURNET, Sr Tho. 3rd Baronet of Leys.

BURNETT, Dr. This is Sir Thomas Burnett, 'Their majesties Physician'. He lived in a large seven-hearth establishment in Edinburgh with his wife and grown-up family (son, and two daughters and their husbands) as well as various other relatives. (Wood p.39)

CARRE, see II 2).

CLERK, Sr John of Pennicook, was created Baronet in 1679, and after 1688 represented the shire of Edinburgh as an M.P. Died in 1722 aged 73. His son's memoirs, 1676-1755, were published by the Scottish History Society in 1891.

COCHRAN, Sr John of Ochiltree, 2nd son of Wm. 1st Earl of Dundonald, married Mary, daughter of Sir William Strickland of Boynton, Yorks. He was a farmer of the Poll Tax, and in 1695 was committed to prison. Died 1695.

COCKBURN, see II 3).

COMRY, Dr. married to Mr. Adam Waddell's sister, as the diarist tells us.

CRAIG, Mr. John, writer in Edinburgh.

CRAIK, John of Stuartone. He bought the estate from Friershaw in December 1695.

CUNNINGHAME, Sr William of Cunninghamhead. He succeeded to the Baronetcy in 1670.

DAICK, A writer in Edinburgh.

DAES, Mr. James. Crossrig (p.39) mentions ' Mr. James Daes of Coldinknows' performing legal duties in 1686, so that the diarist's reference to 'Coldenknows' on 10 March, and to 'Mr. James Daes's chamber' on 20 July must refer to the same person. Earlier in the century the estate belonged to a branch of the Home family. 'Upon Leiderside stands the ancient House of Coldinknows' (Veitch. p.175).

DALRYMPLE, Mr. Heugh, was a writer in Edinburgh who became Commissary Dalrymple.

DICKSON, Mr. John of Antonshill. Though he seems only to have one mention in this section of the diary, he is to become an important figure in it, first as George Home's and later as Marchmont's factor. See Kelsall, where some of his manuscript accounts are discussed. Later on he married a daughter (Katherine Hepburn) of one of the diarist's aunts.

DICKSONE Sir Robert of Sornbeg, co. Ayr. Had only become the 1st Baronet nine months previously. Had 'acquired considerable property in Ayrshire and in West and Mid Lothian' (GEC).

DOUGLAS See II 4).

DUNDAS, Al. Son of Katherine Hamilton, Lady Hervistone and Robert Dundas of Hervistone. She now lived in Edinburgh, a widow with her three surviving children and one woman servant. (Wood p.48) At one time Ann Cokeburn (Cockburn) for whom Crossrig was responsible, had boarded with her (p.65).

DUNDAS Dr.   This Edinburgh physician, Dr. Alexander Dundas, crops up
    everywhere: he even joins a group of people including Crossrig,
    concerned with the 'reformation of manners'.   References to him can
    also be found in Grisell Baillie and Foulis.

ELLIOT Gideon   }
                                           }   See II 5)
ELLIOTT Sir Gilbert   }

ELLISS, Mr. Tho. A son of the laird of Southsyde (Gala Water). On 30 November
    1704, Foulis had 'a mutchkin wormit wine wt Th. Eleis' (p.360). He also
    went hunting with the laird himself in September of that year (p 357).

FOULIS, Lady Anne.   Daughter of Walter Dundas of that ilk.   She married Sir
    John Foulis of Ravelston on 28 August 1690.   On 10 January 1696 Meg
    Home's report of her death is given - she was his 2nd wife, he married a
    3rd in March 1697 and a 4th in September 1705.

FRANK, Mr. John,   of Bughtrig, only son of John Frank, bailie of Peebles.   A
    Writer to the Signet.   Died 1699.

GALBRETH James   }
GALBRATH James of Balgare   }
        It is not clear whether the former, to whose man the diarist paid the
    interest due to Lady Tarsappie on 18 July 1694, is the same as the latter,
    who is part of the Ninewells story from February 1695 onwards.   The
    Galbraiths of Balgair, co. Stirling (the usual spelling) were cadets of the
    Galbraiths of Culchurch.   Foulis had 'a chopin wine wt Ja nicols and
    James Galbraith, etc' on 17 August 1681; he was probably the first of
    the two in the diary, and as there is no mention of Balgair he may have
    been a writer working in Edinburgh.

GARDNER, Geo. Writer.

GREGORY, Mr., the Mathematician.   This is not David Farquharson Gregory
    who came later, nor James (who died in 1675), but David (1661-1708).
    In the DNB he is categorised as an astronomer; full details of his life and
    work are given there.

HAIG, Anthony of Bemersyde. He had suffered a long imprisonment as a Quaker,
    resigned his estates to the Crown, but obtained a fresh charter in 1672.
    He married Jean, only daughter and heir of James Home of Hariheuch
    (Parish of Hume).   AnonVeitch. speaks of 'Beemerside an Old Estate of

the name of Higgins'; he got the name wrong despite Thomas the Rymer's prophesy that 'Tyde what may betyde Haig shall be Haig of Bemersyde'. Antoine Haig's house is assessed for 4 hearths

HAITLY, And. A contemporary of the diarist's father. This may well be the laird to whom Veitch refers in Nenthorn Parish 'The sneep a Gentlemans House by the name of Haitlie'.

HALKET, Sr Charles of Pittfirrin (co. Fife), the 2nd Baronet; was MP for Dunfermline. Died 1697.

HALL, Sr John, 1st Baronet of Dunglass who died in October 1695 and was succeeded by the 2nd Baronet - Sir James Hall. The latter was to marry Anne, Polwarth's third daughter in 1698.

HALYBURTONE, Mr. David (1639-1697). Writer to the Signet. Mr. David never married but looked after the widow (Margaret Rutherford, one of the Rutherfords of Edgerstone) and children of his brother John Halyburton of Newmains who died in 1688. John's elder son, Thomas, succeeded his father as laird; the younger son, Andrew, was only 21 years old at the time the diarist speaks of him; later he became a Writer to the Signet.

HAY, James of Caruber (co. Linlithgow). A Writer to the Signet, second son of David Hay of Woodcockdale. Foulis records on 3 October 1692 ' to Carribers sons Thomas his nurse drink monie 2-18-0'. James Hay had married the daughter of an Edinburgh goldsmith named Robertson in 1672. What must have been an older son, John, was paid a fee by Foulis for a small legal job on 1 February 1701.

HEBURN, Cat (or Ka). She was very friendly with the diarist's sister Isobel. Her mother was George Home's (and Isobel's) aunt - see II 1) a).

HENDERSONE, Mr. James of Pittadro, Writer to the Signet. He was born in 1644 and married Marion, daughter of John Foulis of Ravelston. He died in 1707.

HENDERSONE, Wm of Todrig. This estate, in the parish of Hume in Berwickshire, belonged to a McDougal at the time Veitch was writing. An earlier description of the house called it ' a Gentleman's dwelling pleasantly situate'.

HOPE, Charles of Hopetone. His father died at 32 when the *Gloucester* was wrecked near Yarmouth on 5 May 1682. Charles, born 1681, would only be 14 in 1695, but inherited large and valuable landed property (including Niddery, Winchburgh and Abercorn as well as Hopetone itself, in Linlithgow).

IRVIN, the laird of Drum. Alexander Irvine was 12th of Drum living at Drum Castle, Aberdeenshire. He had married Marjory, daughter of Forbes of Auchreddie, and died 3 January 1696. His wife had a son who died at birth.

JOHNSTONE, see II 6).

KIRKCALDY, Sir John of Grange. He was certainly the last of a distinguished line, and the diarist's attendance at his burial on 14 January 1696 enables the tentative date 1680 in GEC to be corrected. He had married Mary Ramsay in Edinburgh in 1663. Two of his predecessors, Sir James, Lord High Treasurer of Scotland who died about 1556, and his son Sir William, executed 3 August 1573, both appear in the DNB, where it is said of Sir William that 'his chivalrous resolve and the constancy of his courage have secured him a place of honour in Scottish history'.

KIRTONE, Mr. James. He was appointed to the Tolbooth Church in Edinburgh on 23 January 1691. He was George Baillie's uncle, having married his father's sister Elizabeth. George, son of James Kirtone and his wife Elizabeth, became a surgeon (appointed to the Burgh Council as such in September 1699), and not surprisingly appears in Grisell Baillie's accounts in February 1701 as being paid for his professional services.

KNOX, Mr. The one mentioned on 3 May 1695, who seems to live in Kelso, is probably John Knox, with a tax assessment of 4 hearths. The context in the entry for 6 April 1695 makes it likely that this 'Mr. Knox' is the ' Mr. William Knox pettegougie' in the list of pollable persons in John Carre's household.

LAW, Lady. She was probably Jean Campbell who married a wealthy Edinburgh goldsmith in 1663, and was the mother of John Law of Laurieston, the international financier. For further information see Kelsall pp 147-48.

LAWDER, Mr. Ro. Apparently of Beilmouth. No information on estate or laird, unless he is the Robert Lauder who appears in Foulis.

LIVISTON, Sr Tho. Sir Thomas Livingstone, born c. 1650 in Holland. He succeeded to the Baronetcy on his father's death in 1660 and served in Holland in William of Orange's campaigns. He was made Commander in Chief of the forces in Scotland, and created Viscount Teviot in 1696; the peerage became extinct on his death c. 1710/11. The hearth tax for Melrose shows he had an establishment of 12 hearths.

LOCKHART, Sr Geo. Sir George Lockhart was murdered on Edinburgh High Street, 13 March 1689, but the diarist is probably referring to a debt owing to him.

MARTINE, Sandy. Foulis drank with 'andr. martine' and others on a number of occasions.

MIDDELTONE, of Balbigny. His seat was Balbegno Castle near Laurencekirk, S.W. Kincardineshire.

MONCRIEF, Sr Tho. Sir Thomas Moncrief, a writer in Edinburgh, Foulis went with him and others to a penny wedding on 23 June 1702.

MOSMAN, Geo.   George Mosman is described in the Edinburgh Burgh Records as a stationer. The business was clearly a thriving one for we know he was a leading bookseller and also undertook printing and binding. His entry in the Edinburgh Poll Tax Record 1694 shows him as worth between 5,000 and 10,000 merks; wife, Margaret Gibb; children, John under 15, Margaret; apprentices, John Ramsay, Patrick Watson; servants, Robert Johnston at £18 a year, Grisel Aitken at £12 a year. The house had three hearths (Wood p.24)

MURRAY, Archibald of Spot. Eldest son of William Murray and Isobel Douglas. The laird of Spot's house and kilns 3 miles south of Dunbar were rated for 21 hearths (SRO E69/9). Foulis mentions 'spot' and others at 'sealling my new cloathes' on 3 September 1694.

NEWTONE, Sr. Richard. Made a Baronet in 1697, son of Richard Newton of that ilk and Polwarth's sister Julian Hume. This Newton is in co. Haddington.

NICOLSONE, Sir Thomas. The 6th Baronet of Lasswade (Midlothian) who was buried on 8 April 1693. The roup of his estate is described by the diarist on 5 May 1694.

NISBET, Dr. This is James Nisbet, surgeon in Edinburgh, who in 1705 was fined by the physicians for practising in medicine. Earlier, as deacon of the

Incorporation of Surgeons, he had ordered an apothocary, Patrick Cunningham, to appear before the magistrates for having, by blood-letting, encroached on *their* privileges. See Creswell p 114 and p 123.

NISBET of Ladykirk. It is uncertain whom the diarist means when speaking of 'Ladykirk' on 7 April 1696. Philip Nisbet, elder son of Thomas (brother of the then laird of W. Nisbet) was succeeded in 1684 by his son James, who only outlived his father by a few weeks. James' only child Margaret was heir, but did not marry until 1699. Some relative was presumably acting for her at this time.

NORVELL, Michael of Boghall (co. Linlithgow). This is the laird who was living in the Old Kirk parish of Edinburgh with a valued rent of £1000 and one manservant (for poll-tax purposes) (Wood p.58). His father George, who died in 1672, had been an advocate, and the younger son Robert (also mentioned in the diary on 1 March 1695) followed in his father's footsteps by becoming an advocate in 1683.

OSWALD, Ja. Sir James Oswald of Fingalton. Mentioned in Foulis. He was one of 'Their Majesties' Receivers'.

PATERSONE, 'Mr Patersone the great projector for trade'. From what is said in the diary entries for 14, 20 and 25 February 1696 we can be absolutely certain that this was the great William Paterson (1658-1719), founder of the Bank of England, the account of whose life and work extends to almost three pages in the DNB. He was 38 when the diarist first met him and his supreme business talents were already recognised. His reputation, and his major involvement in all the exciting business ventures of the day, mean that when ' he promises us great things in our E. and W. India trade' (25 February 1696), George Home and his friends need no further encouragement to become participators to the limit of the resources they can raise.

PATON, Bailie. William Paton was nothing if not outspoken; in November 1691 he called Sir Archibald Mure, William Menzies and George Stirling 'knaves, rascals and villains' (Edinburgh Burgh Records p 108).

PRIMROSE, Archibald of Dalmeny was a relative of the diarist. George Home's second wife was half sister to this Archibald Primrose, as they had the same father but different mothers. He crops up at various points and the diarist records having supped with him on an anniversary of Primrose's wedding day, 3 February 1695. He had, several years before, in a wedding at St. James's Westminster, married Dorothy Cressy, whose father and mother were both from Yorkshire families. Only a few years younger than George Home, he was M.P. for Edinburgh 1695-1700 and in the latter year was to become Viscount of Rosebery, Lord Primrose and Dalmeny, being made an Earl three years later.

PRINGLE, see II 7).

PURVES, Sir Alexander, 2nd Baronet of Purveshall (only a few miles from Kimmerghame). His father Sir William - thought to be the 'Sir William Worthy' in Allan Ramsay's *Gentle Shepherd* - an advocate, held office in the Court of Exchequer and was Solicitor-General. He died in 1684 or 85, and his son Sir Alexander, married Helen, daughter of George Home's Aunt Ninewells, and was therefore Crossrig's niece's husband (the diarist simply calls him, on 21 September 1695, Crossrig's nephew, the 'Wm' instead of 'Al' being a slip). Sir Alexander's mother, styled Dame Marjorie Fleeming Lady Purveshall, was still living in the family's large 12-hearth establishment in the earl 1690s; her death is reported in the diary on 24 February 1695. Up till then Sir Alexander had spent most of his time in Edinburgh. Veitch speaks of 'Tofts, now Purveshall; where is a considerable House and a large fruitfull Orchard' (p 178).

RAFO in Ireland, Bishop of. This is Alexander Cairncross, who started his adult life as a litster in Canongate, Edinburgh; acquired the educational qualifications needed for a career as a parson and rose to be Archbishop of Glasgow in December 1684. The Lord Chancellor removed him from this post in January 1687, but after the Revolution he was, in May 1693, made Bishop of Raphoe in Ireland, where he stayed until his death in May 1701. His importance from the diary point of view was that his sister Margaret Cairncross was Whytefield's mother. After his death this relationship became of considerable significance because of the estates he owned (he died unmarried).

RIDDELL, Sir John, 3rd Baronet of Riddell (co Roxburgh). He himself is not mentioned in the diary, but his 3rd wife, whom he married in 1669, is. She, the 'Lady Riddle' at Swintone on 10 October 1695, is clearly this 3rd wife, and would therefore be a sister of Sir John Swintone, the present laird. And we are told that with her were her son William and 'one Ridle of Newhouse'. The latter, Walter Riddell, living in a house with only 4 hearths was something of a poor relation to Sir John, with eleven (SRO E69/21).

RIDDELL Mr. Wm.   The diarist owes money to his son, but without other evidence identification is difficult.

ROBISONE, Geo.   This is almost certainly George *Robertson*, keeper of the register of hornings in Edinburgh, a supposition confirmed by the diary entry of 9 March 1696. See also Foulis.

RUTHERFORD, Robert, brother of Andrew, laird of Edgerstone (co Roxburgh). Robert apparently lived at Whytebank. See II 8)

SCRIMGEOUR, Henry of Bowhill lent money to Edinburgh Burgh in June 1693.

SINCLAIR, Dr. }
ST. CLAIR, Dr. }
        Matthew Sinclair (1647-1728). an Edinburgh physician, was tenth son of Sir John Sinclair of Hermieston and Elizabeth, daughter of Sir John Sinclair of Stevenson. In 1705 he married Margaret Home, daughter of the John Home of Ninewells who died in 1695; and after her death married Margaret, daughter of Sir Andrew Carre of Cavers.   He is also mentioned by Crossrig, Foulis and Grisell Baillie.

SINCLAIR, Sir John, 2nd Baronet of Longformacus, co. Berwick. Veitch's description is 'Langfirmacus Place, which is considerable for building, parks, planting, Wood and Bridge'; and we know it had 15 hearths. Sir John succeeded to the Baronetcy in 1678. He married Jean, daughter of Sir John Towers of Inverleith, and was living in 1696.

SKEEN, Mr. Tho. An advocate, he was the second son of John Skeen of Hallyard who was also an advocate. His wife was Beatrix Hepburn, daughter of the laird of Brunston. Died November 1700. Both Crossrig and Foulis mention him.

SMOLLIT, Commissary. James Smollet, listed in the 1694 Edinburgh Poll Tax Record as living in Old Kirk Parish with his wife, 4 children, 2 female servants, a man servant and a woman servant with no pay; some lodgers. The house had 6 hearths (Wood p. 63).

SOUTHERLAND, Mr. James. See 'The Physick Garden', 9 May 1694 in III; see also II 5).

STEVENSONE, Dr. This Edinburgh doctor with whom the diarist drank wine on

16 July 1694 was attending the Foulis household as early as December 1671, and continuing to do so well into the 1690's. Foulis also notes the cost of entertaining him; and in February 1698 ' young steinson' and others join Foulis for a game of cards.

STIRLIN, Geo. This surgeon has frequent mention in the Edinburgh Burgh Records.

STRAUCHAN, Wm, Probably William Strachan, 8th Laird of Glenkindie, West Aberdeenshire.

STUART, John of Kettleston. This 10-year-old laird, whose father had committed suicide before he was born and whose mother was Sophie Douglass, Marie Douglass Lady Hilton's sister, died (as the diarist tells us) on 16 February 1696. See Kelsall pp50-51.

STUART, Sr Rot. of Allanbank. The 7th and youngest son of the Lord Provost of Edinburgh (who died in 1681) by his 1st wife, Anne, sister of Sir Thomas Hope 1st Baronet of Craighall. Born in 1643, he was a merchant in Leith. After buying the Allanbank estate in Berwickshire he was in 1687 made a Baronet; he was to become MP for North Berwick 1698-1702. His Lady, who was, we are told on 13 January 1695, lately brought to bed of a daughter, was Helen, daughter of Sir Alexander Cockburn of Langton, whom he had married nearly three years before as his second wife. His house, a substantial 19-hearth one, housed him and his Lady, his first wife's mother (the Lady Craigmillar), his children (4 boys and 3 girls), his sister, a chaplain, and nineteen domestic servants (8 men and 11 women). (SRO GD86/770A).

SWINTONE, Sir John, laird of Swinton, was one of the diarist's closest and most influential friends. His father John's estate in Berwickshire had been declared forfeit in 1651, and this was confirmed in 1661 when the Stuarts returned. He died in 1679, his eldest son Alexander only surviving his father by a few years. John, the next son, had by that time built up a successful business as a merchant both in London and in Holland. He and his wife Sarah Welsh had quite a large family, all but one of whom (Frances) died as babies or children. Returning to Scotland in 1690 his father's forfeitures were, after a year or two, rescinded, but repairing the damage to the estates was a major problem. However, his business ventures continued to be successful, and he was one of those named in the Act establishing the Bank of Scotland as well as the Act setting up the Company of Scotland Trading to Africa and the Indies. When in Berwickshire he lived at the 11-chimney family seat, Ellbank House with his wife and sole surviving daughter, the domestic staff only being a solitary maidservant.

TOLQUHON. The laird of Tolquhon, in Tarves parish co. Aberdeen, to whom the diarist talked when in Edinburgh 21 February 1696, also owned what was described in 1721 as ' an old ruinous castle called Auchry' nearby, in the parish of Montwhitter.

TROTTER, see II 9).

WADDELL, see II 10).

WINRAM, James, Writer to the Signet, Sheriff-Clerk at Duns 1692. In 1681 he married Agnes Auchinleck.

YEUL, Widow. There is a possibility of her being the widow of John Yuill (or Zuill) who acquired the estate of Darleith in Dunbarton in 1670, a wealthy man whose grandchildren continued as lairds there.

YOUNG, Bailie. Probably Thomas Young, late bailie in 1689. (Edinburgh Burgh Records).

III TOPICS (IN DATE ORDER)

9 May 1694   The physick garden, Edinburgh

Started in 1675, this garden, in the yard of Trinity College, had by now acquired an extremely high reputation. ' For numbers and rareness of plants it is inferior to few gardens in Europe' was the justified claim of its master. And when appointing him professor of Botany in February 1695 the Burgh Council spoke of the garden's 'great reputation both in England and foraigne nations' (p. 168). When again asking someone in Edinburgh to get him some 'slips of Jerry sage' a month later, the diarist gives the master's name, 'Mr. Southerland'. For more on this garden see Cresswell pp.151-3.

4 June 1694   'Pat: Adamsones children'

This story, which can only be understood by supplementing the information in the diary by material from many other sources, is as follows. Many years before, a substantial sum of money was borrowed by George Home or his father, possibly in conjunction with others, from a certain Patrick Adamsone. He was a merchant in Kelso, married to Margaret Ormiston. He died intestate in April 1690 leaving four children who were still minors - Margaret, Agnes, Jennet and Isobell. His widow was party to an arrangement whereby some of these children were looked after by George Home's sister Isobel who was entitled to payment for doing this. By the time of the first report in the diary of the quarrel between George and his sister, the children were apparently no longer with her, but the burden of paying interest and repaying the loan seems to have rested on her in whole or in part, and later on (21 May 1695) the diarist reports that Patrick Adamsone's widow, still demanding what money she was owed, had married again and was now Mrs. Scot. Her second husband was in fact Walter Scott, merchant in Kelso, who seems to have been living in Newcastle at that time.

19 June 1694   '... 8 loads of coals upon my horses... and cobled twice'

To heat even a modest-sized country house such as Kimmerghame meant fetching substantial quantities of coal a long way, fifteen miles or so, from one of the small Northumberland collieries on the English side of the Tweed; this involved crossing the river by boat (cobble) at Norham. Because many of the roads on such a journey were unfit for any kind of wheeled vehicle, the task was a pack horse one. And as each horseload could not be more, in today's terminology, than two or three hundredweight at most, the few horses George himself possessed were insufficient on their own. The terms on which his tenants held their land, however, included an obligation to provide so many 'carriages', and a 'carriage' meant the service of a horse and someone to lead it, for a day. So it was George's servant's duty periodically to organise a convoy of his own and his tenants' horses to go to the coal hill and back again to replenish the coal stocks at the house. There was no question of George himself wasting a day doing this - it was not laird's work - so his servant had to see to it.

13 July 1694 Marriage Contracts

At this time, and amongst people at this social level, marriage contracts were of vital importance. Representatives of the families involved sat round a table with one or more legal experts in this field and after lengthy discussion and much hard bargaining a deal was struck. The contract had to make provision for every possible contingency, looking ahead several generations. The particular marriage contract that kept Thomas Pringle so busy that the diarist had to wait for him to attend to less important matters, was between Peter Wedderburn of Gosford, co. Haddington and Janet Halkett, Pitfirrane, co. Fife. Peter, born in 1660, was son of Sir Peter Wedderburn of Gosford, a Lord of Session styled Lord Gosford. Janet was *sister* and heir in line of Sir James Halkett, 2nd Baronet of Pitfirrane, and first *daughter* of Sir Charles the 1st Baronet. In the event the terms of the contract proved very important. For when the 2nd Baronet died in 1705, Peter Wedderburn (since 1697 *Sir* Peter) inherited the estate of Pitfirrane and took for himself and his successors the name of Halkett.

25 July 1694 Coinage

Coinage, as many entries in the diary show, presented a number of problems. Many foreign coins were in use as legal tender, and there was also continual trouble arising from the malpractice of clipping the coins as well as counterfeiting them. The older hammered coins were easy to clip, but if you were landed with them debased in this way, they could be very difficult to get rid of as they no longer represented face value. Once the newer milled coins were introduced clipping was no longer possible.

4 January 1695 'a parchmt pocket book'

Tragically, this pocket book in which the diarist noted down all that happened to him on his five-month London visit, 4 August to 4 January 1695, has not survived.

11 February 1695   Dying testate or intestate

The various decisions the dying Ninewells is reported in the diary as having taken on this particular day actually amounted to his latter will, written for him by Alexander Home WS, and witnessed by Crossrig and Balgaire, the testament being eventually registered on 1 March 1698.   From his latter will we learn that his wife was Dame Marie Norvell, and that their two children, for whom she was to be sole tutrix, were Michael and Marie.   Helpful as this is (for this information is not contained in the diary and is not readily available elsewhere), so many matters were already dealt with in other documents with legal force that Wills were to some extent superfluous.   Alexander Home himself, for example, died intestate when his time came on 15 May 1702;   for a leading member of the legal profession to do so today would certainly cause surprise, but it was clearly not a matter of great concern in 17th century Scotland.

27 March and 3 April 1695   Linen and Paper Manufacture in Scotland

The background to these diary entries is very fully sketched in by two articles by W.R. Scott (SHR Vol. II pp 53-60 and Vol. III pp. 71-76) under the general title 'Scottish Industrial Undertakings before the Union'.   The first is on linen manufacture, and in the second, on white-writing and printing paper manufacture, we learn a great deal more than the diarist is able to tell us about the activities of the French refugee Nicolas Dupin.

George Home's friends were also interested in these developments.   Grisell Baillie, for instance, bought 10 shares in the linen manufactory in 1693 at 19s. sterling per share, and invested more in December 1695 and November 1696. Foulis also seems to have bought 10 shares in September 1695, attended a meeting on 2 December, bought a further 10 in July 1696, and more for his son in January 1698.   His interest in *paper* manufacture was of rather a different kind, for 'together with the purchase of Woodhall Sr John acquired the paper-mills of Spylaw' (p xxxvi).   In George Home's own account of what was taking place in connection with linen and paper manufacture projects, the interest shown by Polwarth, Blackadder, Swinton, Lady Hilton and others is made clear, though ' blind Will Home' got slightly short shrift from Polwarth on one occasion (4 April 1695).

21 May 1695   'the club talks of great things'

The club was the designation given to a small group of members of the Scottish Parliament whose main objective was to undermine the administration.   Polwarth was a founder member (see Kelsall pp 126-7).

30 July 1695 'Cornwill well' water

This is Cornhill, two miles east of Coldstream, just across the Border in Northumberland. In the *History of the Berwickshire Naturalists* vol. X p.440 this account is given of a meeting at Cornhill in 1884. 'We went to the Medicinal well in the Haugh below the Plantation. This Well, having no connection with the Bathing Well stream, and now nearly obscured by neglect and marshy overgrowth, is mentioned in County Histories as being well known to possess medicinal properties; and it is more than a tradition among old people of the neighbourhood that invalids used to stay at Cornhill, or Coldstream, for the purpose of drinking its waters'. Oddly enough, the massive 15-volume *History of Northumberland* seems to contain no mention of this particular feature, though there is plenty about other aspects of Cornhill.

3 October 1695 Poll tax calculations

The diarist explains in this entry how he calculates the valued rental of his tenants for poll tax purposes. For information on how the amount of tax *all* pollable persons had to pay was arrived at, see the introduction to Marguerite Wood, *Poll Tax Returns for the Edinburgh Parishes of Tolbooth and Old Kirk 1694.* Edinburgh 1951.

31 December 1695 'my Brother has suffered a party to ly on him'

This certainly needs elucidation. The 'party' concerned was Alexander Bruce, writer in Edinburgh, though neither his name nor the nature of the wrong he had done to David Home, appears anywhere in this part of the diary. The wrong he was alleged to have done was betraying the trust and confidence David reposed in him, and stealing money that should have gone to David. The story, of which this remark in the diary on the last day of 1695 is merely the *beginning*, unfolds roughly as follows. Alexander Bruce was agent to the Earl of Crawford's Regiment during David's period as Collector for Berwickshire from early November 1695 until August 1696. Finding that David was seriously in arrears with his tax collecting he wrote letters to him (so it was said) pretending to be his friend, to get details of the people from whom tax had not yet been 'uplifted'. He then sent two of his servants, posing as soldiers, to extort what was owing by threats of quartering, and pocketed the proceeds (plus 'expenses and gratification') himself, so that neither the Regiment nor David as Collector ever received any of it. David, and his elder brother George Home as his cautioner, both lost heavily as a result of this, but in David's case it 'was certainly the occasion of his breaking and undoing' and was ultimately to lead to his abandoning everything and going ' with the last Fleet to Caledonia' (SRO GD158/677).

8 February 1696   Bank of Scotland

For some years before this volume of the diary starts, Scotland had been endeavouring to create for herself a position in foreign trading. It was natural that ambitions for a more prestigious banking system would follow, and in 1695 the Act establishing the Bank of Scotland was passed.   A full account of how the venture was organised can be found in *The Bank of Scotland 1695-1945* by Charles A.Malcolm. George Home and a number of the friends he mentions applied for shares in the Bank, and thus were allocated voting rights in respect of who was to be Governor, Deputy Governor, or was to be a Director. A folio lay in Edinburgh from 1 November to 31 December 1695 for subscribers to sign, then from 1 January 1696 it was transferred to various towns. The diarist kept watch on the progress made while it lay in Edinburgh. On 21 December he noted that 'bussines looks very well and as if it would be profitable', and on 27 December 'I went to the Bank wher the books are fast filling up'. When the Collector removed the folio from Edinburgh he collected the money due from each of the 136 persons who had signed their names in the book.

20 February 1696   ' I went afterwards to a French painters one Eude...'

Nicolas Heude, a member of the French Academy, had been expelled from France as a Protestant and came to Scotland around 1688.

26 February 1696   Books of the Darien Company opened

George Home's great friend Sir John Swinton was named in the Act of 26 June 1695 setting up the Company of Scotland trading to Africa and the Indies. We now know that the distinction of being regarded as the real founders of that company rests with two men, James Balfour and Robert Blackwood, with the second of whom the diarist had contact. This discovery was made by George Pratt Insh on examining the papers of James Balfour, and is reported in SHR Vol. XXV pp 241-54. Over the years so much has been written about the Company and what happened to the venture - from the publication of *The Darien Papers 1695-1700* by the Bannatyne Club, to John Pebble's *The Darien Disaster* in 1926 - that no more needs to be said.

NOTES ON THE TRANSCRIPTION

The three volumes of George Home's diary which have been preserved are small leather covered, blank notebooks ($5^1/_2$ ins by $6^1/_4$ ins), specially bound for the diarist, as is noted in the first entry of volume 2 " Having ended my other diary I caused George Mossman [Edinburgh] bind me up this.''

This is George Home's private diary, written for his eyes only and presumably often in a hurry. Because of this the reader is often unsure whether he wrote a, e or i, especially in the middle of a word. When this indeterminate letter is dotted, we have of course read it as an i, otherwise we have rendered it as seems most appropriate. The same difficulties are found with l and t, where we have again used the more appropriate letter. There are difficulties with two place names Belshile and Betshile (or Bedshile). Both are part of the Kimmerghame estate, Belshile near Kimmerghame and Betshile beyond Greenlaw and detached from the main Kimmerghame lands. George Home however usually visited Betshile on his way to and from Edinburgh (see map) which has helped us to identify which one he means.

George Home's capital L's have given us trouble because he had two versions; where we would expect a capital (e.g. Leith, Lord) he used a florid version with a long tail; we have rendered the less florid ones as lower case l's. To some extent he does the same with capital S; unexpected capital S's are more like long S's; again we have made these lower case letters. He used capital letters indiscriminately to our eyes and these we have retained; we have however given capitals to names and places throughout the diary to make easier reading. Similarly he often omitted periods and commas, and again we have added these, very sparingly.

He usually used contractions for 'which', wch, whc and very rarely whi, with bars above. These bars have been omitted, as have other uses of this indication of contraction. We have added the full word in square brackets where we think necessary. Raised letters, e.g. 5^{lb} (for £5) and Ed^r, have been lowered.

Sometimes we have divided paragraphs to help with clarity, but sparingly as we have tried to retain the 'flavour' of the diary; many of the longer paragraphs still need very careful reading! Trivial mistakes which George Home had corrected have been omitted; but where he had stroked out several words, perhaps indicating a change of mind, we have retained his original words, where legible, and indicated the author's correction,

The dates in the left margin have been standardised, George Home usually contracted the day but not always in the same way. He sometimes noted in the margin names or topics which were dealt with in the body of the diary. These we have not reproduced except on the few occasions where they were afterthoughts for which there has not been room in the main diary.

Diaries such as this often indicate how words were pronounced at the time. George Home often treated names less familiar to him phonetically but one word with which he was very familiar, "Jerviswood", is consistently spelled "Jeriswood". Lady Grisell Baillie in her Household Book and Erskine of Carnock in his Journal refer to "Jerriswood". George consistently wrote his name Home - how did he pronounce it?

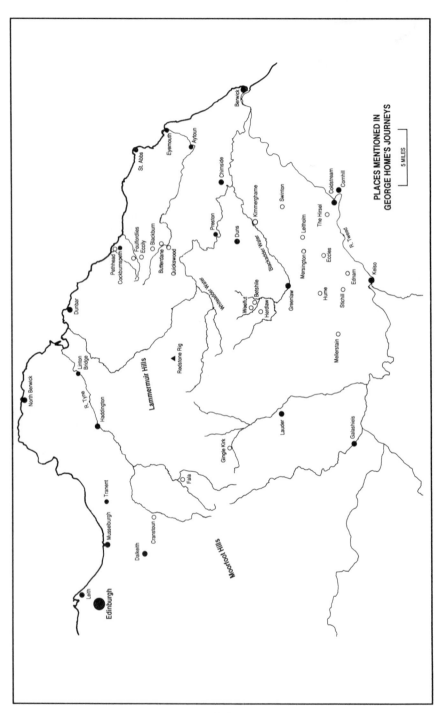

PLACES MENTIONED IN
GEORGE HOME'S JOURNEYS

5 MILES

Berwick

Ayton

Chirnside

St. Abbs

Eyemouth

Coldstream

Cornhill

Swinton

Kimmerghame

Preston

Pethhead

Cockburnspeth

Foulfordlees

Eccily

Blackburn

Buttardane

Quickswood

Duns

Leitholm

The Hirsel

Mersington

Eccles

R. Tweed

Dunbar

Wheelfut

Betshiele

Greenlaw

Hume

Ednam

Kelso

Herdlaw

Stichill

Linton
Bridge

North Berwick

R. Tyne

Haddington

Lammermuir Hills

Redstone Rig

Mellerstain

Lauder

Gingle Kirk

Galashiels

Fala

Musselburgh

Tranent

Dalkeith

Cranstoun

Moorfoot Hills

Leith

Edinburgh

Blackadder Water

Whiteadder Water

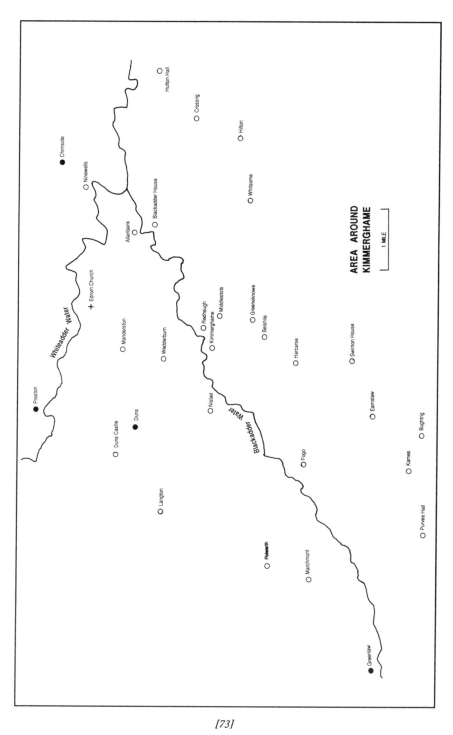

AREA AROUND
KIMMERGHAME

1 MILE

Chirnside
Preston
Ninewells
Whiteadder Water
Edrom Church
Blackadder House
Allanbank
Hutton Hall
Crossrig
Hilton
Whitsome
Manderston
Wedderburn
Redheugh
Middlestots
Kimmerghame
Greeneknowe
Belshie
Harcarse
Swinton House
Duns Castle
Duns
Nisbet
Blackadder Water
Earnslaw
Langton
Fogo
Kames
Bughtrig
Polwarth
Marchmont
Purves Hall
Greenlaw

[73]

1694

Monday May 7th. 1694. Since the Beginning of this month on tuesday last I have writt nothing my other book being ended, Besides since saturday was eight days the weather has been so sowre out of the N.E. that I have been litle abroad only on friday.

Friday 4th. My Lo: Polwarth came here about eight in the Morning and took me to Blackader wt him wher we dined & in the afternoon went to Allanbank and from that to Whitader Bridge whc my Lord is causing repair having a gift of some vacant stipends for that use. from that we came to Wedderburn and thence to Nisbet wher we parted. I returned home The News letters he had tell us the French K. by the mediation of Denmark offers a treaty of peace they report that befor the treaty he offers to restore Strassburgh & Dismantle Luxembourg but I dare not trust all this.

Saturday 5th. My sister Julian Came here from Edr she tells me that that week the Estate of Nicolsone was rouped that Sr John Clerk of Pennicook gives 22 years purchasse for Laswade that Dalmeny gives 24 years purchasse for Nicolsone wt 20,000 Ms for the house and parks and Yards and 2,000 Ms for the Coal that Sr John Hall gives 26 years purchasse and a quarter for Colbranspeth who were the Competitors that raised the price so high I cannot tell.

Sunday 6th. It rained this day whc was very seasonable ther being a great drought but it was cold the wind being still N:E.

Monday 7th. This morning Tho: Pringle came hither wt my brother Da: fro Blackader I spoke to him anent raising ane adjudication agst the E. of Homes Estate he desired me to send him the papers agst this day eight days to Stichell.

Tuesday 8th. Sr John Home and his Lady and his sister Helen and my sister Isbell came here a foot I met them on Blackader muire and returned wt them. I

1

payd Sr John Home 4 guineys I had borrowed from him in I think march last. I
wrote to Mr Al: Home anent the money I oue to Mr Wm Riddells sone to try if
he could put him off till Martimes or get the money.

Wednesday 9th. Andrew Halyburtone designed Chamberlan in Hadden to
whom the late James Robinsone in Kelso has left his means came here this
morning wt one Wm Pringle notar in Kelso to intimat his right to me of the
1,400 Ms I oued to the sd James [and now to him - deleted] and told me that he
desired I might at the terme pay the years interest will then be due and
corroborat the bond payable agst Candlem. next and that at that time I might
ether pay the summe or become debtor to one of those who had gotten legacies
   My sister Julian went to Blackader this afternoon And: Watheret not going for
Edr till to morrow I wrote to Dr Dundas to try if he Could get me any slips of
Jerry sage from the Physick Garden and to send me any of the tomes of Horace
he had read Mr Geo: Waddell came here this afternoon. he tells me the Great
Mr of The Teutonick Order who competed wt the B. of Collogne for the
Bishoprick of Leige is dead. About 7 a clock came my Lord Harcasse and his
sone

Thursday 10th. I bottled the seck I bought in Leith ther was 2 gallons and a
chopine of it wch should have been 33 bottles ther is 28 bottles and one sett by
for present use not altogether full and another thick being the ground of the
barrell. I count I had draun off 3 mutckins befor so ther will be about 3 mutckins
of intake but I think the bottles are some what larger than chopins. I melted
some beewax and rosin together and covered the corks over cutting them closse
by the bottles.
   My Lo: Polwart and Coldenknows came here they had been these 3 nights at
Coldinghame upon Laws bussines wt Morissons tutor. Coldenknows told me he
had spoke to my Lord Home anent our common engagements for his mother and
him. My Lord desired to see what we had given out befor he should condescend
on a locality for our paymt and my Lo: Pol. is to give Coldenknowes a note of it.
But we were all of opinion that my Lady should be further spoke to that we
might have a locality out of her jointure wch she may very well spare

Friday 11th. Mr Auchinleck Apothecary in Dunse having been dressing Da:
Robisons Wifes arme wch she broke some days agoe came here as he went
home. I was talking wt him about the price of the Cortex Peruvianus he says he
sold it last year at 16sh Scots ane ounce that now it is sold and [sic] 3 lb Scots
and he has knoun it at 30sh st. according as the ague is frequent.

Monday 14th. These 3 or four days past have been so intollerably cold wt a
constant surly N.E. wind that I have gone no wher abroad. John Murdo went to
Blackader and brought me ane ansywer from And Watheret but Dr Dundas was

not in toune and he says Ands. wife sd he delivered Mr Al: Homes letter And. himselfe being gone to the coals. Swintone came here in the afternoon and stayd about ane hour.

Tuesday 15th. Geo: Umferstone Millar in Betshile mill being to goe away came here this day and told me Geo: Brack had arrested his beasts. I told him that I would keep still his beasts till I saw what way I should be paid of what he was due and if he did not satisfie me in that I would cause appryse them. Talking wt him he tells me that Halyburtone gets 12 lb for the acre of his land whc is not so good as mine in Betshile and in Longformacus they get 16 lb but they give 3 soumes to the acre and Halyburtone and I give but two but that will not make up the difference

Wednesday 16th. Account of my Linnens. Imp. 6 Night shirts. 4 Holland halfe shirts. 5 pair of slieves. 7 Caps for nightcaps. 8 litle caps. 5 snuff napkins 4 long Muzlin cravats 4 Muzlan cravats wt stocks 4 long Holland Cravats 3 linnen night cravats 5 snuff napkins. 4 pair of linnen thred stockins. These I use at present. I have beside lying in a trunk in the litle study in my chamber 5 laced Cravats 1 point cravat 2 pair of laced Ruffles and ane odde one 2 holland shirts. I gave Margaret Turner my linnens for present use to be washt. I gave her likewise a haggabag table cloath wch is not in her account and some days agoe two pair of linnen sheets and halfe ane one wch I had at Edr wch likewise are not in her account. Mr Adam Waddell came here in the afternoon. he tells me the K. is safe arrived in Holland, that the Fr. K. makes offers of peace to the Confederats and to restore what he has taken this warre provided they will assist him to restore K. James or at least let him follow his oun methods in doing it if these proposalls shall be refused he protests the blame of the warre shall not ly at his door. the Ministers of the Confederat princes are to meet the K. at the Hague ther to resolve whether to hearken to the proposalls of peace or prosecute a vigorous warre.

Thursday 17th. My Brother came here in the afternoon he had been in Polwart house. Robin Broun the Masson came here to see when I would have lime ready for ending the Wall. Ther has been a great drought for a long while till Wednesdays night it raind and it hes continued pleasant showers from time to time allwise since. but the air is not yet so warm as that I can leave off having a fire in my chamber. When It rains any thing heavily my house drops through I know not what to doe wt it. Ther is great promising of fruits all the Country over the trees being all covered wt Blossoms I have gueens cherries and plumes set a week or ten days agoe the apples are setting.

Friday 18th. Sir John Home was here in the afternoon having been at Harcasse.

3

Saturday 19th. My Lord Polw. came here about 12 a clock and I had just dined. a litle after him Sr John Hume came here having been at Polwarthouse. Sr John spoke to me anent the losse his mill was at by Da: Robisons not grinding at his mill because he duells not on the ground. I alleaged that if his servants that dwell on the ground did grind at his mill it was all could be asked for tho Da: Ro: did not dwell on the ground himselfe yet he had servants on it that Laboured the ground. for that he sd he brought his servants off this ground and Laboured it and that his millar was sensible of it. I told him that the difference would be found to be very small tho now his millar might magnify it and that befor his millar alleaged his advantage was litle or none of Redheugh and that the tenants allwise abstracted ther Moulters tho now they alledge great dammage. Sr John alleged that whoever possessed that Room was obliged to grind all the Corns consumed in ther family at his mill by my charter. after he was away I lookt and found that the words are near to that purpose but I can hardly think It will extend to a possessor not dwelling on the ground if he keep as many servants on the ground as will Labour the ground for in that case one man eats as much as another the servant as much as the Master. That wch he would be at is that Da: Robisone should pay dry Moulter to his millar. I think it will be equall if it be considered what was ground one year wt another during Geo: Johnstons stay in Redheugh and that Da: Robisone pay Moulter conforme. Mem. When I was looking over the Charter I find my tenant is not lyable to his court and yet Ro: Gray was fined at it once by James Craw. My Lo: and he went away together to see Whitader bridge. My Lo: came back this way again to ask me about the priviledges the East mill had in this ground I told him them. the reason why he asked was that his tenant had complaind to him that the East mill had casten much fail in the ground wch is common betwixt him and me to wch they had no right ther being no such reservation to them. but being informed it was ther use and wont he sd it went a great length but when I consider the thing I find he has no ground to challenge it but I rather; for in Respect of him the Lands are as if they were still in Wedderburns possession in wch case all the tenants of this ground have right to the common. and as to me I think It were hard to exclude them they having no other place to cast in and ther houses could not otherwise be kept up. tho if it had been lookt to early I think ther being no such reservation to them I might very well exclude them all things considered.

Sunday 20th. This day was rainy and foggy all day the Communion was given at Lantone this day. I was not abroad.

Monday 21st. John Murdo having met with Wm Brack at Lanton yestday and he having told him that Geo: Umferstone would take away his beasts by force wch I had ordered to be arrested for his rent I sent John to Betshile to see them apprysd. he tells me Pat: Knox one of the apprysers is not at home to day but that Wm Brack will cause doe it to morrow. He brought me 11 lb Scots of peat money from Geo. Brack. It has raind very much this day. I spoke to my Lo: Pol: on Sat. anent our bussines wt the Countes of Home. he told me she is so ill of a Gravell at present ther is no writing to her of bussines. And Watheret hes no word to me.

Dr Dundas or Mr Al. Home I fear to be at a losse in Watt Riddells bussines by Mr Als. not geting my letter in time. he must be away wt Ninewells.

Ja: Jaffrey Brought me 24 lb Scots. he made severall complaints of Tho. Rutherfords cuting his meadow of tysting away a maid of his of another tenant of Polwarts cuting his corn upon the march. It has rained most part this day but the day was milde the wind being west.

Tuesday 22nd. This morning is one of the roughest that can be rainy gloomy and a tempestuous wind out of the N.E. consequently cold. I sent John Murdo to Dunse to get notice what was become of my horning agst the E. of Home and to buy me some things. he brought me word that It was given to Geo: Gardner to denounce and that I should have it shortly.

Al. Jeffrey payd me 30 lb of his Whitsondays rent of this present year, Wm Trotter came here & got halfe a years anrent due at this Whitsonday

Wednesday 23rd. This being a meeting of the Commissioners for revising John Home the late Collectors accounts I went to Dunse but all was over befor I came. all was done was to appoint the accounts to be ready agst that day 8 days. My Lo: Polwarth was not ther being at the Synode of Kelso

Will: Brack was at me this Morning & told me the Apprysers had apprised Geo: Umferstons 4 cows 2 to 48 lb and other two to 30 lb being in all 7 lb st or 84 lb Scots. he owes me 9 lb st or 108 lb Scots wch is 3 terms rent but he repaired the house of Weelfit both timber and stone work for wch he demands 27 lb but I must call for David Robisone to know what agreement he made. if I allow him 27 lb I will be due him 4 lb Scots. Wm Brack tells me Geo: Umferstone and a brother of his Robin spoke very bigly to him as threatening him ane ill turn for having apprysed his beasts. Wm advised Geo: to come to me and he douted not but I would give him his beasts at lest two of them again but he refused to doe it so that I resolve to sell them. ther is one I will keep for my oun use being near the calving, another that gives some milk I will keep till the other calve. these are the 2 best

Thursday 24th. This morning the 2 best of the Cows were brought doune hither. Pat Knox counted wt me as per his account in my count book.

Dr Aber[nethy]. came over this morning from Nisbet went back again befor dinner. Tho: Pringle was here yesterday morning. the Dr Got back his book du

Choix et de la Conduitte des etudes this day and got from me a loan of Boils receats

Friday 25th. Wm Grive in Dunse was here seeking his anrents. he showed me his right from his father to him whc Must be registrat. In the afternoon Sr John Home & Swintone came hither Sr John Having dined wt Swintone. after Swintone went away Sr John and I red some of Boileaus letters &c. He went home at night

Saturday 26th. I sent John Murdo to Berwick for provisions for the house see the account book. The Weather continues still sour and the Wind N.E. tho some times it falls to other airths but does not continue

Sunday 27th. This morning was very pleasant I went to Church but as I went I found a cold n.e. Wind Blow. in returning it was south east and raind at night

Monday 28th. The Wind S.W. and Gloomy but not cold. I cut some Asparagus today. I have had 3 or 4 dishes of it this year being the first time it was cut it is 4 years old just now. I have caused plant some chatts of plains this year taken up at Nisbet.
Memo. Pat Cockburn sent me My Letters of Horning agst the E. of Home wt the Execution being of the 30 Ap. and the denunciation by George Gardiner of the 21st May.
I counted this day wt Wm Johnstone George Johnstons sone as by his account.

Tuesday 29th. Receaved from Geo: Broun in Betshile 36 lbs of his Mart. rent. This is a very pleasant warme day but the wind is somewhat high. one of the Bee skeps hived this day. I went and saw the houses in Redheugh whc are in ill condition and must be helped this summer.

Wednesday 30th. James Redpeth in Weelfit payd me his first terms rent for Weelfit. he entered Whits. was a year and should have payd at the Mart. after but Da: Robisone conditiond wt him to pay at the Whitsond. after his entry wherby I got no rent at Mart. for Wm Fogo paying at the Mart. after his entry was clear at the Whits when he removed. only it was not clear whether the 3d and teind was drawn that year he entered so that I agreed wt him for 26 lb Scots and we past the bussines. James told me anent a peice ground that had been common to Weelfit Herdlaw and Rawburn that Rowistone to whom Herdlaw belonged and Sr Robert Stclair to whom Rawburn parted this betwixt themselves but at the parting they decleared that did not prejudge Weelfitts right in both shaires. yet since that time Weelfits possession has allwise been troubled by both. he asked me what he should doe he says he hes been

pasturing ther but they have poinded his beasts. I told him to keep his
possession and I should warrant him in it. he says that Weelfits peaceable
possession may be instructed by men yet alive. I must speake to Wm Vaitch
factor to Sr John Stclair and Sr John himselfe about it. My Brother David
having been at Newcastle brought me 2 pound of sarsa and a pound of China
root. The sarsa is tollerable but the China is ill.

 Ther being a meeting of the Commissioners I went up to Dunse. the meeting
was about Jo: Home late collector his accounts. it was ordered that my Lord
Pol: My Lo: Crosrig Jeriswood and I should meet wt Bayly Home at Edr and
get them in Order agst the 2 Wed of August. Then they Called for the bond of
Cautionry for Jo: & then for my Brothers bond of Cautionry. My Lord Crosrig
and Sr John Home are named in it but not signing. Sr Jo: Being ther My Lo:
Polwarth desired him to signe it knowing nothing but that it was thro want of
opportunity that Sr John Had not signed it. Sr John said he would not be
Hectored to signe it wch my Lo: Polwarth did not understand but Swintone
who had been speaking to him befor to signe it and betwixt whom and Sir John
ther past some words about it askt who had Hectored to it. he said he upon wch
Swintone began to vindicat himselfe and sd that all he had said to him was that
he thought he should not forsake his freinds and Cusen in such a bussinesse. Sr
John was positive he would not signe that bond upon wch my Lord Polwarth
who had signed it calld for it and took it up from the Clerk as not being a
delivered evident and wt all told Sr John that he had forgot himselfe for he had
promised to him to be Caution whc Sr John denyed he had but sd if the
Commissioners would take him alone he was willing to be Caution but would
not be Hectored to signe that bond and the Collector was appointed to find
Caution agst munday. The truth of the bussines I find is this that Sr John on the
one hand tho nominat in the bond thought that My Lo: Polwarth Swintone and
I having signed it he would be overlookt, on the other Swintone having offered
himselfe wtout being desired lookt on Sr John Home not signing as a deserting
him challenged Sr John on it whc he took hottly. We had severall matters befor
us as commissioners of Excise as complaints of Brewers agst James Broun
collector Under Blackburn but we could doe litle in it the law being so
favourable to the Collectors.

Thursday 31st. Was a fast I went to Church. Sr John Home having fallen ill
at Dunse the day befor and fearing a return of his ague came not out.

Friday June. 1st. I went to Blackader to visit him found him better than I
expected. I dined ther and came home at night

Saturday 2nd. I went to Polwart house and finding my Lord My Lady
Jeriswood and his Lady &c were Gone to the fishing at Greenlaw I went on
and stayd wt them till they came home and supped wt my Lord. it was late

befor I came home. My Lord Pol: I found took Sr John Homes not signing my brothers bond of Cautionry very ill. he said of the years he was of he lookt on it as childishnesse but if he had had more experience he would have lookt on it as the hight of pride. that it was a breach of that freindship and Neighbourhood had allwise been intertained in this place of doing things among freinds in concert together &c. When I came home I found Horace translated by Martignac whc I desired Dr Abernethy to Lend me

Sunday 3rd. I went to Church

Monday 4th. I receaved a note from my Sister Isabell from Wedderburn to send her money to Dunse for she had some things to buy. I went to Dunse and she came wt Cat: Heburn ther. she asked money from me. I told her she might remember I was to pay Pat: Adamsones children the halfe of the summe I engaged to them for her at Candlemes last. that the whole being 175 lb 1sh the halfe comes to 87 lb 10sh 6d wt a quarters interest of the halfe whc is 01-06-6. in all 88 lb 17sh 00d. ther remains 21 lb 03sh. she said she beleived if I would count ther would be more due her then that summe considering the 2 years she had been with her aunt Borthwick. I told her that I beleived otherwise but not having account of what she had got It was very fair if I payd her the Current anrent of her portion especially when I was not obliged to it. she told me very briskly that she was sure if I were not obliged to pay her I would never have given her anything and why was I not as well obliged to pay her as my Brother. I told her I might give Da: what I pleased tho I was not obliged to it. wherupon she Broke out in a passion according to her ordinary and said well if you are not obliged to give me any thing I will have nothing from you I had rather win it with my hands. I offered her what was over the summe due to Pat: Adamsones children whc she refusing we parted. For my part I think myselfe very Justifyable if I pay my sisters ther current anrent. especially her wtout being obliged to count from the beginning every farthing they have received wch is impossible for me to doe they having got many times money from me that I did not set doune, When my father left them ther portions he left me in all appearance in a very plentifull condition but it soon changed so that Im sure if he had forseen it he would have restricted ther allouance for he himselfe took a thousand Ms off his brother and another off his sister upon Polwarts evicting the Lands of Peel from him whc was most rationall for him to doe since it was in proportion to his estate. his father left his children ther portions and I see not why I might not have done the same considering my losse by the Estate of Aitone but all I project is a discharge of anrents whc will be very inconsiderable if anything at all. when it is considered that tho Isabell was 2 years wt my aunt Borthwick yet then she got cloaths and when she had the goverment of my house it is well known what neadlesse waste she made both of the furniture and extravagant provisions for the house especially when I was from home. intertaining a number of Idle people who frequented it so that the expenses of my family were greater when I was from home than when I was at home, (as is evident by Da: Robisons accounts) these commerads of hers not frequenting my house when I was at home. Not withstanding of all this I am willing to give them my bond in the terms of my fathers that one halfe shall return to me the other to be divided amongst them or if they will the one halfe to me the other at ther disposall. I doe not make use here of the strongest argument I have in law to wit that legally I am not subjected to my fathers debts he never having been infeft in any of his Lands and his Executry being lesse than his debts. for I never made use of it hitherto nor I hope ever shall ther being nobody can challange me on that account.

Ther was in the afternoon a meeting of the Commisioners for considering of a methode for revaluing the shire or valuing it rather it being pretended ther was never any valuation or at lest no authentick valuation book extant subscrived by the valuators but the Act of Parla appointing a 3d part of the Commissioners accepting to be present. and ther being 31 accepting whereof 11 ought to be present and ther not being present so many notwtstanding of Sr Rot: Stuarts causing send and send again to seek some commissioners that were in the toune we could not proceed. only it was resolved that against the 2nd Wednesday of Augst intimation should be made to all the Commissioners to meet for that effect. The methode my Lord Polwarth seemed to encline to if ther had been a quorum would a been that every gentleman should give in his rentall upon his honest word and the Commissioners to lead probation on it afterward.

My Brothers bond of Cautionry was moved. My Lord Pol. told the Commissioners that it lookt very negligent like that Caution had not been found befor this that he had subscrived the bond In Oct and did not doute but those named in it had likewise signed it but that sr John Home upon what considerations he was not to Judge had refused. yet that for his part he was still ready to continue cautioner. Swintone sd the same and I so the caution was found sufficient and the bond put in Sr Rot Stuarts hand for the behoof of the Commissioners.

I sold 2 of the cows apprysed from George Umferstone. they were apprysed at 18 lb apeice. I got the one sold at 18. but the other was sold at 16 lb so I lost 2 lbs beside about 7sh or 8sh of expenses.

Tuesday 5th. I receaved from Wm Johnstone in his father Georges name 49 lb Scots

It. from James Jaffrey 36 lb Scots.

Ellshy Trotter came here this morning about 3 a clock having been wt his commerades in Dunse fair

In the afternoon we went and visited Swintone and My Lord Harcars.

I called for Adam Forsyth who threshes the teind and asked him what teind was this year. he tells me ther is about 14 bolls of Bear and 30 bolls of oats and 3 bolls pease and 5 furlets of Ry. I asked him whether he thought the teind grew better or worse he said he thought It rather grew worse for he his seen fourty bolls of oats.

I have counted what I have given out for books these 2 years I find it is 172 lb 19sh wch is too much for me. a litle money given out from day to day comes to a considerable summe at the years end.

Wednesday 6th. My Brother having spoken for grasse for my horses in Lantone parks at 2sh Scots a night. I sent my Black and Gray gueldings ther this day but I think John Murdo does not much commend the grasse. yet they goe wher his own horses goe for My Lord Jedburghs regiment of Dragoons have most of his grasse

Thursday 7th. Dr Waddell and is [sic] wife and Mr Adam and Dr Comry came here this morning. The Dr is going over wife [sic] his wife to Wintone the Earl having made him Chamberlaine to his Estate. Mr Ad. returned in the afternoon and stayed wt me till night. he borrowed from me How upon thoughtfulnes for to morrow.

Marg. Turner brought me ane account of what money was given out when I was at Edr this winter for the houses use and ane account of the Kain fouls she has got in and how they were disposed of.

Friday 8th. I wrote on Munday to Mr Al: Home anent Freershaws affair. this morning I receaved one from Mr Al. wherin he writes that Freershaw would delay till Lammas and desired his interest now but he having sd he would write to me and not having done it Mr Al: thinks he may delay till martimes as I desire. I wrote likewise to Gideon Elliot to get me some slips of jerry sage from Mr Southerland and some dryd if he have any and he returns me answer he shall try for me agst next occasion.

And Watheret has brought me a sugar loaf but no bread

Saturday 9th. I went to Betshile and counted with my tenants vid. ther severall accounts. I went along the March betwixt Kettleshile and me wher ther is some difference and wher my tenants all saye he has cast turfs upon my ground wch I caused stop. James Redpath tells me that Robert Winter and Robert [blank] who were present when Rowistone and Sr Ro: Stclair parted the Ground common to Herdlaw Rawburn and Weelfit betwixt them wt this clause that ther parting the sd common betwixt them should not wrong Weelfit nor hinder its giveing thro both parts whc those two men heard Sr Rot Sinclair say. but Weelfit having been now of a long time keept fro the possession by Wm Fogos simplicity and those two men being now dead it will be hard for me to prove my possession. the[y] tell me ther is one Waddell in [blank] who knows something of it. I went to the peet mosse and find it will presently fail and I know not wher another will be found. I went to the Lady Mosse whi is full of holes some advise me to cast a ditch thro it and drain away the water and so the Mosse will grow again, other alleage it is not worth the pains. the peets were the best in Lammermoore. I returned by Polwarthouse and supped ther. I see some gazets and news letters by wch it seems the French have a designe on Barcelona and the fleet at Brest is gone ther. Our fleet is gone to sea wt 10 or 14 thousand land men aboard tis not known upon what designe. Gen Talmash is wt the land forces. the letters talk of a great Scarsety in France, that ther is now great appearance of peace wt the Turks. The Dauphin commands this year in Flanders. The Confederats have in Flanders 160,000 Men. The Weather continues very sharp the Wind alwise easterly or Northerly. we begin to want raine

Sunday 10th. I went to Church

Monday 11th. I sent John Murdo to Softla with the Black Mare to a stallion ther wch was Chattos now belonging to James Hall. I went to the Doucoat and found Many young doues dead wch is for want of food. I Broke all the eggs I could find and took out all the ripe young but they are very lean the season being now that they can find no grain in the feilds.
  Dr Abernethy came over from Nisbet this afternoon and returned me Boils receats he had borrowed from me. I went over to Nisbet wt him. he had been sent for yesterday to Mrs Margaret who was ill. Cavers was not at home being gone to Harcasse.

Tuesday 12th. Mr Adam Waddell came here in the morning and stayd till night. Cavers & Mr Rot Knox came here in the afternoon

Wednesday 13th. I lookt over some accounts and receats of Da: Robisons to my tenants. I went up to him to Midlestots to call for the accounts since he gave in his last. I sent Jo: Murdo to Dunse for bread and to bid Pa: Cockburn come to me. The weather has been extremly cold all may and this month so that on sunday morning particularly the was hoar froast and Ice early in the morning. this day ther has been a pleasant rain from the south east and after it the Wind is turned S.W and it is warme. I hope the Weather shall now settle. They tell me the Merchants in Berwick begin to look out for oats. they offer 4 lb 4sh Scots for them. they had sold at 3 lb 12sh all this spring.

Thursday 14th. Pat: Cockburn came here. he promised to get me a list of my Lo: Homes tenants that I may arrest ther rents. I ordered him to denounce my Lo: Home. having let the last denunciation expire. Geo: Gardener having given his execution wrong to the E. I think it will not be a misse to charge him over again. Al: Taite came here and got his anrent due to him and James Becket at Whitsunday last.

Da: Robinsone gave me in his account of money receaved fro my tenants and debursemts. I got likewise from him 144 lb as part of the ballance due to me. I was all the afternoon upon his accounts wch I find very unexact. My Lady Polwarth and her daughter Mrs Julian came here and stayd a very litle

Friday 15th. I went in the afternoon to Whitsome to visite Mr Adam Waddell. I got from him Bartolines Anatomy wch his brother Mr Androw had borrowed from me. I went from that to Blackader to visite the Lady not knowing Sr John was come home. I found he came home late yesternight. he tells me the French have defaite the Spaniard in Catalonia and tis thought they will have Barcelona befor this. And that some talk that the French have got the Smirna fleet this year again.

Since Wednesday the weather has been pretty good the wind being South west. The strawberries begin now to be for use and the artichoks. I met John Haitly as I came from Blackader coming from Kelso. he says the peas give 7sh st the Kelso boll. They begin to refuse the English pewter halfepennies and farthings in this country. I have 7 lb 12sh scots of them whc I have given to Da: Robinsone to passe for me in Berwick tomorrow. I have sent John Murdo ther to buy a leg of Veal. And Watheret brought me a 6sh loaf from Edr but I gave him 9 pence to have brought a 3 penny one also but I was not at home when he came. I sent to the Doucoat and all the Young ones were found dead for hunger.

Saturday 16th. Tho: Rutherford came to me and told me that ther being some difference betwixt Polwarths Millar and mine the first was threatening to take the others p[ar]t. but that I would not doe well to part wt mine being ane industrious body only the mill might be brought to 200 Ms. we fell a talking of my other rooms he tells me that Adam Turnbull in Ryselaw is allwise saying he will have Kings law it having been possest by his wifes Grandfather & grandmother so that it may be brought to 200 Ms likewise. That the Westfeild hes payd 3 terms rent wt this last crop since James Jeffrey fell on the right way of labouring it whc he had not befor. When we began to talk freely he told me that Da: Robisons thryving at the rate he has done these years past is a wonder to the Country who generally say it hes not been done by labouring but intromitting wt my estate that he hes got his means for when he went to Greenknow he had litle or nothing and now he ferms land to the value othe [sic] 2,400 [changed from 2,600] Ms a year. The truth is I am as litle apt to suspect a mans honesty as any man but when I consider his so sudden rise I cannot but be suspicious especially when I look on the accounts I got in last day wherin severall articles are neglected whc I find he has receaved from my tenants. I find it is a Gentlemans interest who is conversant in country affairs to hear country people especially the more intelligent talk of bussines. they think of nothing else and so are ready to make more solide remarks than Gentlemen who are more taken up wt other things.

Sunday 17th. I was at Home all day

Monday 18th. Peter Broun came here and set off a squair quite about my garden and house making the new wall the principill paralell line the Garden walls doe not at present run paralell to it but I resolve to lift them out 100 foot east west and south and so make the lines or walks parallel to the new wall. he has guessed at the bussines this day but he will return another day and prove the work. I gave him a rix dollar. Wm. Grieve came here and got his interest of 152 lb I oue him from Martimes. 1690 to Mart. 1693. to witt. 27 lb 06sh. On saturdays night it was very sultry so that we expected rain but on sunday it was clear and a high south E. wind till night that it fell cloudy and this morning and all this day it hes been a pleasant calme small rain. On saturday on of the beeskeps hyved and it flew away Westward the wind being south west (the Gardner alleages the[y] fly agst the wind wt a checkwind) He followed it but got no information of it on sunday morning the Wind being south E. a hyve came to the same place or hard by whc the others had gone from so the Gardner alleages it is the same. Robies nurse came here on saturdays night

Tuesday 19th. Being airly up this morning befor 5 the morning being very pleasant I walked out and met wt Ro: Robisone who was at Earlstone fair yesterday wher he says beast sold at a great rate both nolt and sheep. I calld for the smith who tells me he has made and removed shoes for my horses since feb was a year 131 whc at a penny a shoe is 6 lb: 11sh. that he has brought home 10 Loads of Coals upon my horses halfe great halfe small. I called for Geo: Archer who hes brought home 8 loads of Coals upon my horses halfe great halfe small and Cobled twice. this I did in order to the examination of Da: Robisons accts whc I find differ much from this. John Lidgate tells me that in spring 1692 while I was at Edr he got four bolls of oats from Da: Robisone but the year befor he had lost the acct. I caused take doun all the sparrow nests whc spoil my house extremly. ther were above a dozen of them some eggs some young ones. I went in the after noon and visited the Old countesse Douager of Home who has been very ill of a Gravell so they conclude she has a confirmed stone. she is weak and beside is 72 years of age. I stayd wt her a very litle and past about ane hour wt Lady Anne from thence I went to the Hirshell to have waited on my Lord but he was gone to Newtoune wher was a Briddall. I sate a litle wt my Lady. I see my Lord Dunglasse who is a very pretty boy. I went and took a turn in the Garden wt Mr Geo: Waddell who waits on him. he tells me that the Berwick news were that Russell offered to

Land his men in the Bay of Camaret wch is near Brest and put a shore 400 of them but all the coast being planted wt canon ther was a Dutch man ôf war sunk severall English ships disabled and the men that were landed bate back to ther ships having lost 200. that Talmash is shot in the thigh and the Duke of Leeds's sone wounded. that ther were ther attending ther Landing above 16,000 foot and horse so that no doute they had intelligence of the designes. I came home by John Fish of Castlelaws house. he was not at home but I found his wife. I found upon the table Bacons history of Henry the 7th wch I had lent him ten years agoe. I brought it home wt me but he has spoilt the binding of it miserably and besides inked it so in severall places that it is not or very hardly legible.

Wednesday 20th. I went to Blackader and took Robie befor me on the black mare and his woman behind John Murdo. we dined ther and returned at night. James Jaffray payd me 25 lb 14sh . When Blackader came from Edr he brought me a letter from Dr Dundas and the 4, 5, & 6th volumes of D'aicers Horace. I have this day got the 4 & 5. he has keept the 6th.

Thursday 21st. The being a meeting of the Heritors appointed for repairing the Church I went ther. ther were ther Sr John Home Cavers & Brymer of Newtone in Fife or Edrom here. Deacon Rankin a Masson who is repairing the Bridge of Whitater [sic] was brought ther to view it. after we had lookt to it he told us yt he could say nothing till he had taken off some of the thackstones. Sir Rot Stuart being absent we thought it fit he should be advertised of our resolution to help the Church so we desired the Minister to write to him he being in Edr to see if he would concur wt the rest of the Heritors for the reparation and in the mean time we desired the Minister to acquaint the presbyterie that we desired a visitation of the Church. But I fear we will lose this summer for Sr Jo: Home is to be away at Scarborough and probably I may be absent and Cavers will not stir and Sr Rot Stuart will never willingly concur in anything of wch the expense is to be laid on by the Cesse roll. After our meeting was over I came to Nisbet wt Cavers and at night returned home. This has been the warmest day we have had this summer I rose this morning about 4 a clock. I sent Jo: Murdo to Blackader about a stone of Wool and wrote to Blackader to send me a pluvinet whc he did.

Friday 22nd. I was at home all day. Cavers's two youngest boys James & Thomas came over here to see Robie.

Saturday 23rd. I called for Da: Robisone and shewed him severall errors in his accts as that from the 7th of June 1692 to Novr. 7th. 1692 he has given in no acct and yet that he has receaved money from my tenants during that time and his Lammas rent 1692 is not stated and yet he Brings his Ballance of 7th of June 1692 to be the first article of the acct begun on 7th Novr. 1692. He has promised to look out this agst mund. Sr Jo: Home & his Lady and her sister Bethia and Cusen Lilias came this way Going to Stichill. my straberries were fully ripe so I gave them of them. they were very large and good they might have been used 3 or 4 days befor the Verginea if ther were any quantity of them 8 days agoe. I have had Artichoks about eight days agoe. Sr John told me that deacon Rankin had been wt him about repairing the Church. he says ther are 900 stones up on the Church that not one in ten will serve and that most of the stuff betwixt the pend and the stone being Earth must be throuen out and that he cannot possibly think of doing the Church not mentioning the Quear Undir 550 lbs and the Quear and Sr John Homes Iles proportionally the Quear having 600 stones & Sr John Ile 400.

Geo: Brown and Agnes Turner were here. Agnes payd me this terms rent for the Mains of Betshile for her halfe (whc is the Last terme she is due) only she possesses one acre at 8 lb which I knew not off and I beleive has never been stated to her that I remember of she is due me 4 lb for it and 1 lb 1sh short of the Mains whc she has promised me against Wednesday so I gave her a discharge. Geo: payd me 30 lb.

Sunday 24th. Being at Church I told Cavers what Deacon Rankin demanded. he seemed surprised wt he not having laid his acct wt above the halfe so we spoke to the Minister not to desire a visitation as we had befor Concluded till we considerd bett[e]r.

Monday 25th. James Fogo came here and Gave me the 26 lb I had agreed wt his father for in full of what I could Claime as he having been my tenant in Weelfitt of whc I Gave him my discharge. on Saturday was eight days I gave Da: Robisone 7 lb 12sh Scots of English pewter halfe pennies and farthings to passe in England they of late being generally refused in this country. on saturday last he returned me of them 5 lb 13shil. wch will be uselesse the people refusing them in England saying they are cryd doun at London.

Tuesday 26th. I sent my man to Dunse yesterday to my Brother for the kee of the amry in the mid room when he came back he told me the Old Countesse Douager of Home died yesterday morn[in]g. she has been very ill of a gravell the last spring whc brought her very weake beside she was 72 years old. I took the things I had in the litle study as we call it and put them in the Ambry of whc John Brought me the kee and gave Marg. Turner the kee of the litle study for putting her milk ther. the Cow I got from Geo: Umferstone calved the 18th or ther abouts the sam day the old cow should have calved wch is not calved yet. My sister Julian Came here this day from Blackader. I gave her 50 lb Scots. Sunday and allwise since the Mornings have been gloomy and threatened rain but the afternoons clear till night that it fell gloomy again the air sharp in the mornings but warme when the day broke up as it cannot but choose at this time of year. I have been bussie clearing the allmost insuperable difficulties of Da: Robisons accts and have found out many faults in them wch he terms escapes.

Wednesday 27th. I sent John Murdo to Kelso for halfe a pound of tobacco and some bread

Thursday 28th. I receaved from Da: Robisone 144 lb Scots upon acctt of his intromissions. I called for James Forsyth and David and went thro James his accts but they are not all as yet clear.
This day I am entered into the 35 year of my age. Lord teach me to employ the years thou addes to my life in thy fear & service in Christ Jesus our Lord.

Friday 29th. I went to the Old Countesse Douager of Homes buriall from Coldstream to Home Mr Al: Home came from Edr to it I came straight home from thence.

Saturday 30th. I sent John Murdo to Berwick for provisions

Sunday July 1st. I went to Church when I came home I found Mr Al: Home who staid till he supt and went at night to Polwarth House. After I was a bed my Brother came here from Blackader.
Mem: on Monday I sent in My horning and execution therof agst the E of Home to be registrat. Tho Pringle wrote to me wch I receaved on saturday that he had receaved them. I likewise got a letter from Dr Dundas wt the 7th volume of Daicers Horace.

Monday 2nd. Mr Adam Waddell came here in the morning and staid till the afternoon and went to Blackader wt me to visit Sr John Home & his Lady & sisters who goe for Scarborough to morrow. I got from him the 6th volume of Daicers Horace so that now I have 7 volumes of him and Dr Dundas 3. I got likewise Lock of Education.

Tuesday 3rd. This morning Sr John Home sent for my Deck he taking a Sumpter horse along wt him. I was busie most of this day upon Da: Robisons accts.

Wednesday 4th, Having counted what money I have I find it 124 lb 8sh sterlin. I went to the Dowcat and found only 3 pair of eggs in it wch I broke and a pair of doves.
The Weather can only be called not cold sometimes hardly that it is for the most part windy this day out of the S.W. some days agoe N.W.
Mem. Dr Abernethy sent me on munday Pallas Armata a description of the

English plantations in America in french, Esope a comedie in french. Traite du bon usage du lait whc are all the books I know he had of mine. This day the old cow calved a bull calfe the other cows is a quay.

Thursday 5th. Friday 6th. Saturday 7th. I have been at home and seen no body. the Weather has been pretty milde these few days past saturday in the afternoon it was a very pleasant rain

Sunday 8th. I went to Church .Cavers told me that Admirall Russell was dead at sea of a feaver. (I know not whether I have marked that Lieutenant Generall Talmash was dead of his wound he got at the descent at Brest) he told me likewise that the Land forces designed for the descent at Brest are now gone wt the fleet into the Mediterranean. Russels death & yt last are mistakes.

Monday 9th. I caused John Murdo bring me 3 pound of sugar from Berwick on saturday I made this day a bout a pound of conserve of roses. All this day is a very high west s.w. wind, it has shaken very many of my apples and overthrown most of my Artichocks.

Three or four days agoe the cheries upon the flanders cherry tree are ripe the Black Orleans is ripening some allready ripe but I fear the trees are decaying the rest of the Kinds are not yet ripe.

This day was the first time I eat of my peas wch are pretty late by the gardners fault I eat also turnips for the first time

The oats have been at 5 lb & 5 lb 2sh this last week but they are settled Im told peas were also stirring but I know not the rate.

I made 4 bolls and ane halfe of oats of mine oun on Munday was 8 days and got 2 bolls and ane halfe from Da: Robisone in all 7 bolls there was also some peas ground wt the gray shelling for bread to the servants.

Tuesday 10th. Sr Wm Ker of Greenhead his brother Gilbert Young Cliftone Mr Douglas Chamberlane to the E of Roxburgh. Don of Whitslaid. [blank] Scot merchant in Kelso & another came here in the forenoon they staid but a very litle they were going to meet the Countesse of Roxburgh and the E. her sone who are going to Scarburgh wells Sr Wm is going forward to the Wells. I askt him if he heard that Admirall Russell was dead he sd there was no such news at Edr. for he had spoke with one lately come from that. he desired me to tell Julian his Lady desired her to goe to her till he came home.

Wednesday 11th. David Robisone brought me a coppy of his actts from the 2d January 1685 till may 1689. he tells me that ther was no acct. of Russells death in Berwick upon Saturday last but that the French fleet had retired from befor Barcelona upon the News of the English fleets approaching that the English had taken 60 and odde sail of Danish & Swedish ships Going to France with Corn and materialls for ships & brought them in to the Douns.

I sent John Murdo this morning to Wm. Mckall to look to a horse wch he has having none to ride on in the summer but he was away.

I went to Dunse after dinner to look for a Galloway but could see none to please me I saw Will. Mckalls horse but he held him too dear asking 7 lb st. and beside doe not think him well paced. I met wt Swintone and Blackburn we went to Ja: Brouns and talked together. afterward I came to my Brothers chamber wher came Cap: Cockburn. I went to Al: Lorrains and gave them a bottle of wine not having tasted any of this Vintage it was pretty good but 20sh Scots a bottle.

The beasts are fallen of ther price.

Oats give six pund a boll in Lothian, peas as much. Ther is very litle corn in the Country. The wind has continued ever since Munday very high and Cold having turned N.W. it has done much hurt to the bear peas and wheat.

Thursday 12th. I receaved from Da: Robisone 36 lb Scots. I left wt him 15 lb st to give my brother. I am due him this by note beside severall termes cesse. I came from home for Edr and at Betshile receaved from Wm Brack 12 lb scots & Wm Waddell 13 lb 06sh 08d. I dined at Ginglekirk and came in at Night. I lodge in Mrs Romes up Blaires Staire the 4th story upon the street. I visited my Aunt Ninewells & My Lord Crosrig. & Mr Al: Home.

Friday 13th. I payed Mr Geo: Meldrum his anrents due at whits. It Friarshaw his due at that terme. It Walter Burn his due at that terme.

I bought a new Hat. I dined wt My Lord Crosrig. I sent for Mr John Craig who tells me that ther has been nothing relating to me in this session. Tho: Pringle whom I designed to cause raise ane adjudication agst the E. of Home is at Pittfirrin having Written Gosfords Contract of mariage wt Sr Charles Halkets daughter. The News are that de Lorge has repast the Rhine and that in repassing The Prince of Baden defate a considerable party of his men. The armies in Flanders have not acted anything as yet our fleet is gone into the Mediterranean but no certaine acct from it, some say they have blockt up the French fleet in the Bay of Rose's

Saturday 14th. I dined wt My Lo: Crosrig he having invited me to a solen goose after dinner I walked wt him to the Physick garden wher we met wt My Lo: Newbaith My Lo: Presmennen & Wisha. after our walk we went to the Bull & supped. having met wt Blackwood we treated the Lords of the Session. I got this day from Meg Home the Dutchesses of Claves wch she had of me a long time it is Hary Fletchers Ladies

Sunday 15th. I went to the Tollbooth church forenoon and after noon at night I supped wt Mr Al: Home wher My Lord Polwarth also supt

Monday 16th. I spoke to Whytefeild anent my raising ane adjudication agst the E. of Home desiring to try if he knew if my Lo: were resolved to settle wt me but not finding any such inclination by what I could learn from him I resolve to proceed in my diligence. but Tho: Pringle is over the water in Pittffren. I expect him hourly here in toune. I dined wt my aunt Ninewells after dinner I went to my Lo: Crosrigs after yt I visited the Lady Jeriswood and after I went to Mr Al: Homes chamber. he & I went wt Dr Stevensone and drank a glasse of Wine. Saturday yesterday and this day have been very warme It has rained all this afternoon.

Tuesday 17th. Ther is talk here this day that the English are now landed at Diep and beseiging it litle other news. I dined wt Mr Al: Home. this day his been showers of rain up and doune.

Tho: Pringle for whom I have been waiting all this time came to toune this day. I trysted him again tomorrow to get my papers for raising ane adjudication agst the E. of Home. I went to Fennwicks wt Mr Al: Home & Earnslaw

Wednesday 18th. Tho: Pringle Came here to my chamber and got for raising ane adjudication agst the E.of Home the following papers:
(1) Contract betwixt the E. and me dated the 3rd I think of Feb. 1683.
(2) Articles of agreemt dated 14th Decer 1683.
(3) Bond of 2,500 Ms be him to me. Registrat.
(4) Decreit & act at my instance agst the E.
(5) decreit of Circumduction at my instance agst him
(6) Decreit of suspension &c at my instance agst him.

I got up from him my horning registrat. I spoke to him to ask about the Exchange of money he tells me it gives $2\frac{1}{2}$ per cent. This time twelve months giving in 94 lb here one would have got 100 lb at London but the occasion of this was the forces that are now gone for Flanders were payd from England.

I payd this day to James Galbreths man the Lady Tarsappie's interest from sometime in January 1693 to Candlemas last 1694 being 41 lb 8s.

I met wt My Lord Polwarth designing to have gone home he spoke to me anent clearing the acct betwixt him & me so I staid and went to him after dinner he gave me the acct to adjust. I brought it home wt me and made a charge and discharge and went to Him betwixt 7 & 8. after having stated the acct we agreed that my Lord Crosrig should discharge My Lord Polwarth of Henry Douglas's bond & that my Lord Polwarth should grant me a bond for the ballance of the acct.

I caused Geo: Mosman print me some alphabets of the small Character to teach Robbie by.

Mem: Mr Al: Home gave me some days agoe my note of 30 lb Scots, to John Raynolds wch I payd Jo: in Winter last or sometime befor but got not up my note he not finding it at that time.

Thursday 19th. I went to My Lord Crosrig in the morning and told him that I had fitted [sic] my acct wt my Lo: Polwarth and that if he thought it fitt he as assigney should discharge Henry Douglases debt and that I should give him a receate of the money in part of paymt and to acct of what was betwixt him and me. he desired I might cause Mr Al: Home draw the discharge and I should draw the paper I was to grant him. I went to Mr Al: Home and caused him draw the discharge I brought it to my Lo: Crosrig he said he had not yet thought how the paper I was to grant him should be conceaved because that tho he thought it was his oun money he had payd Henry Douglas wt yet he found it was Blackaders and seemed to say as much as that I was overpayd of what Blackader was due me and that he having given out Blackaders money upon my acct I ought to pay Blackader anrent for what was given out on my acct more than payd my sume. I told him I knew not how it stood betwixt Blackader & him but that if he was ouing me the time he payd Henry Douglas as much as would pay him it would allwise be reput that he had given it out of his own money and it would come to the same thing, for the more he had payd out of Blackaders money for me the more he himselfe would be ouing me. He seemed very undetermined but desired he might think on it and that I might stay till tomorrow in the afternoon at whc time he would have more leasure. I told him that I hoped the clearing wt my Lord Polwarth should not be stopt by him. we spoke no more of it. I dined wt him and after dinner went and told My Lord Polwarth that My Lo: Crosrig desired to think a litle on the nature of the paper I was to grant him. I went afterward to Dr Dundas's chamber and from that to my aunt Ninewells's and from that home.

Friday 20th. I went to my Lo: Crosrigs & spoke to him again about my ending wt Polwarth he said he would think on it agst night

Whytefeild sent to me for some books I had borrowed fro him for wch he had my note. I had left them wt Dr Dundas when I went last from this so I sent my man for ym who got them & I retired my note

In the afternoon I caused Mr Al: Home call for the grounds of the Marquis of Douglas's decreit of non entry agst being affraid the executions may be changed because of Blackwoods confidence they are right enough. Mr Al: met wt the young man one Stuart who showed them to us befor in Mr James Daes's chamber. he was very willing to show us them again wherby I beleive they are not as yet changed. however he not being at leasure then I left wt Mr Al: 2 lb to give him and desired Mr Al: might have present famous wittneses to see them in case they should be changed.

I went afterwards to Tho: Pringles Chamber and talkt wt him anent my decreit of adjudication agst the E. of Home. he promised to have it ready agst the next week or the week after. I told him that the E. had payd out for me some money about 40 lb st of anrents to Ro. Dalmahoys children, about 10 lb st to Dr Nisbet he sd it would be fit to mention these things and desired I might send him a note of what was due and what was given out.

I went afterward to look for Mr Al: Home I found him in Fenwicks wt Sr Walter Seatone and Geo. Robisone.

Saturday 21st. I went in the morning to My Lo. Crosrig to see what he would doe in the bussines betwixt my Lo: Pol: and me anent the summe payd to Henry Douglas. he pretended he had been looking for a paper that would have cleared what money of Blackader had been given out on my acct but could not find it yet he sd he was content to signe a discharge to my Lord Polwarth providing I would signe ane obligation to repay Blackader the money given out on my acct wt the anrent therof if it should be found that ther was more given out than he was due me. I told my Lo: as befor that he being my debtor as well as Blackader till both the debts were exhausted I could not pay interest to any of them. he sd he was not my debtor only that I had accesse to his Uncles estate. I was not willing to Urge the argument further only told him that I saw this bussines of mine wt my Lo: Polwarth behooved to ly over till he and I cleared so I took leave of him designing to goe hom[e] this day.

I went afterward to My Lo: Polwarth told him what my Lo: Crosrig had sd wch was the occasion we could not clear. my Lo: Pol: was very desirous some periode might be put to it but it could not be so all we did was to keep every one of us a double of the acct as it stood and mark on the foot that the other had the double of it.

I went afterward and Cleared my Chamber rent went to see my aunt Ninewells & Meg Home took my boots in Dr Dundas's chamber my Horse at the foot of the Kirkheugh & so came from Edr about ten dined at Ginglekirk called at Betshile and came home about 9 at night

Monday 23rd. Since I went to Edr the weather hes been pretty warm wt pleasant showers (tho they tell me ther has been no rain here in this place since) Sunday and this day have been very cold the wind somewhat high and N.E. & N.W. so that at night I cannot dispense wt a fire and would have it all day were it not extraordinary to have a fire in the daytime in July. I went not abroad yesterday.

This morning I sent for Da: Robisone and sent him to Berwick to try what the exchange is ther to London designing God willing to goe ther within a few days

I sent John Murdo to Lantone to bring home my Black horse designing to take him up for my Journey. he hes been ther since the 6 of June at 2 sh Scots a night I gave John money to pay for him

Al: Jeff. payd me ten pund 10 sh in full of Whits: rent last past. see his acct.

I went over to Nisbet in the afternoon Cavers went to Edr this morning. Dr

Abernethy came ther while I was ther he walked out wt me we talkt about travelling in England. I went to the Douecat to have broke the eggs ther because it is lint time I saw a pretty good number and broke 3 paire but thin I began to consider that the feild peas would be ready in a fourtnights time the question is whither the doves can loot them befor they be full ripe and cutt doun for then the cods open easier. till I am resolved of this I held my hand beside I considered the lint bolls will be out of the way in a fourtnight if this be not it will be better to break them for ther is not eating a pigeon fed wt them they have so abominable a taste.

The old Cherrie trees carry still and are but just now ripe they have never been graft yet the cherry is not unpleasant when fully ripe

This day till about 2 a clock has been very cold but since that time warme enough litle or no wind anything ther is is from S.W.

Tuesday 24th. I was at home all day. Dav: Robisone brought me word they will have 2 per cent of Exchange. ther is none in Berwick but Young Comptone can afford it so.

Wednesday 25th. I sent to Dunse for provisions to the house. the Nurse who has been here some time this summer being desirous to be back to Edr I ordered John Murdo in wt her upon the Black mare agst tomorrow morning. I gave her a R dollar & a coat for her husband. I wrote to my Lo: Polwarth to know if wt his convenience he could send me a precept upon one of his tenants of 15 lb or 20 lb. I send my Lo: Crosrig the 3 volumes of of [sic] Abadé and wrote to him he would doe me a kindnesse to send me wt John Murdo 15 lb or 20 lb. I wrote to Mr Al: Home litle or no bussiness only to know if he had seen the grounds of the Marquis of Douglas's decreit. I wrote likewise to Tho: Pringle & sent him in a note of my Lo: Homes debts due to me and what the E. had payd out for me to witt 40 lb st as two years anrent to Ro: Dalmahoy. It a year & ane halfe or 2 years anrent to Doctor Nesbit of 2,000 Ms. Inde at most 160 lb. It upon my acct to Vogry 138 lb. some odd shillings and pennies. I find since he has payd Mr Tho. Gordon a debt he Ninewells & I were bound in I beleive it was to pay the thousand Ms was borrowed when we went to Bothwell Bridge wherin Borthwick & Eccles were also concerned. so that I must cause leave room for all these things. I am also conjunct wt him to Castlehill for my Lo: Polwarth wch he payd I think the summe is a thousand Ms. but I beleive the ane halfe is only Polwarths the other halfe the Es oun. I ordered John Murdo to buy me a totum wt six sides in Wylies for Robie & some bread.

Thursday 26th. Geo: Brown came hither & payed out his Whits days rent all to 3 sh st.

He begins to repine at the price of the tree I sold him by way of roup the truth is it was dear enough.

Wm Brack payed me out his Whits. rent for the acres. James Jaffrey payd me 31 lb of his Lammas rent last & his acct.

This day has been milde but gloomy threatening rain the 2 days past have been cold north west winds, so that I have had a fire evening and morning

Friday 27th. This morning Dr Abernethy came over here from Nisbet. he got Martignac's Horace I had of him & I lent him 7 volumes of Mr Daicers Horace and the Alcoran in French. When I look I find he has not the 4th volume of Horace but if I find occasion I will send it to him.

Geo: Johnstone cleared wt me this day.

Ja: Ridpath was at me seeking timber for repairing his barn.

James Forsyth payd me his Lammas rent next to come

Saturday 28th. I have been all day and yesterday afternoon on David Robisons accts wch It is allmost impossible to cleare unlesse a man had them by heart for he sets down many things twice in different places sometimes puts 2 or three articles in one and then disjoins them wt ane hundred such things but I have taken some pains in them and must take more.

John Murdo returned not till this night. He Brought me the answer of my Letters my Lord Crosrig says he is to pay money at Lammas and cannot answer me. My Lord Polwarth has sent me a precept upon Tho: Rutherfords Elder and Yr of 20 lb st. Mr Al: Home writes to me that the Executions of the Marquis's summonds are just as I saw them to witt vitiat. Robin Pringle and Pa: Home Bells brother saw them. He writes yt Jeriswood takes journey on Wednesday and knows not of any company as his Lady says. The news that all Dieppe is burnt and Halfe of Havre de Grace that Russell has blockt up the French fleet in Thoulon that a battle is dayly expected in Flanders & yet great talking of a peace. Gid: Elliot has sent me the piluloe bulsaemicae I sent for. John Murdo has Brought me the Ivory Totum with six sides I bad him. It hes been a small rain all this day a[nd] foggy.

Sunday 29th. Ther was no sermon at Edrom. I went not from home in the Afternoon Dr Sinclairs Lady and Cavers came here from Fogo Church Cavers was telling me he came from Edr on fridays night he had been in about buying his teinds from Wedderburn by a decreit of the Commission for Valuation of teinds that He was to goe in next day and had cited wittnesses one of wch is Da: Robisone to prove the Value the Lords not admitting ether of the fiars as a rule or 100 Ms the Chalder as the price. He told me likewise that Sr John Cochran had gott the poll money whc was rouped the 25 instant he gives 44,100 lb sterlin.

Monday 30th. I sent for old Thomas Rutherford and shewed him My Lo

Polwarts precept he promised me paymt this afternoon Ja: Ridpath brought me
24 lb Scots of wch I gave him a receat in part of paymt of his Mart. Rent next
to come.

Thomas Rutherfords Elder and Younger came to me in the after noon and
payd me My Lord Polwarths precept of 240 lb each paying 120 lb

Tuesday 31st. I went to Blackader in the afternoon to see the bairns Sr John
& his Lady were just lighted he has been fro home just a month. I got from
him Boileau and promised to send him Lock of Education. I got also Colisons
perfect accountant which I must send to Polwart house it being my Lords.

Wednesday August 1st. I went to Dunse. I got some guineys from my brother
for money. I drunk a bottle of wine wt him Capt Cockburn Mr Comptone
Younger from whom Dav: Robisone is to get me a bill for London I see
Cornette Holburn I returned by Nisbet. There is no news at present.

This day and yesterday have been very pleasant & warme ther is still a great
drought

The old cherrie trees have had very good cherries this year and all last week
have been very good ther are of them still.

Alison Waddell payd me 17 lb 16sh 4d whc makes her Martimes rent 1693.

Thursday 2nd. I went in the after noon to visit Swintone but he was from
home. his Lady is better having been ill since she was brought to bed (the
childe is dead since). I returned by Harcars and missed my Lord he being gone
to Polwarthouse. I saw my Lady. when I came home. I found Mr Adam
Waddell & Mr Androw Guthrie here

David Robisone being returned from Edr brought a letter from Mr Al: Home
telling me Jeriswood was to be at Polwarthouse this night I sent one presently
to know of his dyet he sent me word he was to goe next morning so I wrote to
Sr Jo: Home telling him I was desirous to see him

Friday 3rd. Sr John came hither and a little after my brother whom I had
also writt to the night befor but he was not at home. Not having provided
myselfe of a bill I sent Robin Robisone to Berwick to Young Mr Comptone
whom Da. Robinsone had engaged to give me one but he returned me answer
he could not possibly give it till saturday. I went to Polwarthouse My Brother
wt me when I cam ther Jeriswood told me the horse he designed for his cloack
bag was lame & that he behooved to get another whc would stay him all day.
My Lord Jedburgh was ther. I dined ther & returned home in the afternoon. as
soon as I came ther finding we were not to goe till next day I sent John Murdo
home to cause Da: Robisone goe to Berwick for the bill Mr Comptone is to
give me. My Brother went to Dunse & Came here at night and brought me
some Louis dors. James Jaffrey cleared his Candlemes rent this night.

[The "parchment pocket book" (see below) not having survived, there is no account of the London visit; the diary resumes on the next page]

1695

Friday 4th. January. 1695. I returned home from London having gone from this the 4th of Augst 1694. What has occurred to me since that time till now is writ in a parchmt pocket book I had wt me. that morning I went from this I got a bill of 50 lb st from Mr Comptone Junior in Berwick upon Mr Jos Jacksone Mert in London wherof 40 lb was Da: Robinsons and 10 lb I gave out & 1 lb likewise for exchange.

I left wt Margaret Turner 5 lb 19sh Scots for buying things for the house.

at night I sent to my Brother for the Kee of the presse I sent Him from London wch he sent me

Saturday 5th. My brother came hither in the Morning. he tells me that he sent Mr Alexr Home the gift of the E. of Homes Escheat. I find My Lord Crosrig the E of Annandale & the Countesse Douager of Home are likewise contending for it. the E. of Home himselfe is also seeking it he is at Edr it seems by liberty from the Councill. my Brother says that those yt are seeking the gift say my gift signifies nothing not being presented wtin year and day after the date of the gift. this morning I sent John Lidgate to Berwick for provisions to the house and the black Cloath I bought from Mr Stow and a warming pan 1 ounce of cloves 1 ounce of Nutmegs and 1 ounce of flour of Brimstone all wch he brought me save the Warming pan ther being none to be had.

Cavers came here and stayd till it was pretty dark. he tells me Sr Ro: Stuart has got part of the Excrescence of the Cesse it being divided betwixt the E. of Hadingtone My Lord Polwarth and him. he told me likewise that that division had stopt any further Valuation but that when they were beginning to Value and every Heritor to give in his rentall upon his word and signed by his hand he S.R. [Sir Robert] gave in his rentall at 4,000 lb tho all know it to have been above 5,000 so that ther was no other rental given in.

Mem. I counted wt Al: Jaffrey and got money fro him, and got up some receats of my Brothers and DRs [David Robisone]

Sunday 6th. the day being ill I went not to church

Monday 7th. David Robisone was at me this morning & told me he would have difficulty to get money till Candlemisse. Mr Adam Waddell came here just as I had dined a litle after My Lo: Harcas and his sone & Mr Ro: Sandilands Minister of Swintone. Swintone & his family is at Edr. Mar: Turner gave me in an acct of the 5 lb 19sh I gave her when I went to

London and of 9 lb she got from Dav: Robsone and of 2 lb she got from James Forsyth. she tells me she has got a furlet of meal from James Forsyth the meal made befor I went away being done at Christmasse

Mem: When I was at Berwick I wrote to Mr Home to get 53 Maps Mundi Vit. from Vaillant wch I had given him to get Illuminat that the Illuminating would stand about 2d or 1d^1/$_2$. a peice. to Get fro Mr Brissac next door to Vaillants a perfumer 2 bottles of the Queen of Hungaries Watr 4 soap balls 3 botles oil of Jasmine & A litle bottle of Essence of lemon thyme. It I wrote to him to get ten lbs from Mr Geo: Jacksone having spoke to Mr Comptone Yr to write to him about it whc he promised to doe I counted wt Ja: Jaffrey and got money from him & some receats of my brothers & Da: Robisons.

Tuesday 8th. I went in the forenoon to Nisbet and dined. when I came home I found Mr Adam Waddell who staid wt me till thursday after dinner

Wednesday 9th. having on tuesday sent for the folks of Betshile they came all Here except the smith who it seems had no money. I receaved from them about 162 lb and got up some receats of my brothers & David Robisons as by accts. this last night and all this day is a great N.E. wind and a frost

Thursday 10th. Sr John Home came here this morning going Falside to the buriall of one of the Lady Fulsydes daughtress wt Bellita Called Margaret Home I got a letter but this day is so cold that I could not goe nether would I beleive he have gone if his Lady were not at Stichill. John Lidgate gave me 9 lb Scots wch he says he agreed wt my brother as the price of my fruit I gave him a shiling again he gave me also 6sh. as the price of 3 pints of Honey and 10d as the price of a pound of wax. he has yet a pint of honey and the old honey I gave him he is keeping for feeding the bees. they being as he says very weak. John Denholme sone in law to Wm Trotter got from me 10 lb Scots (Da: Robisone having given him formerly as much) as his father in laws arent due at Mart. last. Mr Adam Waddell went home this afternoon. John Lidgate got from Me some seck his wife being in travell

Friday 11th. Dav: Robisone brought me ane acct of what money his [sic] has got in or given out since I went to London. Petr Broun came here to talk wt me about the English Gardens and gardening and Wyses in particular. And Thos: Rutherford came here and we spoke about setting the Westfeild and Greenknow and Kingslaw. I went in the afternoon & visited my Lord Harcasse and his Lady I saw not the Young Lady she being indisposed. I wrote to Sandy Home (London) to cause Mr Wyse send me 56 dwarf standard pears. 20 aples 10 plums 2 peaches and four plums for the Wall. from Mr Westone a bushel of accorns 2 or 3 hundred Walnuts 2 or 3 ounces of pitch tree seed a pound or two of Lime tree seed as much beech mast. To remember what I told him anent the

E. of Homes affair to try for a good house clock at a 2d hand. to cause Mr
Deyon buy me Kersies arithmetique

[Saturday 12th.] I went as soon as I was drest to Blackader not having seen
the Lady since I returned home and Sr John and she having returned this way
yesterday as they came from Stitchill. It was pretty late befor I returned. It has
freized all this day and yestirday very hard and the Wind S.W.

Sunday 13th. I went to Church. this day is a strong thaw Wind from W.S.W.
yet Blackader Water carried but Wedderburn did not. I came befor the Minister
went in and so Went and visited him and his wife. I see Sr Robert Stuart at
Church his Lady is lately brought to bed of a daughter & is not come abroad
yet. A propos the Young Lady Mangertone is about a month agoe brought to
bed of a daughter

Monday 14th. Wm. Home of Greenlaw Castle sent me a letter this morning
craving his arents betwixt and Candlemes. I writt to him I should order them
agst that time. In the afternoon Dr Abernethy came here he returned me the
Alcoran in Fr. he borrowed from me he went to Nisbet Mrs Blair being unwell.
It has snowed some this day and theres a strong wind from the N.E.

Tuesday 15th. The day being ill wt showers of snow and a north E. wind.
hindered me from going to Church. It became calme and clear in the afternoon
and it freezes

Wednesday 16th. This morning is a frost wt a Boisterous N.E. wind and
some showers of Hail & snow. Al: Jaffrey brought to the loft 4 bolls and six
pecks of oats and sometime last week 2 bolls 2 pecks of Bear wch pays his
teind. Da: Robisone has the [barn - deleted] loft full of his peas. I ordered his
Brother to get them disposed some other way and get over the oats that are in
it. ther is in the loft 7 bolls of the teind bear. Having some old peas in the loft I
cause carry halfe a peck to the doucoat.

Thursday 17th. Mr Adam Waddell sent to me for a French Dictionary for his
Brother George. I sent him Dands Fr: and Lat dict. he sent likewise for Allans
Catechism whc I sent him. I went in the afternoon to Blackader wher I stayd
all night (by the Way I visited Mr Ad. Wad and his sistr Mrs Comry). I sent
home my horses

Friday 18th. Next morning Mr Daniel Douglas came ther and Crosrig I
stayd dinner. Mr Daniel told us a number of stories he spoke by way of
Rapsodie but very pleasantly. Sr Rot Stuart came over in the afternoon I find
the Country is full of the news of Luxembourgs being dead and that his sone

designed Momorency has killed the Duke of Maine a Bastard sone of the Fr: Ks. and is fled for it from France to Brussells [in the margin - this did not hold] and is now at London. I returned at night

Mem: I receaved from Da: Robisone 5 lb yesterday

I wrote to Mr Home at London desiring him to pay Keps acct to buy me Leister for Dr Abernethy and to direct my goods for Mr Comptone Junior and if he can to enter them for Scotland to save trouble of opening at Berwick. I ordered Da: Robisone to buy me a 3d loaf in Berwick a pair of stokins to Robie and 6 ounces of Worsted

Saturday 19th. Alexr Jaffrey payd me 9 lb Scots in full of 160 lb due at Mart. last. It I gave him a receat for his teind and another for a dozen of Cain hens.

I remember among other things Mr Daniel Douglas told us he sd that in the Genesis Bara Elokim Creavit Deus bara is in the singular number & Elokim in the plurall but reading the words backward immediatly preceeding the word bara they make up in Hebrew the 3 persons of the trinity. He quarelld much at the [new - deleted] last translation of the Bible especially of the new testament alledging that they were a company of men sett to please K. James. one of the Instances he gave was that they did not translate the word Eniokopos allwise the same way. sometimes they translated it overseers as take heed to the flock over whom the holy ghost has made you overseers and in other places when it made for ther purpose they translated it bishop so that they endeavoured to by ther translation as much as they could to countenance Episcopacy. He mentioned another text that he sd was not well translated (We have this treasure in Earthen vessels) wheras in the originall it is wiorpaioi whc is in oyster shells and is very emphatick for the oyster shell is ugly wtout but neat and clean wtin. And that the oyster shell was that wherin pearls were ordinarily found in. He alledged that the Nicolaitans spoken of in the Rev. were called so of Nicolas who is called in the b. of the Acts a proselyte of Antioch that it was not for nothing yt was added for near Antioch ther was a temple of Venus wher all the young people used to feast & debauch and that Nicolas being educat ther tho he became Christian yet [afterwards joined - deleted] ether retaind or returned to this way he had been Educat in. He told that Paul was two ways a nobleman of Rome first by birth and 2ly by adoption of Sergit Paulus who after his conversion by Paul adopted him and Gave him his name of Paul and it is remarkable that in that very chap wher Ser. Paulus's conversion is mentioned Saul is first named Paul.

Sunday 20th. It has snowed much and bloun this day so I could not goe to Church. the Weather was out of the N.E. David Rotsone came here in the morning and brought me a note of a letter from my Lo: Polwarth from the post house of Berwick directed for me to be sent to me wt Care and hast but when I lookt I found it written on Sat was eight dayis and ther is only this in it Cusin I wish you wellcome and that you may be here on tuesday if your gift passe not on Wednesday I fear it shall be of no use so that Im affraid my bussines is lost that way. Da: Brought home bread but no stokans nor worsted. Sr John Home and his Lady were at Church as bad a day as it was they sent me word that poor Joseph Johnstone of Hiltone was dead and buried. he was at the Colledge at Edr but I have not heard what his disease was.

Monday 21st. I got from James Jaffrey 50 lb. Ther has a great dale of snow fallen this night so all the ground is covered wt snow.
   I sent up to Dunse to my Brother a note to enquire for any papers he has of mine relating to my Lo: Home affair. I find ether he or Pa: Cockburn must have the Horning raised agst My Lord Home upon my last decreit. but I think rather Pa: Cockburn has it for I find no mention of it since he got it to Charge the E. for Whitsdays annuity. I sent John Lidgate to Blackader to see if And Watheret was going to Edr. He Brought me word that he was gone to Kelso but the snow is so deep that I think he cannot goe
   John Murdo brought me a letter from my Brother wherin he sends me enclosed my Horning agst the E. of Home wch I find to be registrat 25 of June last. ther is likewise ane execution for the term of Whitsonday last dated Augst 13th. last but it is not registrat. I wrote to my Brother to know how the ways were he writes that both Moor way and wester way are impassible and that the way to the post road every step is to the horse belly. he tells me Thomas Pringle has the summonds of adjudication

Tuesday 22nd. Sr John Home came here in the morning tho the wind drives the snow very hard he staid till near sunsett all the afternoon it snowed and blew very hard. in the morning the wind was N.W. and fair but in the afternoon it turnd N.E. again and then It snowd. ther is now a great storm on the ground so that I know not how to get to Edr wher my affairs require me extremly. We were regrating poor Joseph Johnstones death which gave Sr John occassion to tell me that this summer Tho: Pringle riding with Young Abbey now Minaster of Aitone in view of Hutton hall Abbey sd to him I cannot see that place but my heart warms and told him that Mr Jos: Johnstone had evicted it from Sr John Home of Huttonhall (who was I think his Grand Uncle) by ane expird Comprising far below the Value of the Lands and that Gods Judgemts were seen upon his posterity, and having enumerat the misfortunes that befell tha late Huttone and his brother George he sd and as for this young man you shall see he shall not live till he be 25. whether the matter of fact be true that Mr Jos. got these Lands below the Value I know not having never heard it befor And what moved Abby to speake so in relation to this poor young lad I will not determine whether any forsight of the thing or a heat and concern transported him which eventually came to passe. if it was this last it was very unwarrantable but I am no judge of these things, Sometimes we see God punish the posterity of the Wicked and those who by indirect means have acquired Estates sometimes we ill [sic] conquest Estates thrive beyond the 3 & 4 Generation so that it is hard to give a sentence on such matters God acts as seems best to him.

Wednesday 23rd. Ther has much snow fallen this night and it still snows but tis calme ther is now a great storme of snow on the ground.

Thursday 24th. I receaved a letter from Mr Al: Home pressing to be in Edr Wednesday last. It was written on saturday. he tells me all the stop in my bussines comes from the E. of Annandale but Gives me no particulars. He writes that Ninewells and Lo. Polwarth are impatient to have me in toune. this made me resolve to goe for Edr next day so I sent to my Brother to know what travelling he hears it is. John Murdo brought me word that ther was no going the Wester way but that some this day were gone the post road but that it is ill getting to it. I sent to Blackader for a loan of his Black sword & his cloakbag sadle and Maillepillion.

Friday 25th. Rot Knox returned not till I was a bed. he brought me Sr Johns sadle and sword I wrote for and a letter from Sr John wt one to Dr Dundas and another to Tho: Row. My sister Isabel wrote also to me in a very singular way for money. this day blows so hard that they perswade me ther will be no geting thro the Moors so I have laid aside my resolution of going this day. My sisters letter contained a number of reproches for unkindnes cruelty and hatred. that since Whitsonday she had not had a farthing of me and was forced to be obliged to Sr John Home for mentenance &c and in the Conclusion desired money. I wrote to her that her reproches did not surprise me &c but that I was much surprised wt her complaint of my not giving her money remembering she refused ye superplus of what was due to Pa: Adamsones children. that she could not expect that I should offer her money wtout seeking that I was still the same as to my opinion of gratuity. Yet that I had allwise dealt wt her as if it had been obligation till this bussines of Pa. Ads fell out whc it was fit should be paid agst that tho the superplus was 39 lb I had ordered Da: Robisone to give her 5 lb st.
I writt likewise to Julian that waiting every day for a good day to goe to Edr I could not send my horses for her.

Saturday 26th. It has been sometimes calme sometimes windy but still it snows. the snow is soft whc hinders it to blow. it comes now from South East

Sunday 27th. I went not out It was foul in the morning but the afternoon was very pleasant clear and a hard frost.

[in margin - Receaved fro Jamy Forsyth 40 lb fro D.R.24.]

Monday 28th. I took horse in the morning betwixt seven and 8 being resolved if possible for Edr. it snowed all the time as we went to Dunse. I called my brother who had sent me word he would goe wt me but he could not goe having a party quartered on him for cesse. Capt Cockburn told me I would have ill travelling and advised me to get a pair of light boots. I got but [sic] good luck a pair from my Brother. I went to Prestone and ther took a guide one James White. we had very deep snow and very oft were forced to walk above the knees in snow whc toild me very much. yet God be thanked we had a clear day and no blowing so that we mist not the way. We came by Quickswood and Butterdane & Blackburn and Eccily and Foulfordlies Cockburnspeth and so to the posthouse in Pethhead. Dav: Robisone and Rot his brother were wt me.

Tuesday 29th. I came forward to Haddingtone. by the Way I lighted att Lintone bridgs [sic] to warme my selfe it being extremly cold and drunke some warme ale. I met Bishop Woods corps going to Dunbar he died at a place near Hadingtone called the Abbey. I din'd at provost Lauders and fear to spoil the black mare I left her at Hadingtone & hird horse ther for John Lidgate. I came to toun about 5 a clock the way was extremly well paved and good so that I told them that askt me that the sands of Musslebrough was the worst way I had got and they were as good as they use to be. I alighted in the Kirkheugh and went up to Dr Dundas's chamber. he was in my aunt Ninewelles. I went up and sat wt her and Meg and sent to look for a chamber but ther was none in the stair. then I went and visited my Lord Crosrig and from that to Ninewelles chamber. he has been ill of the Cold for some time. I sent and sought a chamber in the Stair wher Ninewells lodges in the back of the court of Guard and found one in one Mrs Johnstones but it is young Stevensones and I must goe out of it as soon as he comes to toune but I could find no other so went to it. the[y] ask 14 sh Scots for it anight. Mr Al: Home came over to me to Ninewells chamber. I have got but a lame acct of the bussines as yet for wch I came to toun

Wednesday 30th. I sent John Lidgate home wt the horses and sent Robie a pair of shoes and writt to Sr John Home, and to Da Robisone to send me what money he could and try to sell the 2 cows. James Forsyth had been speaking to me for one of them and offered me 14 lb
I went in the forenoon to my Lord Polwarths lodging he gave me acct of my bussines of the E's Escheat. that Annandale had procured a letter from the King discharging any gift to passe till the case of all pretenders were represented to him. that it would be necessary we gave in our pretentions to a committy appointed for that effect but that we should insist as little as possible in reflecting anything upon Annandales title but fortify our oun the best way

we could and leave the rest of the Creditors to invalidat Annandales pretences as much as could be. I gave Gilbert Somervail my clothes to make. I dined wt Ninewells in his chamber and sat wt him till about 7 a clock. that I went out wt Mr Al: Home to meet wt Earnslaw in Bouchans. I got ane acct from him of the ground of Annandales claim agst the E of Home wch because I am not distinctly informed of I omit at present. he told me likewise that ther is past since my first wifes death ane adjudication of the Estate of Aitone at Mr John Bethuns instance wch is now passing the privy seal and to wch I would doe well to take heid. Mem. to consider about the teinds of Eccles parish.

Thursday 31st. I went to My Lo: Polwarths and dined. he told me he had got the Comitty that is appointed for taking in our Claims putt of till twesday. In the afternoon I met wt Whytfield who spoke to me in the Bussines of the E. of Homes Escheat. he pretends if this bussines had not fallen out that the E. had laid doun such Methodes as would have cleared him of debt in 7 years. I told him it was ill luck this should have fallen in at such a nick of time but that it was but a cloack to cover his former unjustnes to his creditors. I went afterward and waited on my Lord Crosrig. we came to talk of the Es. Escheat he told me he wondered I had never acquainted him wt my having the gift of the Es Escheat that by his offering to take it he had brought a great dale of odium on himselfe and got no benefit by it and that if he had knoun of my having it he would never have sought for it. I sd that all my designe in taking it was to bring the E. to a reasonable agreemt and that no body knew it save my Lord Polwarth & Ninewells who were concerned in it & that if he had told me he had a mind to take it I could allwise have told him I had it allready. he showed me a coppy of the Kings letter in favours of Annandale and told me that he had a list of the debts Annandale Charged upon the E. of Home but being bussy wt his informations I left him and went and visited My Aunt Ninewells and from thence to Ninewells chamber and so home

Friday February 1st. I got my cloaths from the Tayler. Meg Home came here and I desired her to get me 2 muslan cravats. she told me of some differences were betwixt her as factrix to her Brother Will and Ninewells who oues Will 500 Ms by bond but that Ninewells thinks to compensed [sic] that summe by his mothers letting doun the house of Ninewells and a Mault killn and barn and cutting planting for whc he may get praetium affecttiones. I think it would be fitt such differences were taken away.
I went to My Lord Crosrigs who had invited me to dinner wher Ninewell's also dined. we went after dinner to my aunt Ninewells's and from that I went to visit the Lady Jeriswood who told me she had a letter from Jeriswood wherin he writte she wishes the gift in my favours of the E. of Homes Escheat had never been given. what sense to put on this I know not yet. I went afterwards and visited the Lady Hiltone and mett wt Sandy Home & Earnslaw

and went to Will Toms together. Earnslaw told me severall things relating to the Estate of Home particularly that E: Alexr pursuing his fathers creditors in Annandales name upon Jossys [?] apprysing it was found by Witnesses that this debt was payd and satisfied out of the price of Dunglasse but the depositions will be ill to be had tho I beleive he may know wher they are

Nota for ought I find the E. of Home has no good title to the Teinds of Eccles parish

Saturday 2nd. It his been a great thaw these 2 or 3 days wt a south west wind wt out rain. I dined wt my aunt Ninewells. My Lord Crosrig spoke to Ninewells yesterday to look to himselfe and not to neglekt his health being under appearing symptoms of a decay. he prest the thing a little too hard wherat Ninewells beginning to Canker as people in sicknes use to doe I interposed and told Ninewells he should not say too far in refusing to take phisicians and advice and desired my Lord Crosrig not to presse him too hard but to give him time to consider. I spoke to him in the afternoon and told him that tho I hoped his condition was not so ill as his freinds apprehended yet it being visible his strength & vigour were abated and that he was become much leaner than ordinary yet it was fit to satisfy them so far as to ask advice of a physitian. I proposed Dr Dundas as understanding that disease particularly as being much inclined to it himselfe but wt all desired him to pitch on any other in whom he had more confidence. he yielded to my desire as to advising wt a physician but ballanced a litle about the Choice but after consideration he resolved upon Dr Dundas whom he advised wt this afternoon. This day or yesterday I was walking up the street wt Mr Al: Home and met wt Capt Cunninghame my fellow traveller and afterward was attackt by my old freind Paton who in short told me he would be relieved of Mrs Yeuls debt and that he had given up wt the Lady Hiltone and now gave up wt me and that he would put the Caption agst me in Execution. He had one agst in K. James's time but I had a protection but I knew not whether it be upon his relief from Polwart &c or upon Mrs Yeuls Bond that he had it for if it was upon the last I am informed by the Lady Hiltone that he has no commission from her and if one the first the bond of relief was granted to George Mosman and not to him so that he cannot persue on it. I acquainted the Lady Hiltone wt it and desired her to send for Mrs Yeul. I went afterwards to the Lord Polwarths but he was not to be found so I came home

Sunday 3rd. I went to the Tron church fore and after noon and supped wt Dalmeny it was his Mariage day

Monday 4th. I dined wt my Lord Polwarth and talked wt him about our gift of Escheat and resolved to advise wt Mr Heugh Dalrymple in it. I went to Mr Heugh and spoke to him he sd he was in no wise Engaged yet pressed me to

Concert wt my Lo: Crosrig wrby I suspect that he has writt to Secretary Stair in Crosrigs favours. I went afterwards to my Lord Crosrig and spoke to him about the E. of Hs Escheat. he seemed undeterminat in the thing. I met wt Coldeknows who says it was never heard that any person was preferrd in the gift of Escheat but the Rebells oun Creditors. I advertised him it was the E. of Homes concerne to look to it that that were well represented to the Committie. I went afterwards to Burrells w Sandy Home & Earneslaw and from that to my Lord Polwarths and so home.

Tuesday 5th. I went in the morning to Mr Heugh Dalrymple and spoke to him to appear for me at the Committy that was to meet in the afternoon about my Lord Homes Escheat. I dined wt my Lord Halcraig and Mr Walter Pringle and Mr Cunninghame Sr Wm Cunninghames Brother in Arnots. In the afternoon I found the Committy was to meet so I went and gave Mr Heugh Dalrymple two guineys. he came to the Comitty wher was My Lord Tarbet & My Lord Hatton. Annandale had for him the Advocat. I had Mr Heugh Dalrymple and the E. of Home caused appear in name of his other creditors Sir Pat Home & Mr John Frank. the main debate was whether the King could prefer ane extraneous person to the Rebells lawfull & personall Creditors. the Advocat alleaged that the K. might very well doe it out of Equity wher the E. of Annandale was a creditor to the Es father Especially when Annandale was content to cede the Estate of Aitone to this Es Creditors. Mr H. alleaged that tho he did not plead what the King might not doe yet the King never did dispose of a rebells Escheat but to the rebells [himselfe - deleted] Creditors. after a dale of Wrangling the Lords appointed us to give in our claims in writt to the Clarks agst Thursday next. then My Lord Annandale made a discourse and told he had been at a great losse by the family of Home and that he was very ill requited for that the family of Coldenknows would never have succeeded to the Earledome of Home without his assistance. Mr John Frank sd that after a fair count the E of Home would be found to be ouing nothing to the E. of Annandale. He sd he would give him 5,000 Ms Merks [sic] & 50,000 Ms to the back of it if he would make that good. After the Committy young Stevensone being come to toun whose room I lodged in I went to find another room but finding none I went to Robert Campbells who now has the stable and house Thomas Cesford had formerly. I met wt My Lord Home &c at night and talked a little but not of bussines then I came to Ninewells chamber and so home.

Wednesday 6th. I went and visited my Lord and Lady Polwarth and fro thence to the Lady Hiltons. I spoke to her anent Patons bussines she told me she had been wt Mrs Yeul who told her Paton had no power fro her to doe any more diligence but the Lhe [?] telling her we would not be any more troubled wt Patons noise and desiring ether to take her money or free Paton of his engagements she desired to consider of it. I went from thence to Ninewells chamber and thence to the house. I dined wt Sr J: Pringle Mr Walter & Mr Rot Pringles & Mr Arch: Douglas in Arnots. after dinner I went & visited my Lord Crosrig and from that went to see Caruber (whom I had not seen) Mr Al: Home & Earnslaw in Burrells. from that to Ninewell's chamber wher I found his sister whom I conveyed to Dr Dundas's chamber. from thence I came home.

Thursday 7th. I went in the morning and got Commissary Dalrymple to Draw my information for my bussinesse about my Lo: Homes Escheat. I dined in Ninewells chamber and after dinner went to the Exequer wher the Committy met. all our claims were not ready so they adjourned till munday at 3 a clock. the E. of Annandale was ther who behaved very imperiously he offered again to free the Estate of Aitone but when he was askt by my Lord Polwarth whether he did not mean by the Estate of Aitone parks apprysing as a part of it he refused to allow it. I went afterward to Ninewells chamber from thence to My Lord Polwarths wher I supt and thence to my chamber.

The Weather hes been very warm these 3 or four days past wt a South west wind

We hear litle news. they say the Dutch have taken a colony of the French in the East Indies.

Friday 8th. Mr Al: Home came to my chamber in the morning and borrowed from me 14 Rix dollars. I went up to Ninewells chamber who continues still ill.

I went to Mr Al: Home and gave him a note to extract My old Lady Homes bond and this E.s out of the Register

I dined in Ninewells's chamber

After dinner I went to Dr Dundas's chamber wher I found Sr John Home of Bl[ackadder]: and his sisters and mine come from the Mirse they had brought John Lidgate wt them. I heard from them my sone was well. I got a letter from Da: Robisone telling me he had sold one of the Cows and a calfe at 18 lb scots whc he had given my my sister Isabell. he says he could not goe to Berwick last week wher he expected money because of the waters. I wrote to him to provide me money to kill the geese that were feeding and salt them and to agree wt the Betshilers for ther cain fouls.

I bought some garden seeds according to my account and gave the gardner them.

Saturday 9th. I went to Ninewells chamber I found him more feavirish than formerly and much troubled wt shortnes of breath, I went to Mrs Heburns wher sr Jo: Home and his Lady staid all night and visited him and his Lady and went to my Lord Crosrigs wher we dined. I went after dinner to Ninewells's chamber his sister had been speaking to him to take further advice which she having told me he referred to me. I spoke to him & told him it was thought necessary he should call further advice to whc he condescended and Sandy Home & I went and found Dr Stevensone and took him to Ninewells chamber wher Dr Dundas was we went afterward out together and they 2 resolved together what to doe.

I went wt Earnslaw to Will Toms. he told me he was suspicious some of E's advisers were upon some new project because of a question they had askt him. he sd he would not tell me what it was but if he found afterwards it should tend to my disadvantage he would advertise me he not being charged wt secrecy and they not fancying he could drive into ther designe. He told me likewise If I upon my debts due be the E. to me should charge him to Enter air to his father & Brothers considering the losse of papers ther might be in many dilegencies agst the Estate of Home he douted not my Adjudication might become a good right to build on. He likewise promised me a coppy of E. James the last mans adjudication upon Waughtons inhibition whc he says comprehends all the lands ever the E. of Home possest and Beatons adjudication of the Lands of Aitone. Mem. Beatons adjudication is of consent of the E. of Home upon sinistrous designs for the debts that I payd of the Estate of Aitone and wherof I took blank assignations and wch I delivered up to the E. of Home. Bethuns name is filled up in them and he adjudges for the whole. I went to Ninewell's chamber and then to Sr John Homes and so home

Sunday 10th. I went to Ninewells's chamber whom I found very ill of a shortnes of breath and a feaverish pulse so that his physitians are affraid he will last very few days. I went to the Tron church and after sermon went again to visit Ninewells and from that to visit my aunt Ninewells who is extremly concerned for her sone and would have gone to see him tho she has keept the house for severall weeks but I told her we had some thoughts of Bringing him to her house yet after ward we found it could not be done for his weaknes. I supped wt my Lord Polwarth who was all day indisposed.

Monday 11th. Ninewells was very ill last night and continues so. he has left his Lady sole tutrix to his and her 2 children. he signed a note declairing yt a bond wch was assigned to him by Sr Thos Burnet of Lyes was payd out of his pupills money or something to that purpose. he signed a declaration that the debt I payd to Sr Geo: Lockhart of the Late Aitons of 1,000 Ms and to wch I took assignation in his name was to my behoof. & a note to Geo: Home his factor declairing that Daniel Darling was not payd of 40 sh he oued him. I went to the Committy of the Exequer in the afternoon anent the E. of Annandales Escheat. the Competitors gave in ther claims. the Committy sat upon Annandales from 5 to halfe ane hour after 7 and adjourned till wednesday at 3 a clock. and say they will not have done wt it on wednesday. I drew out my claim and the debts Polwart Hiltone & Ninewells & I stand engaged in for the

E. My Lord Polwarth gave me a decreit as a claim upon the estate of [Aitone - deleted] Home of 6,000 Ms he And Blackadder had engaged in for Al: E. of Home. When the Comitty mett the K's advocat who was ther for the E. of Annandale shund having our claims read openly and when the Clerk was going to read the claims and had taken up the E. of Annandales claim proposed all pties should retire and leave the Committy to consider the Claims. I proposed all our claims should be red openly and that I was content they should begin wt mine. but it seems My Lo: Annandale had no mind his should be so read. he was called in when his claim came to be considered befor the Committy mett. he and I talkt about the Estate of Home what of it the E. might be in posession of and severall things to that purpose. I came afterwards to Ninewells chamber who is very sensible but grows weaker

Tuesday 12th. I was called about 3 a clock of the morning to Ninewells his sister and those about him thinking he was adying. he had taken a kind of fainting fitt but came out of it. Mr Meldrum being sent for spoke to him and prayed he spoke very religiously & sensibly. we sent for his other freinds fearing he might slip away. about 8 in the morning he begun to rave a litle but soon recovered himselfe. I came home at 9 and lay doune above the cloath till 12. I went to Ninewells's chamber again he continues very weak yet sometimes is better sometimes worse. I went out and in ther till ten a clock that I came home

Wednesday 13th. I went in the forenoon to Ninewells's chamber who continues still alive beyound expectation I returned afterward to my chamber and payd Wm Clerk his anrent from Mart: 1692 to Mart 1694. I dind wt my Lord Polwarth who has been troubled wt a pain in his head just such ane one as I remember I had at London when I had my fitts of the ague so that he thinks his distemper tends that way. I had a pain in my head this afternoon whc I think also to be aguish the weather being at present very foggy and the Wind Easterly. In the afternoon I went to the Committy of Exequer and after my Lord Annandales bussines was over I was called for & gave in my claim and the Instructions therof. the Committy went thro them and marked what they had seen. I went afterwards wt Earnslaw & Sandy Home and supped & came to Ninewells's chamber & visited him he wears still on. Earnslaw askt me if I would give the E. any ease if we came in terms and told me the reason why he askt was that one whom he named not said to him that I would be very ill to deal wt. I told him that I knew he would not make ane ill use of it but that if I saw good security I would give doun and he having desired me to show him the [ground - deleted] of my claim and It amounting 36,012 Ms in all I told him I would give doun the interest of the soumes that bore interest whc would be about 6,000 Ms.

Thursday 14th. I was this morning called at 5 a clock to Ninewells. I rose not so airly not thinking he would die so soon and being indisposed I sent my man to waite in case he should fall weak. he calld me about halfe ane houre after six I put on my cloaths and went up but he was dead befor I came and in him one of my best and most intimat freinds. he was sensible to the very last and just slipt off allmost befor those about him were aware. he died in a very devote and resigned frame wherin he was all the time of his sicknesse. his son Joseph came to toune yesternight and his brother David. His freinds resolved to transport him to the Tron church friday at 3 a clock and on wednesday to carry him out of the toune to Dumbar and from that next day to Chyrnsyde. he forbid to open him and Dr Stevensone alleaged he will not keep but Dr Dundas is of another opinion so he is to be put in 2 Cirecloaths. Tho he seemed not to desire a Scutcheon we have ordered one wt his 8 branches to be put over the door of the Church.

I was surprised when Daick came to me this day and told me that one John Giles to whom it seems my brother David oues 624 pund Scots has given him a note to put up his Escheat. I wrote this night for my horses to be in on Munday and a note to my brother to take notice of himselfe

Friday 15th. I forgot that yesterday I consulted Mr Walter Pringle in my reduction agst the Marquis of Douglas. I went this day to the house expecting it should be called but I found it would not be in this week and so not this session ther being no outter house to be the next week. I went up this morning to Ninewells chamber who was put in cirecloaths about 11 a clock and in the Coffin about 2 and transported to the Tron church at 3. at 4 I went to Sophia Cockburns buriall who was daughter to I think Anne Nasmith daughter to Mr James Nasmith and my grandaunt Sophia Home Lady Hiltone. she died in my Lord Annandales lodging having stayed wt his Lady & her mother who is her aunt rather as a servant than freind and yet they say of the small portion she had they made her at last pay board whc troubld the lasse extremly.

after the buriall I went to my Aunt Ninewells's who is very Melancholy at present from that to Blackaders chamber and Stichill coming in ther Blackader Stichill his Brother Walter and Rot and I went to Rosses and supt.

Saturday 16th. I went to My Lord Polwarths lodging in the morning ther being a meeting of the Commissioners of the Assesment of the shire of Berwick because they were quartered on for the deficiency of the cesse. Mr Alexr Cockburn was ther and we ordered him to cause the party quarter upon the deficients and to order that that [sic] the party should goe to the country and intimat for we were informed they would not take the pains to goe to the Country to quarter but out of ther oun head would goe and intimat quartering upon the commissioners. Mr Alex Home Earnslaw and I went to Leith & dined. at night I went to my Lord Polwarths Lodging. Ninewells as a mark of

February 1695

his kindnesse left me his cane his man brought it to me this night his Lady came to toun yesternight but I have not seen her as yet

Sunday 17th. I went to the Tron Church wt my Lord and Lady Polwarth and dined wt them and went to church wt them. in the afternoon after sermons I went and visited Ninewells Lady wt Mr Al: Home and after went and supt wt him at his house. at night I went to visite Cavers who came to toune and lodges next doore.

Monday 18th. I dined wt Dalmeny and Lieutenant Colonel Winram in Steels. I visited my Lord Crosrig my aunt Ninewells who Im afraid is going into her old disease of Melancholy. Meg Home told me severall discourses she had wt Ninewelles's Lady about Ninewelles's childrens affairs. I went and visited Ninewelles's Lady. At night I went to My Lord Polwarths. I spoke to him anent the E. of Homes Escheat and told him that I was now of opinion that if Mr Johnstone and Annandale would prefer me to all the E. of Homes other Creditors, I would restrict my selfe to the Estate of Aitone. he sd he would speake of it tomorrow wt Annandale. When I came home to my chamber I found John Lidgate come to toune wt my 3 horses he brought me 27 lb st from Da. Robisone

Tuesday 19th. I dined wt my Lord Crosrig being invited ther. Sr John Home dined ther likewise and his Lady and Sisters. I went after dinner to my Lord Polwarths lodging and spoke to him anent the E. of Homes Escheat he sd he would write this night about it And that Annandale would doe so likewise. he has spoken to Annandale and he desires that his gift and mine may be in one. I told my Lord that In all probability his might be stopt and mine passe in declarator if they were seperat wher as if they were joint the one might hurt the other. I spoke this night wt Earnslaw again and he told me that he thought that E. was upon some project but he knew not what it was and that he was affraid my Lord would not solidly make any settlement. I payd Mr Stirlin the Dalmahoys anrent and gave my sister Julian 5 lb st. and lent the Lady Law 2 Rix Rollars [sic]. I visited Ninewelles's Lady who when I was coming away told me she would doe anything that would be for the good of Ninewells's family and that she hoped the old Lady would give good Example.

Wednesday 20th. Ninewells's body being to be caried from the Tron church to Dumbar this day and next to Chirnsyde I went in the morning about 7 a clock to the Tron church. I met with my Lord Polwarth who told me he thought it would be neccessary I should stay for that Annandale and he had spoken together about drawing my gift in relation to the Estate of Aitone and that it were fitt it were done this day that it might be signed in Johnstons month but the difficulty was to get Annandale persuaded to separat the gifts. I went afterwards to my Chamber and put on my boots not being able to resolve not to accompany my Dear freinds body to his buriall place. when I came up I found that My Lord Polwarth had spoke to Annandale to separat the gifts and that he had condescended therto so I went presently to Tho: Pringle and desired him to draw a new gift for me taking all my hornings agst the E. both those containd in ye former gift and those that I gave him. those contained in the former gift are (1) a horning at my Lord Polwarths Ninewells's and my instance upon the E. and his mothers bond of releive and inventary of debts (2) a horning for 2,000 Ms in lieu of the jus mariti and 4,500 Ms as the halfe of the Expense of the mariage twixt me and the Lady Aitone. the hornings since are (1) a horning upon the bond of 2,500 Ms the E. granted me in lieu of several debts I had payd for the Estate of Aitone. (2) a horning for my annuity of 1,800 Ms for the 1683 and subsequent years. I took Tho: Pringle to the E. of Annandale and told the E. what I had ordered Tho: to doe wt wch he was satisfied and promised to send it up wt his oun. We lifted the Corps about 8 and came to Dumbar about 3 few meeting us by the way. my Lord Polwarth went in his Berlin all the way wt us. My Lord Sr John Home & I lodged in Bayly Rutherfords. after we had put the Corps in the Church and put off our boots we walked out and see the old Castle of Dumbar whc belonged to the Earls of March all ruinous standing on the Rocks of the sea on the north East of the toun. we could discover nothing remarkable save on ane old gate the E. of March's arms whc is a Lion rampant wt a border of Roses. On the right side of them was the Mans arms 3 legs on the left a coat of Arms My Lord Polwarth sd was the Bruces. Mem. when we were in the Church of Dumbar we saw the E.of Dumbars tomb whc caused Erect for himselfe befor his death all of Marble wt ane Iron Rail about it a very stately fabrick. he is designed E. of Dumbar Lord Howme of Berwick Lord High Thesaurer of Scotland and Knight of the garter. His statue is ther in a praying posture and a book befor him they say the face is very like, a bold grim man black short hair and a long Black baird &c. The bayly wher we lodged could not tell us how old the Burgh Royall of Dumbar is. my Lord Polwarth was alledging it was about King James the 2ds time. I think it has been erected upon the forfaulting of the E. of March that the toun having a greater liberty might not be desirous of the return of ther old master. this I think they were saying was in K. James the 2ds time. The toun as allmost all the old burroughs of Scotland is much decayed. the Herring fishings was its greatest trade and since the fight of Dumbar ther has been no such tack as formerly they made red herrings whc they smoak in great houses wt the wood of Ash and [blank] but they bring most of the timber from abroad the Country about being quite bare. my Lord Polwarth told us of ane old saying you shall be Like the toun of Dumbar and have the Ward of Ste Beé you shall never want you shall never hé and frost shall never your corn slae (for it is very air harvest about it and ane excellent corn country)

Thursday 21st. We lifted about 8 came by Pethhead and so by Eckily Edge to Chirnsyde about 3 a clock to Chyrnsyde. after the Buriall Sr John Home Boghall Balgare Mr Al: Home &c and I were invited by Da: Home Ninewells's Brother to Ninewells and ther Eat some cold meat. I proposed that Sr John Home & Mr Al: should put their seals on Ninewells Charter chest whc they did his Lady has the Kee of it. Sr John Home took the rest of the Company home wt him. Mr Al: Home went to Dunse. I went wt him to see my Brother he is better but his leg is not fully well as yet. he told me he had pay[d] John Giles his money. I parted wt Mr Al: Home & he going to Billy I came home. these two days past have been very pleasant. when I came home I found Roby troubld wt the Cold and his feet so scabbed he is not able to walk.

Friday 22nd. Was a very boisterous windy day so that I went not out but to the garden wher I found the young trees all eaten wt the hares. I wrote a letter to Mr Home at London discharging any trees this season and desiring him to send me doun for my Lord Crosrig 8 of Mr Flemins books called the ground work of religion Printed by Tho: Parkhurst at the signe of [blank] at the lower end of Cheapside

Saturday 23rd. James Jaffray Will Brack Pat Knox James Forsyth Brought me some money according to their severall accts. this day was very pleasant and I walked to the Redheugh haugh wher Da: Robisone takes out Marle for gooding his Land. I went also into the house of the Heugh whc is quite out of repair

Sunday 24th. I went to Church tho the day was very rough and windy. Sr John Home and I trysted to goe together to Edr tomorrow. At night he wrote to me that he had heard from Purvishall that the Lady was dead and so was in a doute whether to goe to Edr or not till the Buriall was over whc was to be on thursday and desired to know what I designed. I wrote to him that my affairs calld me be at Edr that I resolved to goe ther and if my affairs permitted to return agst the buriall

Monday 25th. I took horse for Edr and Blackaders boy came to me to goe in to the Lady and brought me a letter from Sr John telling me he resolved to stay till the buriall was over and the more because he thought by his being ther my absence would be the more excusable. he sent me likewise a rentall of the Estate of Ninewells. I came by Betshile and spoke to the tenants that I would have 12 lb ane acre for my Land and 20 Ms more for the Whiteknows so I desired they might consider on it. Geo: Broun and James Ridpeth gave me some money. I dined in Ginglekirk from that I came to Edr and Lodge in Robert Cambells. I had a very rough day. It was a high wind and raind sometimes and from Ginglekirk to Fala mill I had snow

I saw Sandy Home my Lord Crossrig and my Lord Polwarth who came to toun this day.

Tuesday 26th. I find my gift of the E of Homes Escheat in so far as concerns the Estate of Aitone was writt by Tho. Pringle as I desired him and given to the E. of Annandale who has sent it up wt a gift in his oun favours of the Earls Escheat in relation to the Estate of Home and the Exequers report anent the Claims of the Earls fathers creditors and his own were likewise sent up. I visited the Ladies of Ninewells Elder and younger. My aunt is very Melancholy. I dined wt My Lord Crosrig. I met wt Wytefeild and Mr Al: Home Mr Al: told me that Whytefeild had a commission to treat wt me from my Lord Home and so left me. Whytefeild said he had but yet did not talk of treating so I heard no more of it and meeting wt Earnslaw afterward He asked if I had seen Whytefeild. I told him I had he sd he had a commission to treat wt me from the E. of Home and when I told him what had passed he seemed surprised. Whytefeild did not make me any proposals.

Wednesday 27th. Mem. that on the 19th instant I got a charge of Horning at Blackburn Brouns instance for the anrents of the 1,000 Ms Ninewells & I stand Engaged in for the E of Home to him. the money was got from Al: Martin but we gave the bond blank of the Creditors name and it seems it was keept so by Sandy Martine for Blackburns name was filled up in it because it seems Martine was his debtor at Candlemes 1690 or 91. Blackburn assignes this bond to Mr Robert Lauder of Beilmouth and the E. Ninewells and I gave a bond of Corroboration therof in favours of Mr Robert Lauder and Ninewells and I have payd the Interest of it from Candlemes 1691 to Candlemesse 1693. Now when the Escheat was agitating befor the Exequer Mr Ro: Lawder has given me a charge of Horning that I might give in this debt in the list of debts due by the E.of Home to me and Much about the same time I got the above mentiond Charge at Blackburns instance so that I took them both to be from Mr Ro: Lauder the one upon the princapill bond the other upon the bond of Corroboration till I spoke to Mr Ro: who told me he had given me but one charge and told me to take notice that the other was not for the anrents due befor the assignation granted to him. I lookt and found it so and gave the charge to Mr Al: Home to be suspended on this ground that when the bond of Corroboration was signed to Mr R. Lauder we were told that the E was to allow the teinds of Ryselaw wch Martine was in possession of. I know not yet whether it be Tho. Calderwood or Blackburn that Causes charge me

Thursday 28th. Mr Al: Got the charge suspended this day. the session rose. I dined in Arnots and afternoon met wt Whytefield he told me he had a commission from the E. of Home to treat wt me. we went into Danets. his proposition was that what I had ether given out for the E or had his bond for they were content to allow me Only the Expected defaulkation for the by gone annuities and in time coming, and that for the bygons they would give me 700 Ms and 1,000 Ms in time comeing yearly. Whytefield was very free [Ingenuous - deleted] wt me as to many particulars relating to the E. of Homes Estate. he told me the E had paid near 15,000 Ms of Debt last year, that for our relief of the debts Polwarth Ninewells Hiltone and I stand Engaged in for him and his mother he would communicat to us such rights as would be effectuall for our releif particularly a right upon the E. of Dunfermlings Estate for 10,000 lb wch was now in Linthills persone as trustie for the E. ther being ane old Inhibition whc would prefer us to most of his other Creditors or he would show us other rights wch if we liked bettr we might have. He told me also of a debt due by Buckcleugh to the E's father wch would now be 36,000 Ms and sd that if it were not for his Escheat the E. would persue many debts By wch he could recover considerable summes. As to my particular I told him I would have possession out of the Barony of Aitone for as much as we could agree and whc he offered the bear at 5 lb the oats att 4 lb. I was a litle to forward to accept this offer as also to to [sic] offer to restrict my whole summes to 30,000 Ms and my annuity in time to come to 1,200 Ms. he told me he had gone all the length he could goe and that he had taken much pains to bring the E. the length he had offered his affairs not suffering him to goe any greater length. Earnslaw was not wt us so we resolved the E. and I should meet in the Country and talk further about it. I went and visited the Ladys of Ninewells, The Younger is Earnest to meet wt my Lo: Crosrig. Sr John Sinclairs' sone Ro: Sinclair is dangerously ill of a feaver. Dr Abernethy came to toune this day

Friday March 1st. I payd Widow Galloway 2 years anrent of 200 Ms due at Candlemes last. I dined in my Lo: Crosrigs being invited ther. I went in the afternoon wt my Lord Crosrig to the Lady Ninewells Yr her chamber wt My Lo: Crosrig wher we lookt on some papers of Ninewells's brought from English Mauldy and put them into the Coffer he had in this toun and sealed them and delivered it to Baylif Home who was present conform to ane act of sederunt appointing all papers to be lockt up and the kee to be delivered to the Magistrat of the place till tutors or curators accept under pain of Embezelment. after we had done we went to Grahams and sat a litle & Sr John Home who was come in came to us. Baylif Home treated My Lo: Cr. sr J & me Boghall & his Brother Mr Rot. and Ja. Galbrath of Balgare was wt us in the Lady Ninewelles. Sr John and I went to his chamber and from that I came home. Dr Abernethy came in at sat wt me till after 11.

Saturday 2nd. I dined wt Mr Walter Pringle and Whytefeild. I got up from Mr Tho: Aikman my fathers bond of Corroboration to [blank] Stuart for John Home of Bell Sclathouse having payd the debt as having given bond for it being Bells tutor Curator and factor and he having taken assignation to the Bond. but it is to be remembred that Mr Aikman gave him considerably doun of his anrents that Sclathouse in counting may not state the whole upon Bell.

Sunday 3rd. I went to the Tron church in the afternoon and supt with my Lo: Polwarth.

Monday 4th. I dined in Michells wt Sr Wm Cunninghame 2 Mrs Cunninghams a brother of Cesnocks and one Moore. in the afternoon I went to the Lady Ninewells yr and ther found My Lo: Crosrig who spoke to her anent the bad Condition of the affairs of that family and gave her ane acct of the Estate and debt wherby the debt as affairs stand at present Exceed the Rentall in 1,400 lb yearly. We are to meet wt her tomorrow. Meg Home came to toun this afternoon and her Nephew came wt her.

Tuesday 5th. I went wt My Lord Crosrig and Blackader to the Lady Ninewells's chamber. My Lo exposed again to her the Condition of the family of Ninewells and we pressed but wt all discretion that ther might be some thing put in writting of what she would doe and that I might by way of Contract betwixt the old Lady and her. she was rather of opinion it might be done betwixt Ninewelles curators and then she did not condescend on any summe but In generall sd that tho her jointure was lesse than the old Ladies she would goes shares wt her. I went to Leith wt her she going ther in order to her journey home. This day the Castlie [sic] and some men of war that are in the road of Leith dropt shots all afternoon it being the Queens buriall. the bells likewise tolled.

Wednesday 6th. Tho: Pringle told me the E. of Annandales gift & mine were come of the E of Homes Escheat mine of the Estate of Aitone & his of the Estate of Home. I sent Tho: 7 lb and 5sh to get up the gift from Henry Douglas whc he did and Daick promised to put it up on the Wall to be past next Exequer day. I met wt Androw Halyburtone Exer to James Robisone whom I promised ether paymt or further security against Whitsonday next and to advertise him a month befor the terme

Thursday 7th. I dined wt my Lord Crosrig and after dinner met wt Whytefeild who told me he had spoke to Sr Pat Home for bying the Estate of Aitone. I went to Tho Pringle who shewed me the gift of Escheat come in my favours of the Estate of Aitone. I was in the afternoon wt Pa: Johnstone and Mr Alexr Home he agreed wt Pa: Johnstone for Ninewells's bay Mare for 100 lb Scots wch he payd, and Da: Marshall Ninewelles groom was ordered to deliver her to him wt a snaffle bit and ane hunting stock.

Friday 8th. I went in the morning to my Lo: Polwarths lodging to tell him that my Lord Annandales gift of Escheat and mine of the Estate of Aitone were to be past this day he promised to be in the Exequer house at 10 a clock. I went up ther wt Tho: Pringle and gave in my gift to Daick and 2 Rix Dollars wt it and Tho: gave his sone halfe a croun. I saw Annandales gift wch is only of the E[arl]s. liferent Escheat as is also mine his single Escheat being in none of them and the E. has taken his gift upon the Hornings narrated in my gift. My Lord Polwarth spoke to the Lords in my favours. the Thesaury being met revised the gifts and put ten mark of Composition on them. I dined wt Mr Al: Home wher Carubber dined also. After noon I waited on at the Exequer. ther were severalls solliciting to be in the backbands particularly My Lord Crosrig Blackader for the debts due to the Lords of Session by the old E. of Home in wch he is bound. Whytefield gave in a bill for this present Countesse of Home for ane aliment and desired that the E. of Annandales gift be burdened therwith. he is content his gift be burdened wt the Countesse Douager of Homes liferent. ther was such a pother keept about this that the Lords put off passing our gifts till Wednesday next.

I signed yesterday a bond for my Lord Polwarth as Conjunct cautioner for Him wt Ro: Johnstone of Hiltone to Geo Pringle of Greenknow for 2,000 Ms wch was employed for paymt of a debt of the same summe due to Widow Yeul wherby we are freed fro the noise of Bayliff Paton who was bound to widow Yeul for late Geo: Mosman who was Cautioner in the bond for Polwarth. we got likewise a bond of releif of the sd soume from My Lord &c.

Saturday 9th. I thought to have taken my horses to goe take the air in the feilds but the day was sour and ane easterly wind. It has bein very bad weather ever since I came to toune great frosts and snow all the hills about are covered so that ther is litle or no labouring in the country only about Edr and near the sea yet the price of the Victuall is low. Sr John Home sold a bargain of wheat this day to Deacon Andersone at 8 lb but it has been at 9 lb this year and now the price is declining. oats they say are giving 5 lb and some 10sh more at Dalkeith. I was invited to My Lord Crosrigs this day to dine and found ther at dinner Sr John Home and his Lady and Bailif Home. I walked to the Castle Hill wt My Lord and the Bailif and came from thence to Danets and sate with them. Sr John Home came to us and then Mr Al: who had been selling Ninewells's horse to Boussy for 18 lb 10sh. I could not meet wt him in the forenoon else he should not have sold him for Capt Johnstone of Westerhall came to me and told me that Pollock would give 20 lb for him but would not be in toune till tuesday. After we parted I went to my Lord Polwarts he was not wtin from thence I returned home.

Sunday 10th. I went to the Tron church in the afternoon and supt in my chamber at night.

Monday 11th. I went up to Mr Al: Homes chamber and wt him met wt Dr Irvin who is pursuing his father Dr Irvins relict and her children as adulteresse and adulterous bastards befor the Commissaries of Edr to get free of a debt his father has burdened the Estate possessed by the Dr in Ireland. he is now Maried to Sr John Home of Castle Humes sister In Ireland. I dined wt Sr John Home of Blackader and visited My Aunt Ninewalls after dinner & from that I returned to Sr John Homes Chamber and sat wt him and his Lady till night he not having been abroad this day being troubled wt the cold.

Tuesday 12th. I went to My Lord Polwarths about 11 a clock but found him not my Lady engaged me to come back and dine wt them whc I did. the Lady Jeriswood and Mr Meldrum Minister of the Trone church dined wt us. I went in the afternoon and visited my Lo: Crosrig & My aunt Ninewells. at night Whytefeild came to my chamber and sat wt me he told me severall passages of his travells in Germany at Vienna Presburgh &c and how his Landlords sone in Doesburgh poisoned him wt a designe to get some money he had receaved from his factor how he overcame the poison wt difficulty and went to the Baths of Akin upon that acct he alledges it still sticks to him. I met wt Daick this day who expects that to morrow ther will be ane Exequer.

Wednesday 13th. I went to my Lo: Polwarths in the morning and talkt wt him about our businesse to be this day befor the Exequer he told me that the E.of Annandale now after calculation was beginning to think that this gift he has been pursuing so hotly will be of so small value to him for he has consented to burden it wt the Countesse Douagers annuity and it seems the Exequer Inclines that he be also burdened wt ane aliment for this countesse. I went up to Mr Al: Homes Chanber and then returned to my Chamber and dined. after dinner I went to see my Aunt Ninewells and from that to the Exequer. I spoke to most of them and My Lo: Polwarth came ther and spoke likewise to them. My Lord Crosrig was there and my Lo: Annandale told me he had given in a bill to be preferred in respect he was the first discoveror and had given in the first gift but I found the Lords did not lay much weight on that. After I had attended some time I got notice my gift was past wt My Lord Annandales but the Lords of Session being Creditors to the Estate of Home in 23,000 Ms tho they have lands to pay them and sufficient security had commissioned my Lord Fountainhall one of the Exequer to desire they might be preferred in Annandales back bond, and the Lords of Exequer having refused it he refused to signe the passing and so ther was not a quorum signing Hatton having gone out befor. I spoke to my Lord Fountainhall and told him that tho upon that acct he had refused to signe My Lo: Annandales gift yet the Lords not desiring any burthen on mine as having nothing to doe wt the Estate of Home I hoped he might still signe mine he sd that having denyed to signe Annandales he might look on it as too much favour if he should signe mine. I sought Daick at night to have desired him to carry my gift to my Lo: Hatton to make up the Quorum. Thomas Pringle promised to look for him & to get him to doe it. I went to My Lord Polwarths at night and sat wt my Lady and supt. My Lord came in late he had been ending his bussines of Northberwick wt Commissary Dalrymple to whom he has transmitted his right and has got 11,000 Ms for it and my Lady is to get 20 guineys.

Thursday 14th. I dined in my Lo: Crosrigs being invited ther wher Sr John Home & his Lady &c dined. after dinner I met wt Daick who had been out at Hatton and got my Lo: Annanadales gift and mine signed which made up the Quorum. I find It has been represented to the Lords of Exequer not only that the 23,000 Ms due by the E. of Home is a debt upon the Estate of Home but that also Aitone is bound and so the gift upon the Estate of Aitone ought to be burdened therwt, this was a scruple that I knew not my Lo: Fountainhall had tho I was affraid of it. however the gift is past wt out that burden. at six a clock I met wt my Lo: Crosrig Dalmeny and Mr Al: Home. Dalmeny had frequently desired to drink a glasse of wine wt my Lo: Crosrig he took us to Steels and entertaind us. after we parted I went and visited Sr John Home & his Lady and so home. The weather has been Easterly these many days it presents fair this day and the recruits are sailing out of the firth. I went up to the Ship taverne wt Swintone Mr Al Home Earnslaw &c to look to the road the ships were falling doun from Borrowstounnesse

Friday 15th. I met wt Daick at Sr Tho: Moncrief and saw the Exequers Interlocutor relating to my backbond wherin is only containd my Lords Crosrigs debt to be in my backbond after I am payd. Daick promised the bond should be ready agst to morrow at nine a clock.

Saturday 16th. I saw my back bond to the Exequer it was all as I desired only my annuity of 100 lb was not mentioned as it will be fit. I dined in my chamber after dinner walk to the Castlehill and Heriots wark yards wt Mr Alexr Home. at our return we met wt Caruber and Mr James Hendersone and went to Janets from that I visited my Lady Polwarth and so home. Julian brought me a sugar loaf and 2 lb of Raisins and 2 lb of Currans I gave her money to buy me.

Sunday 17th. I went to the Tron church in the after noon and after sermon went to the Coffee house and red the news That one Capt Killigrew had engaged 2 French frigats and other English frigats coming in took them. Killigrew was killd in the Engagement it was in the Road of Maltha. the Confederats designe to beseige Casal. the fleet of Scots ships wt 2 Dutch men of war sailed from Leith road yesterday wt the recruits.

March 1695

Monday 18th. I walked up to the Castlehill wt Earnslaw and Geo: Robisone and dined in Rosses wt the last. I have seen my bond upon the gift of the E. of H[ome]s Escheat but have margined it to make it more speciall as to my life rent.

Tuesday 19th. I met with Daecks sone and signed my Backbond to the Exequer in wch after my being payd of my debts and annuity of 100 lb my Lord Crosrig comes in then Sr Pa: Home then Binny of Deburnnen I know not his pretensities only he has made agreement wt the Heirs of Aitone and insists for the Estate and has raised a declarator agst the E. of Home as having incurred the Irritancy for having taken the title of E. of Home but the Es. debts will affect the Estate in wch case ther will be litle to the airs of Line. I was wt Meg Home who tells me my Lord Crosrigs opinion is that Joseph Home Choose My Lord Polwarth Sr John Home and me his curators. I have spoke to Sandy Home to get the Edicts proclaimed wch he has promised James Winram shall doe when he comes to the Country. I dined wt Tho: Pringle & Mr Gregory the Mathematicien. I visited my Lord Crosrig and My aunt Ninewells. standing in the parla closse wt My Lord Crosrig one Robert Home came to him whom my Lord receaved very kindly tho a country like man but my Lord had been formerly acquanted wt him when he was made prisoner by Claverhouse at Haick. his father called John was then alive and died in the 103d year of his age. I was at night wt Earnslaw and Sandy Home.

Wednesday 20th. I got my gun whc I had given out to dresse and get a new dog head. I visited my Lord Polwarth Lo: Crosrig &c and came from Edr that night about 3 a clock and to Ginglekirk. that night Swintone and his Lady were in the Upper house I visited them and Swintone came to my quarters and sat wt me sometime.

Thursday 21st. I came from Ginglekirk betwixt 6 & 7 and came to Betshile and told my tenants I would have 10 lb Scots for Every acre and those of Whiteknows 10 Ms a peice more but they demurr. I got from Geo: Brown 14 lb 03sh 10d wch clears his Mart rent. I came from thence about 12 having viewed the mill wch is in pretty good condition having got a new Axle tree of an ash tree growing in Da: Youngs yard. but the wall is ill and must be taken doun. I lookt to the Yard wher the trees are growing and find I must ether wall it or ditch it that the trees that are cutt may grow up for now they doe not being destroyed by the beasts. I am like to be in some difficulty for a mosse.
 Just after I lighted came Mr Guthry from the Synode at Kelso he had no news ther was litle done in the Synode. He had heard the E. of Home was ill of a Rhumatisme. At night came my Brother

Friday 22nd. I walked out all the forenoon the day being as pleasant and warme as if it were in July. all this week the weather has been very pleasant but this day very hot so that I could not allmost stand in the sun. In the afternoon my brother and I went to Blackader Sr Jo: Home told us Sr Fr: Ruthven had sent and poinded him as one of the Commissioners for not payment of a precept he has upon the Shire of 54 lb st. since January last. he poinded also Sr Robert Stuart. We resolved to meet next day at Dunse my Brother returned wt me

Saturday 23rd. After dinner I went to Dunse and my My [sic] Brother ther were Sr John Home and Sr Robert Stuart. we met to Examine the matter why the Commissioners were quartered on. My Brother being Collector told us that as soon as the party came to him and intimat ther Quartering he gave them a list of the deficients wch they refused as not having the summs wherin they were deficient, the Collector answered them that yt had never been the Custome and that was the same thing to them. We afterward Called for Sr Wm Ruthven a very honest ingenuous Gentleman who said as befor that he had got no list of the deficients Only a roll wt out the summs at the persons names and that he gave as one reason of his quartering on the Commissioners besides he produced his order from Ro: Rutherford for quartering on the Collector and Commissioners, We told him that was only to be Understood according to Law that the Law appointed that the party sent upon the Shire should intimat quartering to the Collector and the Collector should give ye partie a list of deficients upon whc they were to quarter but honest Sr Wm stuck by his warrant from Ro: Rutherford knowing no better. however he sd he had intimat quartering upon the deficients according to the list tho he had befor sd the list was not sufficient. then Sr Wm went away and we made a long deduction of the matter in our court books and concluded Sr Wm had acted agst law in poinding the Commissioners. But wtall gave order to the Collector to cause presently poind for deficiency for we have all along out of tendernesse to the shire hindered poinding for deficiency wch has been a great losse to the Collector he paying the party and never getting it in again. we met afterward wt Sr Wm and told him the danger he was in by law he sd he was not affraid and that he had been abused for his lenity but it would be a pitty to persue according to law so honest hearted a man. we parted very good freinds Lt Collonell Hill whose troup it is that Sr Wm is Lt to came ther from London the night befor but we did not see him he being walkt abroad.

Sunday 24th. I went not abroad the Weather being much changed this day and the wind East

Monday 25th. Wm Home in Betshile came here this day as I had ordered him he is still plagued wt Gardener the messenger who having Bowhills

Caption still in his hands comes every nou and then on purpose to get a litle money from the poor people and about 3 weeks agoe got from his wife 4 lb Scots to let the Cow goe he had poinded. I gave him a letter to Mr Al: Home for a suspension. Geo: Brown was at me seeking land for his Brother Rot he would take the Mill but I know not whether the Millar in it designes to stay he would also take Acres and offered me 12 the acre for Wm Homes 2 but I will not turn him out having offered them ther acres at ten lb but told him that if any of them did not accept of that offer that then had should come next agreed wt him at last that in case of any of the possessors of Whiteknows did not give up ten Marks more than they pay he should have ther room. Will Waddell makes the greatest difficulty but I beleive they will all agree still. Old Davie Broun died yesterday and was Buried this day. Mr Adam Waddell came here this afternoon.

On Saturday Mar Turner spoke to me that she was going away being to be Maried and Mar Johnstone likewise desired leave to goe to Edr for a week but is not yet certain till she meet wt her father and mother whither she stays after the terme or not.

Tuesday 26th. Yesternight Mar. Johnstone got from me six lb Scots she went away wt the Cariers this day. I have been troubled wt the Emroides yesterday and this day & can get no wher abroad.

Wednesday 27th. This has been a very pleasant day. I have been most of it in the Garden pruning trees and setting some prunings of Elmes to try if they will grow. I got a lettr to a meeting of the Commissioners I wrote my excuse to my brother my trouble continuing still. I have cut severall slips and joints of the willow come from Nidery set some wt tops some cut at both ends to see if they will hold. The apple trees I brought from Nidery are most of them pilled wt the hares and sheep the Gardner denys the last tho it is evident by the wool on the bushes. At night Dr Abernethies man came here from his Master who is at Nisbet wt Mr Christian who is still troubled wt fits of his ague; and to give Lady a vomit to morrow. I bid him tell his master to meet me at the waterside. I went and met him and talkt about halfe ane hour wt him.

Ther was a boll of malt brought in to the house this day and Masked.

About six a clock Whytefield and blind Will Home came here from Wedderburn going to the Hirshell. Will told me that ther is on Du Pin I think must be his name and the Call him Manes who have undertaken paper manufactories in Scotland and ther are severall that enter into a society and advance so much they have tryed white paper at Wills Mill and have made it very good. they are also Engaged in the Linen Manufactories in Scotland England and Ireland and are the directors of them and have a gift of all the Royall mines in Scotland and that the Lady Hoptone is concernd wt them. Whytefeild told us the Emperor could not mantaine this present war if it were not that he has Mines of silver in [Germany - deleted] Hungary in whc he has been whc enter in the top of a mountain and goe doun 400 and odde steps and 200 more doun is the mill for grinding the ore wher a river under ground makes it goe. that the have a fourth pt of silver out of the ore they told us likewise that these French had sent ore from Scotland into England and upon tryall it was found good Silver but could not tell whence it was digged.

Whytefeild spoke to me anent my bussines wt the E. of Home and sd if he found the E. still inclinable he would send me word. But seemed very averse from Sr Pat Homes having Aitone he did not tell me why. he proposed to me if I could get the money advanced on it and take it But I told him that was Impossible he sd he could wish some would Join and buy it and raese the money and take my security, but I am not for that. I had rather have my money.

Friday 29th. Wm Home in Betshile came back from Edr and brought me a letter from Mr Al: Home who writes that Bowhill is not in toune and that the man not having got a charge he cannot present a bill to meet the Caption but he has sent me out letters of publication of deprivation against Gardner to be Execute on Wednesday next upon a Sentence passed against him in the Lyons court in Novr last. He has not as yet past my suspension against Blackburn but promises to doe it and likewise to look for money to pay Friershaw. This is a cold day and a northe east Wind ther was about a quarter of ane hour a Shower of snow.

Saturday 30th. This last night and this day Tis very cold wt a strong n.e. wind. This morning Tho: Rutherford came to me I told him I had to long a coming to the country to change the rent of Westfeild and Greenknow. he tells me if I had been here in time he could have gotten me as he thinks tenants that would have given the old rent for Westfeild to witt 740 Ms and 500 Ms for Greenknow and Kingslaw. I told him also that I had called for Ja: Forsyth who had refused to give me 200 Ms for the mill he sd he should warrant he should give it rather than quitt it to Sandersone. He tells me that he pays now 900 Ms for Dunse Mills wheras he payd formerly only 750 Ms and that his sone who payd only 900 Ms pays now 1,000 Ms. That the Mill pays 215 Ms wt a Cain swine or 10 Ms wch makes 225 Ms & that the mains 9 chalders of Victuall 2 parts oats and a 3d bear. that this year My Lo: befor he went to toune agreed wt the tenants in the mains for 7sh oats and ten sh and 6 pence bear to be payd all at Candlemis last but for this crop only that whc induced the tenants to this is ther victuall lying long on ther hands. Tho: is now very old being past 77 on pasche last his sight begins to fail him.

The tenants of Whyteknows and the Acres came here wt whom I have agreed for the Whyteknows for 330 Ms and the Acres at 10 lb the acre. Wm Waddell made some litle work but took the rests advice and settled as they. The smith complains of Ja: Redpeth that he does not work wt him. I have promised he shall ether work wt him or pay him as Will Fogo payd which he says was 5 furlits of oats and a days yoking of a plough.

Will Home of St Ebbes came back this afternoon from the Hirshill and brought me a note from Whytefeild wherin he writes that he found the E. indisposed for bussines both in regard of his health and also because of ane advertisemt he had receaved from the Councill to enter himselfe prisoner to the Castle of Edr on friday next so that our meeting must be delayed till both Meet in Edr. Will tells me he has sent for his physitian and Chirurgeon to give an attestation that travelling would endanger his health. Will told me also he heard they were on a designe to sell Aitone and that Sr Pa: Home was the man was designing for it.

I got a letter from my sister Julian wherin she wrote she had sent out my trunk and Candle. my man had been at Blackader about it and tells me Androw has not brought me my candle from Edr and being unwell did not come here today wt my trunk. Julian Writes ther is 29 Cotton and 48 rag week candles.

Sunday 31st. I went to Edrom but ther was no sermon ther of wch Locky had neglected to advertise me our Minister was preaching in Dunse and he of Dunse was at Eccles Mr Lau being sent to preach in the North as is ordered by the last assembly that every presbytery should send so many quarterly ther. My Brother was not in the toune. I went to Sandy Lorane betwixt sermons and sat wt Sr Will: Ruthven and Will Turnbull and after sermons I went ther wt Sr Wm and sent for Mr Al: Cockburn who is lately come from Edr. he tells the Duke of Queensberry died thursday last. That Sr John Trevor who was speaker of the house of Commons and turned out for taking a bribe of 1,000 lb from the Chamber of London in the matter of the Orphans money has accused the E. of Portland of Bribery.

Monday April 1st. Mr Borthwick Minister of Greenlaw came here this morning he tells me the Generall Assembly wch was to sitt on Thursday next is adjourned by proclamation wch will give great offence to many. he went to a presbytery at Chyrnside this day. Tho: Rutherford came to me and told me he had spoke to James Forsyth who he says would be content to give me 200 Ms but that he has the Mill to repair whc he will not doe for 40 lb for that I offered him a 7 years tack wch Tho: says he thinks will satisfie but James proposed to be free of his teind wch In Effect were to take with the one hand and give wt the other the teind being if not worth 20 Ms yet wt More than the halfe of it

Mr Borthwick told me ther was a report that Sr John Cochran who was at Greenlaw church yesterday was going to see his daughter the Lady Morisone at Graden she having been caried out of her bed by women and laid in the dining room supposed to be Witches among whom she knew one in Birghame. melius Inquirendium. I took out of the Doucoat 9 pair of pigeons this day. Yesterday I got a letter to a meeting of the Commissioners on Wednesday next. And Watherhead brought my trunk clockbag this morning.

[Tuesday 2nd.] I was at home and see nobody as I remember. I cutt some more willows and sett them. I wrote to Mr Al: Home to try further for money for paying Friershaw and And Halyburtone

[Wednesday 3rd.] I went to Dunse in the morning the Lo: Polwarth having appointed a meeting of the Commissioners but he sent his excuse being troubled wt a sore throat so ther was no meeting ther being only in toune Sr Rot Stuart and I all we did was to hear Bruce the aquavitie man make his complaint yt he had not gotten up his poind wch was taken from him for not paying to the Commissioners his excise of the annexed excise to the farmers of whc we found him free by act of parlia and so that his poind ought to be restored. Will Home was at Dunse to have met wt My Lo: Polwarth to see in my Lo: could help him in any way to get forward his mill. he showed me a project of 2 French men Du Pin & De Manis of a paper manufactory for writing paper here in Scotland severalls have allready signed. the project is ther shall be 4,200 lb st of Stock by subscriptions in a company wher of the halfe shall be lifted in England the other half in Scotland. 3 lb st is a share but 5 lb has only a vote and no one man can have above 20 shares. wt this money ther will be made 4 paper mills and when the stock augments ther is no money to be taken out by the proprietors but as it increases more mills are to be built. yet tho one gets nether principill nor interest they may sell ther shares when they please whc as Will counts will increase to double the Stock in 2 or 3 years and so furth for he says the paper company in England begun wt 1,000 lb in K. Ch. the 2ds time and no[w] is 98,000 lb. I brought him home wt me. I caused execute the precept of depravation agst Geo: Gardner tho much sollicited to the contraire but when he saw it done he gave his letters to Pa: Cockburn to apprehend Wm Home. Pa: Came to me and I promised to make the man furth coming to him but ordered him to keep the letters wch he promised to doe.

Thursday 4th. I went to Polwarth house wt Will Home. my Lo: tho better came not out of his chamber the day being very sharp. It seems My Lo: and the Lady Hiltone out of kindnes to Will had given bond to Ja: Winrame to get Will 500 Ms to advance his affairs of wch Will has only gotten 10 lb st and cannot get the rest. my Lo has the gift of the Vacant stipends in the shire for repairing the Bridges and a year of the stipend of Aitone lying in the heritors hand. Will spoke to me to speake to my Lo to see if he would let him uplift some of the stipend to make up the 500 Ms. Especially My Lo: & the Lady Hiltone Expecting to get in as many new subscrivers to his contract as will reimburse them of the 500 Ms. My Lo: told me he could not get that done because the Masson that had repaired Whittater Bridge was still unsatisfied and that ther was difficulty to get as much as would satisfie him but if after he was satisfied ther was as much to be had as would doe Wills bussines he should have it. we came away together Will went to Aitone and I came home. I went at Polwarthouse into the Garden and see the peaches and Apricock trees begins to flourish they fear the losse of ther Artichocks.

Friday 5th. I went to Blackader sr John complains still of the cold he got in Edr a pain in his back wch looks like the gravell. I dined ther Mr Robisone the Viccar of Berwick and his father in law Broomhouse dined ther likewise after Dinner Mr Guthrie came ther I returned home at night

Saturday 6th. I went to Nisbet in the forenoon. Cavers was gone to the Hunting he going now every twesday and saturday to hunt wt Young Harcasse he came home about 4 a clock. They told me ther they Heard the King of Poland was dead & that the Queen of Spain was wt childe. Mr Knox gave me the Bishop of Canterburys sermon at the Queens funerall wch I read. Mar. Johnstone came home yesternight and this night told me she was going away but had engaged one of her sisters in her place I told her that I did not desire to have servants till I had seen them and agreed wt them my selfe. This day and these severall days past has been very cold the wind blowing from N.E. the season is dry and good for the seed but ill for the lambs.

Sunday 7th. I went to Edrom Church Cavers and his Lady were ther. the day was very cold. The Lady Blackader was ther but Sr John is not througly well of his cold as yet as so came not

Monday 8th. I got a letter this morning from Wm Home of Greenlaw Castle for his anrent due at Mart. He desires it for going to Edr agst Munday next. I wrote to him I should doe what I could to get it. It has snowed this day and the day is very cold.

Mem. on sat. James Forsyth agreed wt me for the mill for a nother year at 200 Ms and to doe what he would to get my rent advanced to Candlemes after the Entry. And: Watherhead brought me a stone of Candlle wch Julian bought me. Julian writes ther be 48 rag weeks & 29 Cotton ones he has brought me only 44 Rag weiks and 30 Cotton. The Lady Hiltone came here in the after noon and went att night to Nisbet. she came to the Country upon Ja: Torys acctt who is her sones factor & has been very ill of the Gravell.

Tuesday 9th. I went in the after noon to see Swintone he told me that the Councill had sent out Dr Burnett and Gideon Elliot to see what Condition the E. of Home was in he by ane order from Court being ordered to enter himselfe prisoner in the Castle upon wch he sent in his Dr and surgeons testificat that he was not able to travell so they say the Councill allows him to stay in the

Country providing he give double bail. Swinton is bail for him at present
and Killmaronock is to be joind wt him. I came home by Harcasse and saw
the Old and Young Ladies and Y. Harcasse my Lo: being gone to Edr wt his
daughter Barbary to Schools. I found when I came home a letter from Mr Al
Home 5th Ap. wch he sent out wt Gideon Elliot who it seems designed to
have seen me. he writes he has payd Ninewells funeralls all but Gideon
Elliots acct and that I should try what he would give doun. I wrote to Mr Al:
and sent him precept agst Gardner and told him I knew not what he would
give doun but desired him to show him money and that would be the most
effectuall way to get doun. I wrote also that he would informe me if he could
get me the money I formerly wrote of agst the terme

Wednesday 10th. I wrote to Wm Brack to get me 10 lb st fro James
Redpath and What other money could be got amongst the other tenants of the
toune.
One from Earnslaw come to me and told me Earnslaw would gladly have
spoken to me. I went after dinner to Earnslaw and from that to Lithome and
heard he was gone to the Hirshill. I saw at Lithome Sr Al: Purves who came
to the alehouse wher I lighted he spoke to me of his bussines of Lambden
and anent a bill given in to the Councill in name of his sones friends of the
Mothers side among whc I was named desiring they might have power to put
a factor on the Estate and that they might have liberty to grant alim[en]t to Sr
Al: Because of his inability to govern his affairs. he was very troublesome wt
his bussines I waved it as much as could be. from thence I went to the
Hirshill. My Lord was in the dining room wt Earnslaw. while we were ther
Mr Geo: Waddell came from Edr and brought acct yt the Councill had
dispensed wt My Lords' imprisonment in respect of the acct Dr Burnet and
Gideon Elliot gave he doubling his caution. Earnslaw promised if he went
not away to morrow for Edr to see me on friday. It has snowed very much all
this day wt a s.e wind

Thursday 11th. This night it has snowed very much all the hills about are
quite covered and here snow lying on the tops of the houses, and the day
continues to be cold and boistrous. Ja: Redpath came here and gave me 23 lb
Scots

Friday 12th. Da: Young came here and I showed him méy fathers acct
wherby he is due 90 lb 09s. he gave me 10 lb Scots but this summe must not
be exacted from him but a moderat composition.
Earnslaw and his sone came here just as I had done wt dinner and not
having dined I caused get them some meat. his sone who is ane Ensigne in
Maitland formerly Levens Regiment told us severall passages of the last
years warrs. he says the occasion of the losse of Landen was their not casting

up trenches for wher it was done the French could never get over. among severall other things he told us the Flemings set their hedges crossewise like a trelisse or as we make stake & ryce

Saturday 13th. It has been pretty pleasant this day but still cold. in the Afternoon Swintone and Mr Al: Cockburn came here Swintone told me the E. ol Home had written the news were that the parlia was to sit and after 3 or 4 days to be dissolved and a new one called wch was to Establish superintendents &c. Cavers & Deucher came after they told that the Sophie of Persia is dead. I sent Wm Home of Greenlaw Castle 10 lb st in pt of 15 lb st due to him at Mart. last he sent me a receat of it. I counted wt James Forsyth & cleared wt him

Sunday 14th. I went to Church Sr John Home and his Lady were ther he says he is much the better of the flower of Brimstone he has taken. Da: Rotsone brought me a letter from the post house from Mr Home he writes he has got no ship for Berwick as yet but has sent my seeds in a cask wt my Lo: Polwarths aboard of Mr Graham for Leith.

Monday 15th. Sr John told me yesterday he would come in the morning yt he and I might goe see My Lord Polwarth but it rains and the day is stormy so I suppose he will not stir abroad this day. John Jamesone came here I showed him my fathers accts of his arriers wherin he is due me 93 lb. 3sh. 6d. he produced me a receate of my oun of 35 lb upon that acct and gave me 10 lb so he is now resting 48 lb if get me 24 lb together soon I think I will discharge him.

Tuesday 16th. I went to Blackader and dined and sent my man to Berwick to get me some powder and lead and 2 donons of Pill. de duobus and a loaf. I wrot likewise to Mr Home at London to try if he could get my goods aboard of the ships coming home wt the Chancellours goods. I returned at night the day was rainy but warmer than the days befor.

Wednesday 17th. It rains still and is rainy like this morning. I payd Geo Archer for bringing some loads of Coals send to Dunse for some things for the use of the house it has raind a small rain all day

Thursday 18th. Being troubled these 2 or 3 days past wt a weight in my veins and having passed some sand I took this morning a full scruple of pil. de 2bus mixing wt them 5 or 6 grains of salt of Tartar whc wrought very well & gently about 6 or 7 times Da: Robison having a sisters daughter (Jany Robisones daughter) to be married this day and it being very rainy and the water very thicl Mr Moody married them in this toune Capt Cockburn My Brother & Sandy Loran were at the Wedding and Came here. Cornet Bennet was also ther but hearing I was under physick he did not come in. Cap. Cockburn tells me that

Cap. Lockhart and Cap Drummond have accused my Lo Jedburgh of encouraging a mutiny in the regiment when some of them were condemned to be shot last year and my Lo should have given Countenance to the soldiers to set them at liberty and for Keeping up ther pay. it will go high on one side or other. It has rained all this day out of the north East.

Saturday 20th. I was no wher out yesterday it still raining. I sent John Murdo to the Wedding for Roby. It rains still this day but it is not very cold the rain is small not heavy and ther is a mist from the East.

I got a letter from Mr Al: Home he only promises to get me money but it seems he not lookt out for it yet. I got a letter from my sister Isabell anent her debt to Pa. Adamsons children the bond she has granted to Pat Adamsone the 82 lb 14sh in it whc was due befor I went to France and I think I granted him bond for all any of them was due at that time but I cannot remember who gave Patrick Adamsone the bond for when I went away I gave it to somebody to give him and I remember not who whether my Lo: Crosrig or Da: Robisone.

Note. I find my sisters debts have not been included in my bond.

I got likewise a letter from Julian wherin she writes she had sent me a quarter of butter but it is not come yet. Meg Home writes to me that after a great dale a doe she has caused Sandy send out ane edict for Joseph Homes choosing his curators I have heard no more of it.

Sunday 21st. I went to Church ther was a collection for a harbour at Kinkell in Fife.

Monday 22nd. Sr John Home came here in the morning and dined and I went wt Him att night. I played a game at Chesse wt the Lady she defeat me.

Tuesday 23rd. Earnslaws man came to Blackader to me to ask if I had seen my Lo: Polwarth and spoke to him anent Crummie in Dunsteils and Wait in Keilshill. I told him that I had not but that I should give him answer this night or to morrow. Sr John & I resolved to goe to Polwarthouse. we came ther about 12 a clock my Lo: was gone to Bartleshill we see my Lady and dined wt her. I spoke to her of these 2 men she told me Waite deserved to be sent away but was not worth the while being and [sic] old dying body. I returned hither wt Sr John and writt to Earnslaw and told him what I had done and told him if he pleased to let me know I should waite on him next day at Polwarthouse. I went to Bl: wt Sr John

Wednesday 24th. In the morning I got a letter from Earnslaw wherin he says he would goe to Polwarthouse and wisht I might meet him ther. I likewise receaved one from My Lo: Crosrig of 11th. Ap. wt a letter from the Master of Polwarth. My Lo: it being directed to be left at his Lodging had not read the back of it and broak it up but finding it was for me read it not. My Lo: desires me to bring in all bonds Count books and papers that we may clear when I come to toune. The Master excuses his not having writt to me befor a[nd] says he hopes to be at home the end of the Campaigne. the dat. 2. March our stile. I went to Polwarthouse after dinner my Lo: was at home but no news of Earnslaw I spoake to him of Earnslaws bussines. He says that the councill has ordered that if any officers informe of any fellows who have been pickers or stealers they must prove it befor the sheriff or his deputs befor they can carry them away. my Lo: and my Lady are going for Edr tomorrow the Parlia is adjourned to the 9th of May. the Commissioner came off on thursday last and most of the Scotch at London. Mr Carstairs is come to Edr and tis sd has engaged to get the Parlia to give the K. 8 months Cesse during his life. this is a drift of Stairs's &c to ingratiat themselves wt the King yet it seems tho the parlia will hardly doe it, it being of evill consequence to grant cesses of soe long time and so to make parlias uselesse besides this were to Entale 8 months cesse upon the nation for the Argum[en]t is you granted it to the Late K. James and so ought far rather to grant it to this and whoever comes after will say you granted it to my predecessor why not to me. I stayd wt my Lo: till about 7 and came home Mund. Tuesday. And this have been tollerable drying days particularly this has been warm.

Thursday 25th. This day is pretty warme but it is gloomy and has raind. on tuesday was eight days were seen the first swallows. I see none till tuesday the dotterils whc they say come much about a time wt the swallows are also come. I ate of them yesterday at Blackader. This time 12 months the Asparagus was for eating now they are not halfe ane inch above ground Blackaders are all lost for ought I see. Yesterday I told My Lo: Polwarth I had got a letter from Mr Home at London telling me he had put my Lords seeds aboard of one Mr Grahame for Leith whc my Lord not having heard of him took note of.

Friday 29th. [26th] Mr Adam Waddell came here in the afternoon and staid all night. he was in Lothian all last week and could not get home because of bad weather. among other discourse we were talking of a story that goes that when This Laird of Innis's grandfather was in Italie going up to see Vesuvius wt other company and a guide he sees as he thought the Lord Drumlanrig on a black horse ride at full tilt by them wt a red night cap on his head and up to the mouth of the gulfe and so in. he askt his guide what the matter might be and the guide said it was a vision such as they used ordinarily to see. he marked this in his notebook and found upon search that that person died about the same time. this they say is yet to be seen in Innes's book as Collenden reports the Duke of Queensberrys death has occasiond this story to come abroad. Mr Adam told me that one Mr John Somervail minister of [blank] in Teviotdale maried a woman who had some houses in Jedburgh when she died she came

back to those houses and the people acquainted Mr John wt who went there.
and it seems see her but lived but a very few days after it.

Saturday 27th. Mr Adam [Waddell]went away airly in the morning. I was at
home all day.

Sunday 28th. Yesterday I got a letter from my sister Isb. telling me Julian
would have sent me some Irish butter but that she knew not how to secure it so
as And: W[atheret]. should not come at it. I got one also from Meg Home still
full of fears of her sister-in-laws doing nothing for her Nephew &c. I likewise
receaved one from Mr Home telling me he had shipped my goods for Berwick
aboard of one Mathew Linten. My Brother was at Edrom church he came
home and supt with me and tells me that Edicts are served for Joseph Homes
choosing his curators thursday next and that Hiltone is to be served air to his
brother that day.

Monday 29th. I got a letter from Sr Jo: Home telling me he could not come
hither as he designed yesterday his horses being gone to Kelso about Js: Home
of Rowistone and desiring me to come ther. I went and dined at dinner I
receaved a letter from my Lo: Polwarth telling me he designed to be in
Berwick att night to meet the Commissioner not knowing whether he was to be
at Berwick or Belford. I returned the sooner home thinking he might call here
as he passed but it seems he is gone in coach by Manderstone. I hear Mr Al:
Home is at Polwarth house. saturday yesterday and this day have been foggy
the Wind being N.E.

Tuesday 30th. I went from home in order to meet the Commissioner. On the
road going to Blackader I rencountered Sr Wm Ker Sr Wm Bennet and young
Lintone and a number of Teviotdale people going to met the E. of Roxburg at
Aitone. they told us they did not Expect the Chancellour sooner than this night
at Berwick or to dine ther tomorrow. I went to Blackader and he told me My
Lo: Pol's man had been ther and that my Lo: was come back from Berwick the
Commissioner not being expected till tomorrow at Berwick. I staid ther till the
afternoon Sr Jo: Pringle & Mr Walter came ther befor dinner and Dr Abernethy
Sr Jo: & Mr W. staid all night. the Dr & I came west and he went to Nisbet.

Wednesday May 1st, I went airly in the morning to Blackader. Sr John
Home Sr Jo: Pringle Stichill Mr Walt & I went to Berwick. we could hardly
get room for our horses and the fodder is so scarce ther that they aske a shilling
for the stone of Hay and Mr Robisone told us he usually gave 9d for it. we
dined in the post house after dinner My Lo: Polwarth came doun ther. we got
notice that the Commissioner dined at Belford about 4 a clock. the E. of
Roxburgh and all the other gentlemen took horse (My Lo: Polwarth was in his

berline) and went the lenght of the Sands (about 4 miles from Berwick) wher a litle on this syde the sands we met the Commissioner. he came out of the Coach and we quitt our horses and saluted him after whc his Grace went into his coach again. My Lo: Yester & Mr Baird were in coach wt him the Justice Clerck Ricardtone Drummond &c were in another coach and Sr James Ogilby and Dirletone &c were in a 3d. after the Commissioner was come to the posthouse the Mayor and Aldermen came to him and complimented him in name of the toune and presented him wt a burgesse ticket as also my Lo: Yester and the Chancellours other sons My Lo: Roxburgh my Lo Polwarth but they give tickets to noblemen only. the Chancellour is a Marquis wt the same title of Tweedale. so his sons are now all Lords. after we had paid our compliment I took my horse after 7 and came home betwixt 9 and ten. The day was pleasant enough but a north east wind yet when I came home I[t] was n.w. When we came in to toune in the morning the Mayor and Aldermen were going to ride the Marches as they use to doe every 1st of May. Notwithstanding of Da: Robisons search on saturday I found that tis above a 14 night since Mat. Lintin arrived and that my two boxes were standing in the Mayors court. when I came home I sent to And. Watheret to be ready to morrow to goe to Berwick and to Geo: Archer also. And sent to Da: Robisone to goe wt them.

Thursday 2nd. I receaved from Al: Jaffrey 5 lb St in part of his Whit: rent next to come. This day is clear but a cold n.e. wind. I went to Dunse My Lo: Polwarth came ther from waiting on the Commissioner and held a court by a license to serve Rot Johnstone of Hiltone air to his brother & father Sr John Home was chancellor of the Inquest the late Josephs retour was produced but no seasine some declaired to the Inquest they had seen it so the Inquest voted service but on condition the Chancellor should see the seasine befor he signed the Verdict. They say that when Jos. was served air John Bain gave the Inffestmt that the seasine is ether in Hiltons or Ninewells charter chest but was never registrat and that John Bain was exorbitant in his demandes for a new extract. It might be objected that The seasine unregistrat does not signify anything to qch lawiers answer it is sufficient enough except in a competion wt others pretending right.

Jos Home came ther and Chose My Lo: Crosrig Sr John Home & me Curators Sr Jo: & I gave our oath defideli and signed ane act of Curatry. the Gentleman of the Inquest dined in Sandy Lorans after dinner I returned home

At night Da: Robesone Came home wt my two boxes from Berwick he payd 10sh for fraught and 6sh 6d To the English Customers. I find everything I expected but my pocket glasse I gave to Mr Home to mind and Abbrige de la Methode Latine and retraite de dix Mille instead of whc it seems Vaillant has put up a litle book called Ecole du monde and another le Character dun parfaite ami

Friday 3rd. I went to Kelso alighted at Dr Abernethies went and called for Mrs Ormstones books and find I have been in a mistake in affirming my sisters accts were in my bond wch I granted when I went to France for I find my acct avises otherwise so that the accts they granted bond for are not included. I met wt And Halyburtone who is content to supersed paymt of his money till Candlemes but expects his anrent at Whits. I dined wt Abernethy saw Elshy Trottor who is very ill of the Scurvey got the Scholars the play and went wt Dr Abernethy Mr Knox & Mr Kirkwood and talked together in Wm Handysydes. after I took horse at James Duncans

Saturday 4th. Dr Abernethy sent his man for Ray de plantes Lister de Morbis chroniers and Helvetius de la guerison de fierres whc I sent and some queen of Hungaries water to Elshy Trotter and 4 pair of pigeons he longing for some.
Sir John Home came here and stayd most of the day wt me he got Payrard Lait and his Lanterne but I have keept the bible in sheets. he got also from me a loan of Methode Greque & the Conte of Payans relation of the River of the Amazons. My Brother came here at night

Sunday 5th. I went to Church Mr Al: Home came home wt me

Monday 6th. He went from this about 10 to dine at Nisbet and a litle after, my brother David. Mr Al: is going from that to the Hirshell and from thence to Gallasheils to see his sone and thence to Edr. He knows of no money but what is in Sr Jo: Foulis hands wch he says he will try.

Tuesday 7th. This day and yesterday have been both very ill days the wind allwise East or north E.

Wednesday 8th. Sir John Home and his Lady came here in the forenoon and took me over to Nisbet to dine after dinner we went to Wedderburn from that we went to our severall homes. When I came home I found Mr Ad: Waddell here he staid wt me all night. the day was somewhat pleasanter but the Wind still N.E.

Thursday 9th. Mr Adam staid with me till after dinner he borrowed from me La Veritable Histoire de Calvinisme

Friday 10th. I was at home all day the day was clear but cold

Saturday 11th. I wrote to Mr Home at London I told him I had got all my things safe only that Vaillant instead of Abbrige de la methode Latine and La retraite de dix mille had sent me Lecole du monde and charactere dun parfait ami wch I desired him to acquant him wt and that I would send them to him if I found the occasion. I told him also I found not my pocket glasse but twas no great matter. I desired him to write the first occasion. I went in the Morning to Blackader and from that sent John Murdo to Berwick wt the Letter and for some bread. I found Sr John somewhat indisposed. I returned at night the wind has been still in the n.e. it raind toward the Evening. At Blackader I observed the Gueen trees breaking into florish ther is no flourishing here as yet.

Sunday 12th. I went to Church Sr John Home being indisposed was not ther. Dr Abernethy being at Nisbet the night befor was ther

Monday 13th. Dr Abernethy came over here in the morning and got from me Blunts translation of Apolloneus Thyandus Voyage du Levant. Rays discourse of the Creation and Lart de sa conserver la sante. he had been here on sat when I was at Blakader and brought back Lister & Helvetius. Yesterday Having got a letter from the Lady Hiltone to search Ninewells's charter chest for her sone Josephs seasine I went to Blackader and from yt to Ninewells but when I came ther I found the kee My Lo: Crosrig sent me out in his letter I receaved on saturday by And Watheret (desiring me to send him his books first occasion) wch my Lo: had gotten from Meg to send me was the wrong kee. I saw the books that Ninewells has ther David says one [blank] had prevailed wt John Ninewells sone to give him many of them while he was alive. I returnd and dined at Blackader. I returned at night And: Watheret had brought away the trunk. I wrote to my Lo: Crosrig and sent him the kee of the trunk and the kee he had sent me instead of the kee of Ninewells charter chest. I wrote to Dr Dundas & told him to receaved Pool & Venerons from my Lo: Crosrig & Lister I sent by And. I wrote to Mr Al Home anent Ridles affair & to let me know when Whytefeild would be in the Country. I hear the secretary is past yesterday morning at Berwick. This day was very pleasant and warme yet in the afternoon ther arose a wind occasioned I fancy by the Moorburn.

Tuesday 14th. This day was very pleasant in the morning but the afternoon was windy from the same cause as the day befor. I cut this day the first of my asparagus and sent it to Blackader theirs being all destroyed. I find I have some of my artichocks pointing up the flourishing is but just now breaking whyte I have had a peach & ane Apricot flourished sometime agoe but the florishing is gone. Mr Adam Waddell came here and dined he tells me that the English Parlia is prorogued and the King was to goe on thursday. that the A B. of Canterbury the Duke of Shrewsbury the Duke of Devonshire the Lord Keeper who he says is to be made Chancellour and ane Earle [blank] are to have the Cheife managemt of affairs till the Kink [sic] return. The A.B. of Canterbury the B.of Worchester the B.of Eli the B. of Salisbury are to Manage the

Ecclesiasticall affairs. I got alone of Quintince in English from Sr J. Home. Sr John Came here about 5 a clock on his journey to Stichill and from that tomorrow to Edr to the parlia.

Wednesday 15th. I went after dinner a[nd] visited my Lo: Harcars who has been ill of the Cold. Mr Adam Waddell was ther. My Lord gave me a loan of the Kings letter to the parlia the Commissioners speech the E. of Annandales president of the parlias speech and the Kings speech to the parlia at the prorogation therof on the 3rd of may. We hear not as yet of ye Kings being gone, The Lo: Yester Tweddales sone is to vote in parlia in place of the Thesaurer. Secretary Johnstone who past at Berwick on sunday last is to vote as secretary. As I returned home I came by Greenknow I saw the houses wch are in pretty good condition only the Gavels are to built wt stone no higher than the syde walls after that being of fail and so settle and yeild and spoil the roof that leans on them. I went also and saw the Quarry at the Stanefald burn I gave liberty to my Lo: Harcasse to win ther is a great many stones already win but they are not yet at the good stone. I came to Midlestotts and see Will Robisone Davies sone who got his thigh bone broake on saturday or friday last by ane oxes trampling on him in the bire. he recovers pretty well Mr Guthry was ther he came home wt me and staid a litle.

Thursday 15th. [16th] I receaved from Al: Jaffrey 40 lb and James Jaffrey 20 lb. Tho. Rutherford came in the afternoon among other things Tho: told me he has seen the bear a[t] 20 Ms the boll and the pease at 18 lb the boll and that also other times he has sold the oats at 2 lb 3sh. the boll. Peter Broun came here and brought a note from my Lady Polwarth desiring him to ask me if I had a bill of Loadening for the seeds that Sandy Home writes has put aboard of Grahams ship for de [sic] denys the having them. I wrote to my Lo: I knew no more than I told him. Peter has promised 4 dozen of Artichock setts

Friday 14th. [17th] I receaved a letter from my Lo Crosrig he tells me ther are severall committies appointed, for trade &c Dr Dundas writes that the Councill has past ane act discharging Eng. clipt money

Saturday 19th. [18th] Meg Home sends me another kee for Ninewells_ charter chest. The Lady Hiltone wrote to me to break it up because ther would not another kee be found. I delayed till I got ane answer from Edr so having got this kee I went this morning first to Blackader (wher the Lady told me Sr John Had written the French 3sh 6 were cryed doun also) thence to Ninewells wher Da: Home & Aymouth were both present and trying the kee I got from Edr and that it would not doe I caused break up the Cabinet but found no such paper ther we need. naild and seald the Cabinet wt Aymouths seal & my brother Das: who was ther I having forgot mine at home. I returned home befor dinner. Wedderburn and Da: Simsone came here about 7 a clock at night & stayd a litle. these three days past have been extremly cold the Wind blowing strongly from N.E.

Mem: Yesterday I sent my man to Kelso and paid And Halyburtone his anrents due at Whits. last

Sunday 19th. [Saturday 18th - deleted] I went to Church At night a servant of my Lo: Polwarths brought me a proclamation discharging the passing of English clipt money except by weight as our money goes by 24th act of Murrays parlia (for I see they take ther rule from that tho in the proclamation it is not exprest ther is nothing in it of the French 3sh 6ds.

Monday 20th. I went to Dunse fair the proclamation agst English clipt money wch was published this day spoilt the Market so that ther was litle buying tho were many English ther and beasts would have given great rates. some that took English money got good prices. I see Capt: Cockburn who tells me he got 27sh for guineys [a page is torn out here] at Newcastle and that for a shilling on the pound at Edr they will give Scotch money for the Clipt English. I spoke to Will Turnbull about my poll whc Da: Robisone has been so negligent as Not to pay all this time. Will tells me he is content to pay but yet delays to take it when offered but he tells he had spoken to Hadden who told him to take it wtout the deficiency of the quadruple so that I think he will take it. I met wt Sclatehouse and Bell as they were making a minute of agreemt wt Mr Nicolsone late minister of Prestone for the house of the Bell. Jo: Home Sclatehouses brother going now to the Sclatehouse in Aitone He gets it on the same termes that Jo: had it which I thought allwise ridiculous for he pays Bell but 50 Ms and the Casualities he gets as Cains, Cariages, grasse, strae are worth 50 lb at least, tho you reckon the house set for nothing. I spoke to Sclatehouse anent my bussines wt Bell and offered him 100 lb if he would pay me the money now the summe being above 700 lb he sd he could not doe it. I see Hary Borthick of Pilmor Sandy Homes sone in law who promised to come to my house.

Tuesday 21st. Mar: Turner came and told me her mariage was bloun up at this time and that she would be content to stay that she met wt Ka: Neilsone who was to come here in her place and she sd that the Lady Blackader would be content to take her. I wrote to the Lady and told her what Mar: had said and if she had noe use for Ka: her selfe to see if she could dispose of herselfe otherwise if not that I would keep conditions. Ro: Knox met the Lady going to Stichill who promised me ane answer to morrow or thursday by her woman. I went to Betshile and took Engl: money from my tenants rather than none see ther actt, of this days date. befor I went away Mrs Scot once Adamsone came here about the bond I stand bound in for my sister I designe to send her the

English money whc she says she is to send to her husband at Newcastle. At Night Mar. Johnstone brought me a letter from Sr John Home she had got at Blackader. he writes the Club talks of great things of removing ill men from the Government (namely Lithquo, Braidalban, Tarbet secretary Stair) of Granting no more cesse than what will just doe the present bussines at that only for a year but that befor that the money allready given must be given acct of many wholesome laws to be made. so many ships of warre out reikt as will keep our ships from needing any other Convoy. That the regulations of the session (what they are I know not) are past the K,s hand Long agoe. This night Mar: Foord came home to keep Robie

Wednesday 22nd. Kath: Neilsone came hither from Tho: Roucheads in place of Mar: Turner who is going away but her mariage is Bloun up and she would willingly have staid but Kat: being entered home I could not send her away again so I called for Da: Robisone who took up a list of the furniture and delivered it to Kath. I find all the linnen is quite gone. I sent John Murdo to Kelso wt 188 lb 2s 6d due to Mrs Scot by my Sister Isabell. she sent me back 12 Halfe crouns and 3 sh st. and he gave her out 3 lb 10sh I gave him in case she challenged any of the money and and [sic] 2sh scots of his oun so ther is due her still 27sh st. for wch she took his note. While I was sitting at dinner Hary Borthwick of Pilmer Frank Home Rot: Home a sone of Erlie's who stays wt the Lady Plandergaist Da: & Geo: Rentons came here. at night Young Wedderburn and Mr Geo. Waddell came here and staid a litle. They wer saying the parlia was designing to look into the affairs of the McDonalds of Glenco who were murthered by a party of Argiles regimt commanded by GlenLyon they say ther was ane order for it from the King but I hear not how it was procured. they say Stair got it but upon what representation I know not Bradalban Tarbat and Lithquo ar Blamed for it. &c. Mar: Johnstone who I hear now is going to be married to a Tayler in Dunse one Douglas told me this night she goes for Edr tomorrow so I cleared wt her. I wrote to Sr John Home and to Julian that the markets being stopt by the discharging of English money I could get none to send her or her sister as she desires.

Thursday 23rd. This day was pretty pleasant, but the wind continues still easterly and the mornings and evenings cold. Roby begins to be acquaint wt his new woman he was strange to her at first but durst make any noise about it.

Friday 24th. I payd Jamie Denholme sone in law to W. Trotter 20 lb due at Whit. he had a note from Wm. Empowering him to receave it. This day was pretty pleasant but wind.E

Saturday 25th. Wm Brack came here and told me that they knew not now wher to fall on for a mosse. That Geo. Broun and his mother have never paid ther 3d peets notwtstanding yty[?] call peets to Dunse and James Ridpeth likewise has paid none so that I must of necessity goe up ther and hold a court. I receaved a letter this day from Baylif Young for a year 1/2s anrent due him at Whit: last

Sunday 26th. I went to Church the day was clear but the Wind Easterly

Monday 27th. I receaved a letter from Mr Al: of 17th Instant. it seems it has come out by Swintone last week and lyin ther till this week he gives no good ground to think I will get the money for Friershaw.

Mem. My Lo: Harcasse was here on Saturday last and he borrowed from me the history of Cardinal Richlieu in 2 Vol. his sone & Sr James Don were wt him. ther is now a great drought and the Weather clear but the East wind makes it so cold; out of the Wind the Sun is very hot this morning for the first time. I rose wt out a fire tho I had one at night. The Lady Blackader came this way from Stichill about 7 a clock at night

Tuesday 28th. This being Swintone fair I sent my two cowes to it but was offered no money. I had given Da: Robisone 12 halfe crouns & 3sh st to get them changed in Berwick on saturday he says ther is no Scots money in Berwick the English money coming ther from Edr and they having sent ther Scots money to Edr he got off only 3 halfe crouns for shoes to his servants. In the afternoon Young Wedderburn Whytefield & Da: Symsone came over here from Wedderburn. Whytefeild has been in the Country he says these 3 weeks he tells me Sr Pa: Home designes to buy Aitone & that Hoptone would also buy it & Ladykirk. he is going to Morrow to talk wt E. about that bussinesse, I halfe promised to goe to the Hirshill on thursday but I hear ther is company (Colstone & Spot) wt my Lord. this has been one of the pleasantest days we have had the Wind S.W. we expected rain but the Wind turnd high. My Brother came here at night he told me that Cuthbert Brady was content to supersede the 29 lb st he oues him provided I would give my note to see him payd at Lammas next wch I did by way of note to him and my Brother gave me a note obliging himselfe to free me of the samine. He tells me that oats are giving 7 lb Kelso boll at Kelso.

Wednesday 29th. Cuthbert Brady came here this morning. my Brother met wt him yesterday it seems he came only to know of my selfe if it was truly my note. he tells me that he got 27sh st for guineys & and 20sh for pistols and Luis dors. he says he goes for London on Friday come eight days. My Lady Pol[warth]: came home yesterday and writt to me this morning for a cradle for Ro: Baylie whom she hes brought out with her.

I writt this afternoon to Mr Al: Home to try still for money for Friershaw and to try at Sr P. Home because he has a mind for Aitone. to borrow 1,000 lb or therabouts to pay me what I payd out for him to Sr Geo: Lockhart. To send word by Mr Tho: Aikman to Bayliff Young that I designe to be shortly in toune.

I writt to my Lo: Crosrig wishing him joy of his Knighthood and if he could conveniently to let me have some money.

Thursday 30th. I was at home all day It was some rain and the Wind is turned to the S.W.

Friday 31st. I went to the Hirshill and by the way I went to Earnslaw and took Mr Jo: Douglas wt me. I dined at the Hirshill. I returned by Harcasse and found ther Wedderburn Whytefield & Dr Stevensone who had come that morning from the Hirshill and dined ther. I spoke to Whytefeild in the bussinesse I have wt the E. of Home he says they are doing what they can to get things in readinesse for a sale of Aitone. This day was gloomy and some rain. I found a letter Sr Jo: Home had brought me from Edr from Meg Home wherin she offers me 300 Ms in Loan to make up 500 Ms.

Saturday June 1st. I went to Blackader and visited Sr John whom I found indisposed whc he thinks aguish yet does not take the pouder. He tells me the parlia is to lay one 120,000 lb st. wherof the excise annexed to the Croun is reput 30,000 lb. they have not thought full how the rest shall be listed but tis thought by pole and excise and to keep the Land as free as can be we are to have 5 frigats for convoys to our merchants.

Sunday 2nd. I went to church this day was very cold the Wind N.E.
Mem: I got a letter on saturday from Cavers containing that now since Ninewells was dead I would grant further security and Corroborat the anrents

Monday 3rd. I went to Blackader and finding Sr John not going for Edr I gave my letters to And. Watheret on to My Lo: Crosrig in answer to one he sent me wt And Watheret of thursdays date telling me he found a bill of Cap[tion]: at Blackburns instance agst me. In my answer I told him it was suspended, & Entreated him to let me know if I might expect any money from him. I wrote to Meg Home I accepted of her offer and to Mr Al: Home to know what he had done anent Friershaw I misdated my letters calling it Mund 4 ins. of 3d. This day was pleasant in the morning but the wind arose n.e. in the afternoon

Tuesday 4th. Da: Robisone put me up some shelfs in my study of one of the Boxes that came home wt my books. Mem; Yesterday morning Dr Abernethy came over here from Nisbet he gave me again some of the books he had borrowed and got others by the parch. books wher the list of my books is I got

15 lb 4sh from James James [sic] Jaffrey. he brought me 20 lb but I gave him back 4 lb 16sh Scots of English money that was light.

Wednesday 5th. I went to Dunse in the afternoon but found not Sclatehouse ther as I supposed he might I designed to have spoke to him in Bells bussinesse: I only read the Regulations neuly published of the clerks and advocats. I heard no news. Will Turnbull told me he had got from Blackwood a summonds of nonentry agst Wedderburn & me to cause execute. This morning Sr John Home went for Edr and sent me wt his boy Child of Trade and I sent him ways and means.

Thursday 6th. I went to Whytefield in the morning and took him wt me to Aimouth. we dined in one Philip Hoods & after dinner visited Aimouth his mother died on wednesday and from thence went to Linthill and saw him and his Lady And Linthill went wt us to Aitone to John Home Sclatehouses brother who is now come to the Sclatehouse and sells wine. I parted wt them ther and came Straight home.

Friday 7th. I was at home all the day. Tho: Auchenleck was here going to see Will Robisone. I met wt Tho: Rutherford to whom I offered his anrent he sd he had now got money and hearing I was going for Edr he would not have it at this time. I went over to Janie Robisons wt him to give him a drink of Ale I found ther Mr Auchinleck & Da: Ro: I never was in Janies befor. I receaved in the afternoon a letter from Sr John Home wherin he tells me one Mr Duncan Robisone had given in a bill agst My Lo: Stairs complaining of some malversation in a processe of his but he wrotte his letter just as he came to toune so could give me no distinct acct of things. Meg Home writes to me the 300 Ms waite for me

Saturday 8th. I went to Aymouths Mothers buriall who was caried from Aymouth to Hutton to Hiltons buriall place. I stayd wt Wedderburn Wyhtefeild &c and met wt Sclatehouse. I spoke to him anent what Bell was due me he protested they had no money. I told him my bussines prest me & that if it was possible The money could be got I would bind Caution for Bell provided he would also bind whc he promised. I had spoken to Wedderburn anent Bells Entry. he sd that he had agreed wt Sclatehouse for 400 Ms payable at Candlemisse but since Sclatehouse had not performed he would not now stand to the Condition. I spoke to Sclatehouse who told me he had allready payd some of it to Wedderburn and would have been satisfied to have allowed Wedderburn the rest in a debt due by Wedderburn to him whi he would not. But Wedderburn and he spoke together & Wed. desired him to take of Cuthbert Brady for 10 lb st. Whi he promised to doe. I came away from Hutton wt Wedderburn and parted wt him on the road.

June 1695

Sunday 9th. Ther was no sermon at Edrom the Minister of Dunse being at Chirnsyde Comunion and our minister at Dunse so I went not abroad. This day as also Thursd: &c have been very windy & ther is a great drought and the grasse riseth very ill.

Monday 10th. Mr Adam Waddell came here & stayed all day Mr Arch: Borthwick came this way as he came from Chirnsyde wher the Communion was given yesterday. My Lady Pol: was at Nisbet & sent her boy over here to see how we were. This has been the best day we have seen this summer the day very warme and some wind from S.W.

Tuesday 11th It was very warme I was no wher abroad.

Wednesday 12th. I went to a meeting of the Commissioners of Excise to hear the Complaints of severall Brewers who are much wrongd by the tax men of Excise particularly one Wood in Lawder who had taken the Whole excise of the parish of Lawder from James Broun and yet James had set One [blank] his oun excise befor and had quartered on the first for not paying him the whole wheras he would have paid him what was due defaulking what the other Brewd & whc James refused. the Commissioners decided agst Jas Ker was a complaint by Mr Al: Cockburns wife agst Ch: Emiltone for wrongous quartering but she succumbed for her husband would not make ane entry and referred the matter to the gadgers who deponed according to the Rolls they had signed. I went from that to Polwarthhouse and visited my Lady. I see ther James Home and his Lady.

Thursday 13th. This day being appointed for a fast I went to Church. Sr Rot Stuart came from Edr and told me ther was litle resolved as yet in parlia. This morning I got a letter from Sandy Home telling me The Young Lady Ninewells was dead the Lady Blackader told me at Church it was of two days sicknesse of a fever and a flux. Meg Home is over ther at present.

Friday 14th. I got some money this morning from Da: Robisone. James Jaffrey & Al: Jaffrey. And going for Edr caused him give 3 lb Scots to the Woman for the Houses use. I went to Betshile and got some money from John Millar & Pat Knox and Jo: Knoxes peet money. I could not stay myselfe so left Da: Robisone to look for mosse and to see what houses wanted timber & cause cutt it. I came to Ginglekirk and dined in the upper house the lower being full. I came to toun and took my Chamber in Mrs Hepburns. I see my aunt Ninewells (who is still very ill) My sisters & sir John Home. This day was extremly hot and I was very weary having ridden in the heat of the day Sr John Home told me what had passed about BraidAlban and the history of his

69

treaty wt the Highlanders and the occasion of his committment. He told me
also of a project of a plantation.

Saturday 15th. Sandy Home came here. he says If I pay Friershaw at
Lammas it will be time enough. he promises to doe what he can to get 1,000 lb
he oues me. I spoke to him anent Bells bussenes and that Sclatehouse is
content to bind for it if the money can be found.

Sunday 16th. I went to the Tolbooth Church morning and afternoon I supt
upon invitation wt Jeriswood.

Monday 17th. Ther is litle news from abroad the K is lying near the French
lines and the say dessignes to attack them or else to beseige a fort they call
Knok; & Ypre. Sr Jo: Home & I dined together in Rosses. I went in the
afternoon to visite my Lo: & Lady Polwarth who came to toune this morning.

Tuesday 18th. I went wt Sr Jo: Home and waited on the Secretary I came up
and went into the parlia. ther was past ane act for 6 [?8] Months cesse and
retention allowed of one of six anrents. the E. of Roxburghs affaire agst the E.
of Lothian about the precedency was brought in but delayed the bussines of
Glenco motiond but delayd. I dined wt Whytefeild in Will Thoms.

Wednesday 19th. I dined wt My Lo: Crosrig Sr John Home & Meg Home
my Lo: & I talked after dinner anent Ninewelles two Children that are at
English Mauldy. Da: Ninewelles brother being tutor in law to them we agreed
he should be spoke to not to medle because of his unskillfullnesse in such
affairs. the rest we delayed till Boghall & James Galbreth should come to
toune. I went after dinner wt Whitefeild to Errols court wher Mr Al: Home sits
judge and wher my sons nurses husband had a plea agst one John Scales who
had beat him. Scales was found guilty and fined in 10 R. Dollars but Mr Al
exacts no fines. After I went wt Whytefeild to Woods bouling green, he
bouled. from that we went and took a drink and sent for Mr Al: Home and so
home.

Thursday 20th. I went wt Whytefeild to waite upon the secretary & addresse
him to him he delivered him a letter from his uncle sometime Archbishop of
Glasquo now Bishop of Rafo in Ireland about a plea the Bishop has agst B.
Patersone (who was intruded upon him & he turned out in K. James's time
because he was agst taking away of the penall statutes) for refounding the
Emoluments of the Bishoprick of Glasquo. After I went wt him to My Lo: Pol:
and adrest him to him. Mr Al: Home has made me Expect the 1,000 lb Scots
he oues me & in the mean time promised me 300 lb to help to pay Sr Ja:
Oswald but in stead of that he has spoke to Whytefield In my name who has

lent me upon my bond 300 lb. payable the 1st of July wt anrent from the date. & having got from my sister Julian 200 lb wch Meg Home left me when she went to Inglish Maldy I payd Sr James Oswald 512 lb being 2 years anrent due to him at Whitsunday last. My Lord Polwarth sent for me in the afternoon & I went to Leith wt him to get our cask of seeds whc Sandy Home sent home in one Grahams ship but got nether bill of Loading nor did he Mark the Cask so that our seeds are I suppose quite spoilt. We see the Cask but left it ther till occasion be found to send it to the Country

Friday 21st. I payd Bailif Young a year and ane halfes anrent due at Whits. last. I spoke to Mr Al: Home if he has got the 1,000 lb he promised he says he is sure he will get it but yet knows not where. I went in the afternoon to Geo: Mosmans shop wher was my Lo: Crawford. We fell presently upon Gardening he told me he preferred English Asparagus seed to the Dutch because the Dutch is sooner at the White tho it be greater he manors them much wt Cow dung. he told me himselfe what I heard severalls say of him yt he knows all the different kends [sic] of the same fruits as the different kinds of apples by the Bark but most certainly by the leaves. And upon that the Surprisall the Duke of Lauderdails Gardener at Ham was in upon his telling him the severall kinds of pears apples &c he had in the Garden. He tells me likewise that a tree from the seed will partake more of the stock than the graft and that the stock corrects the graft so that he grafts a mellow apple on a sharp stock and the very sweet pears on Portugall quince stoks whc he says are better than our common quince. he shewed me a list of his fruits wch are very many of all kinds. I dined wt Whytefeild in Alex Bellchesses. I win 7sh Scots from him at the Tables I met wt Boghall who is earnest that Ninewells freinds may met anent the papers that are at English Mauldy belonging to Ninewells and in order to dispose of his 2 Chilren that are there. Balgaire will be in toune this night so I think we may meet to morrow.

Saturday 22nd. I met in the morning wt Balgair he told me he was going to Leith but we might meet on Munday. I received a note from Mr Tho: Aikman wherin he tells me he has found the money I spoke to him of to wit a thousand Marks on Bells Sclatehouses and my security. I met wt Geo Robinsone and dined wt him in his chamber. after dinner being in my chamber my Lo: Crosrig came and sate wt me some time at night I went to Mr Al: Homes house

Sunday 23rd. I went in the morning and afternoon to the Tolbooth Church. at night I supped in Mr Al: Homes house and walked wt him to the Castlehill we see the fleet from Holland coming up

Monday 24th, I went to Mr Tho: Aikmans Chamber to cause him draw the bond of 1,000 Ms I spoke to him of Bell wt consent of My Lo: Polwarth and

Sclatehouse his curators Sclatehouse himselfe and I are bound principills. Mr Aikman got the money from Widow Levistone upon his oun bond I receaved the money and granted my bond to Mr Aikman to get the rest to signe betwixt and the 10th of July he designes to have as much money as will pay off Widow Levistone at Candlemes and so he has given her his oun bond & taken the bond in his oun name. The parlia has been all this day on the bussines of Glenco and it is continued till Wednesday. they sat from ten to six it will they say ly at Sir John Dalrymples door. I went at night to my Lo: Polwarths and was ther when his 2 sons Sandy and Andrew who came over wt the Hollands fleet came ther. The Weather has ben very warme since I came to toune this day has been windy and some small rain

Tuesday 25th. I payd My sister Julian some money according to her acct and receate to wit what was due her at Mart and 50 lb of what is due her at Whits. last. I sent wt her My sister Isabells acct to be considered by her. I dined wt Whytefeild and gave him the bond of 1,000 Ms to be signed by Bell and Sclatehouse to get Sclatehouse to signe it he going to the country this day. I went after dinner to my Lo: Polwarths and came again to the street wt Mrs Al: & And Homes I went into Grahams wt them. one Mr Scot and Mr Ro: Patersone went wt us and Mr Al: Home came to us. I went home wt Mr Al: and after a litle went to my aunt Ninewells's and supt & from thence home.

Wednesday 26th. I payd my sister Isabell 77 lb 14sh in full of what is due her at Whitsonday last 1695. The parlia met this day at 10 a clock and sat till 7. still upon the bussines of Glencoe it is not yet done. I dined wt my aunt Ninewells. Sr Jo: Home came to toun this day I supt wt him and Stichill &c in Pat Steels It rained some this day.

Thursday 27th. I think it was yesterday Bailif Home invited Me to dine wt him on Saturday his Daughter being to be married on friday. I went wt My Lo: Crosrig and his Lady in the afternoon to the Sheens to see ther sone Sandy. the pole bill was passed this day in parlia. I dined in my chamber.

Friday 28th. I dined wt Mr Walter Pringle and Stichill Geo. Homes daughter was this night Maried to Will: Elliot a brother of Stobs and Merchant in this toune. I put in order the Maps I have binding in Geo. Mosmans. Lord teach me to improve to his Glory the years and days he addes to my life.

Saturday 29th. I went to the Mariage ther was a great number of people I staid and see the Bride and her Maidens daunce after dinner and supt wt the Company.

Sunday 30th. I went in the morning and afternoon to the Tolbooth Church and supt wt my Lady Polwarth My Lord was sent for by the Commissioner.

Monday July 1st. I went to My Lo: Polwarths lodging he gave me a paper he had got out of the Exequer containing a charge and discharge of what is due to the Mr of Pols. troupe. as also some notes left behind by the master of what he has receaved. they differ very much at least 800 or 900 lb st. If the Master has receaved what the Exequer discharges themselves wt he has receaved much more yn I knew of. I saw Earnslaw who came lately to toune. I dined in my chamber

Tuesday 2nd. I met wt My Lord Polwarth and desired him to speak to Sr Tho: Moncreif to get him a sight of his sones receates he sent me word that he had spoke to Sr Tho: and I went to him. instead of shewing me the discharges he told me the Exequer book was sufficient for them and that ther could be no error because they never booked a precept till it was given out and then they lookt on it as payd unlesse the precept were returned unpayd. Yet he took the Acct from me and said he would doe what he could to satisfy me. I dined wt My Lady Polwarth My Lo: being in Parlia and to dine wt the Commissioner. The Parlia had in Bradalbine befor them yesterday and have given him a fourtnight to prepare himselfe for his tryall. This day the XV E. of Melforth the XV E. of Midletone and Sr Adam Blair of Carbery were forfaulted being in France wt K. Ja: It raind some on Thursday but still ther is a great drought. Al: Dundas sone to the Lady Hervistone brought me this day a precept from Wedderburn of 300 Ms. I refused it & told him Wedderburn and I had a count and reckoning depending befor the Lords of session and till that were cleard I would not pay any thing. I supt wt Mr Al: Home Earnslaw and Geo. Robisone in Rosses.

Wednesday 3rd. I went out in the morning to the P[arliament]. Closse. I see my Lo: Polwarth and told him I found a great difference betwixt the notes the M[aste]r Had left and the Thesaury accts and that it was necessary to get a sight of the accts. I dined in my chamber and after dinner went and heard the debate befor the Committy betwixt the Officers of the Army and the pole mongers the ground of the debate was that the Officers urged the taxmen were now lyable to them for 44,100 lb st for whc they had formed the pole they on the other hand alleaging they had nothing to doe at present wt the officers but having taken the pole of the Exequer they might very well apply to the parlia. for ane case the officers alleaged they had a jus quasidium and that the taxmen having agreed wt the exequer for such a summe ther could now nothing be rebated of it. the committy resolved nothing but are to meet to morrow. I proposed to my Lo: Polwarth that the taxmen should be obliged to pay the soldiers and that the parlia should grant the taxmen releif another way wch he seemed to relish

Thursday 4th. I got in by And: Watheret 9 lb st from Da: Robisone I wrote to him for my horses agst munday. We hear the Spaniards have obtained a victory over the French in Catalonia and killd 2,000 of ther men. I dined in Rosses wt Hyslesyde Mr Tho: Pringle & Sam Cockburn. The parlia. past some acts anent Manifactories and fell on the Glencoe bussines and Called for Lieutenant Collonill Hamiltone who did not compear ther passed a vote ordering him to be apprehended wherever he can be found. The act anent succession to predecessors estate was in and a debate betwixt Mr Heugh Dalrymple & the Advocat whether it should look back or not. the Advocat was for it Heugh agst it. I supt wt Carubber Earnslaw Mr Al: Home & Geo Robisone.

Friday 5th. Dr Irvins Lady sir John Home sometime of Northberwick now of Castle Home in Irelands sister came to me this morning. her husband has a processe here befor the Commissaries for declairing the mariage betwixt his father late dr Irvine and Elisabeth Car null and ther Children Bastards in respect the late Dr did cohabite wt El: Car while his first wife this Drs mother [blank] Wishart was alive. the reason why he pursues this is because his father gave a right to the Children of El. Car upon ane Estate he had right to in Ireland in Defraud of this Dr and he is labouring to declaire his fathers Mariage wt El: Car null to save this Encumberance. El: Cars children pursuing him in Ireland and the Whole bussines ther depending on ther processe here. the Commissaries upon clear probation of the Drs fathers cohabiting wt El. Car and her bearing children to him even while his first wife was in the house wt him have pronounced Sentence agst her and her children but they have given in a bill of advocation to the Lo: of session wch is befor My Lo: Crosrig. The Drs Ladys desire to me was to speake in her favours to my Lo: Crosrig and give him ane information in the bussines wt all to tell him yt the reason why they prest so much for ane advocation was that thir affair being to be decided in Ireland next terme of Lambmas and the Strenght of the Drs defence depending upon the nullity of the Mariage. if he obtaind not a decreit for that effect he would losse his plea in Ireland because there they would not delay their sentence till the Lo: of Session should determine the matter. I went to my Lo: Crosrig and gave him the information. I dined wt My Lo: Polwarth after the parlia was up. The busines about the toune clock of Edr was in befor tha parlia this day, but I doe not well understand it.

Saturday 6th. This morning came ane expresse from the K. remitting the E. of Braidalbine to the sentence of the parlia. his sone the Lo: Glenorchy & the Mr of Stairs were gone to the K.to try to stop any further procedure agst him but it seems they did not prevail. We hear likewise that the K. has invested Namur. I dined in my Lo: Crosrigs and after dinner he Sr Jo; Home & I went to

Lieth in Coach Sr Jo: being to buy a teirse of Wine from Mr Wm Areskine My Lo: Cardrosses brother after we returned sr Jo: And I visited my Lady Polwarth.

Sunday 7th. I was in the Tolboth Church morning and afternoon and supt at Night wt Mr Al: Home

Monday 8th. I got from Geo. Mosman the books I gave him to bind. this day the parlia past the act anent apparent heirs possessing their predecessors estates and ordaind it to look back to the 1st of January 1661. Rot Knox came in wt my horses he tells me the Straberries being ripe were carried to Blackader that ther are no cherries and very few apples. it raind a litle this afternoon. He brought me 24 lb- 12s- 8d from Al: Jaffray. My Lo: Crosrig was this afternoon in my chamber. I spoke to him about our accts wch I think we will not yet cleared at this time I expected he would have given me 1,000 Ms at this time but he says he can only let me have 100[200?] lb.

Tuesday 9th. I sent my horses to the Grange park. I dined wt Earnslaw Ge: Robisone In Gs. Chamber. the parlia had a debate about the adresse they are to send to the King in the Glencoe bussines but it is delayed till to morrow. our news are that the King has laid siege to Namur.

Wednesday 10th. I payd Geo: Mosman 12 lb for binding Samsons maps Geo: Valies Hornij Schiopps minerva petasy Ration. tinys & Horny Hist Eccles. I dined in my chamber & in the afternoon receaved from my Lo: Crosrig 100 lb Scots giving him my receate therof in part of paymt of what he is due me. and I payd Tho: Pringle 112 lb -12sh -08d for expeding my Lo: Homes Escheat.

Thursday 11th. Yesterday the parlia drew ane addresse to the King in relation to the bussines of Glencoe wherin they give act of what they have found in the matter and that Sr Jo: Dalrymples letters to Sr Tho: Levistone doe exceed his majs. instructions and therfor desiring his maj. would dispose of him as he in his royall wisdome shall think fitt and in respect the Glencoe men have suffered much in their goods &c recommends them to the Kings mercy. ther was also past ane act in favours of the Linnen manufactory. I went this morning out to the Street it has raind for the most part since twesday morning but the rain is greater this day so that ther was no walking and I returned and dined in my chamber. It thundered and raind heavily and tis very gloomy. we have no forraigne mails. Sr John Home Gave me acct that the parlia. had been on Rothimays bussines wt Abernethy of Moyens and had found that Mayens predecessors taking out of the Register Rothemays Chest as I remember was a theift and found damages and remitted to the session.

they also horned the late pole to a collection and are to take the formers oaths how much is uplifted

Friday 12th. I dined wt my aunt Ninewelles. the parlia this day made ane act anent the Ep. Clergy assigning them the first of Septr to take the oaths. I supt wt Mr Al: Home; & Earnslaw who told me severall considerable passages of the late goverment in K. Ch: the 1sts time relating to the remonstrators & publique resolutioners.

Saturday 13th. I payd Mrs Marg: Home 10 lb Scots as the anrent of 200 lb for a year 1/4 from Candlem. 1694 to Whit last and gave her my bond for 500 Ms wt Anrent from Whit: to Mart. and payable then. I likewise payed Sr John Home 20 lb as my part of the interest of a 1,000 Ms from Candle 1694 to Candle 1695 due be Sr John & me equally betwixt us to my Lo Edmistone.
Note Sr Jo: Has the disch. and it narrates the money to be receaved from him but has promised to write on the foot of it the halfe to be receaved from me. I left 8 Rix Dollars wt my sister Julian to buy me some things of whc she will give acct. I got this day the proclamation whc was yesterday for raising the money the bank dollars to witt the sword or Dutch dollar. the Wyld man the Wyld horse and the Castle dollars are 3 lb. the Scots crouns and English mild Crouns are 3 lb 6. the Doucatoon 3 lb 14sh. the 4 Mark peices 58sh and their halfes and orles proportionally. but it seems the 7sh peices & 3sh 6d are the same. as also the mild shillings wch I think are forgot. the French Crouns and Milrains are 58sh. it would seem the money is not raised according to its intrinsik value. I had almost forgot that a 40sh peice is 44sh and the 20sh & 10sh peices proportionally. I see not how they have omitted the milnd shilling. I came to Ginglekirk and dined and came home late it being past 12 befor I came from Edr I got a letter from Sr John Home for his Lady he told me he had on thursday proposed the Accts of what money the parlia had given and the president ordered it to be put in the minuts wch was done on frid. when they were read Sr Jo: Challengd its not being ther and desired to know how that came. the Advocate stood up and sd he had put it out. Sr John upon this sd he craved the Advocat might have the Censure of the house for puting out that wch had been ordered to be insert in full parlia by the president but no body seconded him and so he was forced to let it fall.

Sunday 14th. I went not abroad

Monday 15th. I went to Blackader in the afternoon Johny Home being ill of a feaver the Lady Hiltone came ther and wt her Elshy Trotter who is walking on a stilt he has a paine in his knee whc troubles him. Johny is better. At my return from Edr I find litle or nothing done in my garden and it all overgroun wt Weeds. Robin Broun was here to see when I would build the rest of my wall but Da: Robisone promised to have me stones laid in wt his Cart but it is not done he says Ant Comptone has had it at Berwick when I came from Edr it rained North and East and thundered but it came not so far south and west as my road I[t] had been a great rain they tell me here when I came home the weather is gloomy and the Wind in the E. and tis somewhat cold.

Tuesday 16th. In the afternoon Tho: Rutherford came here he tells me the oats are at 6lb the boll in Hadingtone & the pease at 8lb. Mr Adam Waddell came here and Ja: Smalet a sone of Commissary Smallets a Bageant who is staying wt Mr Adam. My Lo: Harcus and his sone came afterward. I wrote to my sister Julian to send me my box wt the maps and some butter. Walking thro my Garden I find about halfe of the Artichoaks hold but few I suppose will carry this year the two trees wt the Limon apple or white apple of Coldenknowes are very full I find them great bearers as also the Cowtail their are a great dale on the foulwood. the rest have not many but they say ther is litle fruit in the Country. The Virginia straberrries are done being sent to Blackader on friday was a sevennight the common big straberrie is now full ripe and has been for some few days. the first pease we had yesterday but they might have been eaten 8 days agoe. ther are few Cherries some of the Cherries begin to be ripe.

Wednesday 17th. Dr Abernethy came hither from Blackader he tells me Johny Home is better. he returned me the 2 vol: of La Conqueste de Mexique and the 2 vol: of Alyssons Voyage of Italie. And Got 2 Vol: Memoires de Pontis and Voyages d'Avrile. I got from Ja: Ridpeth 40 lb and counted wt him it raind this night this day has been cold and windy from the S.E.

Thursday 18th. I counted wt Al: And James Jaffreys as by their acct Hiltone and his Brother John came here from Nisbet & dined. It raind much this day and was so cold that I put on a fire in the afternoon.

Friday 19th. Mr Trotter came here from Huttonhall at night I gave him S.V.G. for the pain in his knee he goes on a stilt.

Saturday 20th. he staid all night and went for Kelso this morning. I went and see Ja: Jaffreys barn. the wall is fled from the cupples and must be taken doun. the millar of Belshile mill was wt me for a new outter wheel. this day was pretty pleasant it raind some

Sunday 21st. I went to Church wher I got a letter from my sister Isabell telling me Sr John Homes horses were to go in to morrow and telling me Julian expected a horse from me as I had promised.

Monday 22nd. I sent the Gray horse to Blackader to goe about Julian I wrote to her for butter Geo: Home in Chyrnsyde mains came here to tell me Mrs Mar: Home had writt out for six lb st to bring over Ninewells 2 children. I went no wher this day.

Tuesday 23rd. Da: Home came this way early going to Kelso and told my man that he was going to see his Nephew who was ill. as soon as I was up I went to Kelso to see him he had been ill since thursday but was better I found Nether Dr Abernethy nor Elshy Trotter the first was to Gallashiels he being as they say past recovery of a dropsy the other to Hartrig. I see Mr Kirkwood. It raind all the way as I returnd

Wednesday 24th. My Brother came here in the Morning but did not stay I sent John Murdo to Dunse to buy some provisions, he tells me the beasts sell very ill

Thursday 25th. This day is cold windy & rainy the Wind N.W. so that I had a fire. Afternoon Whytefield and St Abbs came here going for the Hirshill. I payed Whytefield the 300 lb I borrowed from him at Edr in June and got up my bond. I got also up the bond of a thousand Ms I sent out wt Whytefield to Sclatehouse to signe wch he has refused to doe upon Bells acct but says he will signe Cautioner for me. I see a news letter of Whytefields from Edr giving ane acct of some particulars of the parlia ther is laid on other 3 months cesse payable at Lammas 1696. We hear ther has been a hot attaque upon a fort at Namur wch we have caried but wt Losse whc has all fallen on the Scotch & English, for they made the attack. I had a letter from Sr John Home who came home yesternight. Julian came wt him & my horse is returned. he writes he had spoke to Secretarie Johnsone for Ninewells's ariers & mine. he promised to doe what he could in them. Sr John desires I may goe to toune for ther is a comitty of Parlia to appointed to Roupe the old pole and it were fitt accts were cleared befor the roupe. I am not as yet resolved whether to goe or not. I spoke to Whytefeild in the bussines of Selling of Aitone he pretends the Greatest impediment will be he cannot get a rentall now since John Weild is dead who was factor ther. I told him that was very easy if he would but call the ten[an]ts and take their oaths in a court.

Friday 26th. I went to Blackader in the morning and staid till night Sr John told me that the taking of yt fort at Namur was a vigourous action as any has been heard of in our days. the Scotch and English commanded by M. Generall Ramsey made the attack. the French were so confident we would not cary it that they say Marichall Bouflair who is in the toun sent word to the Garrison in the fort to give good quarters. our men went on till the officers pikes crost on another befor they fired a shot. Prince Vaudemont has narrowly Escaped wt ane Army of 35,000 Men under his command. Villeroy called out of Garrisons and wt his oun army made 80,000 Men and came so near Vaudemont befor he was a ware that it was thought impossible he Could Escape. yet he made his retreat in the night time befor the French were aware of it and got to a passe wch he was able to defend. the K. hes writt him a congratulatory letter upon it wher he says his retreat is well worth a victory. Sr Jo: told me of severall things done in parlia since I came from Edr but the minuts wch he has brought me will contain all. he was causing dig for a quarrry east from the Greenloan but I thought it was very deep. 14 foot and a halfe befor they came to the rock. he resolved to try further west the stone raising that way. When I came home I found My Lo Harcas had sent me back the Hist. of the prince of Conde

Saturday 27th. I sent John Murdo to Berwick for bread and severall things. Dr Abernethy dined here having been at Blackader to see Johny Home who is now alltogether recovered. he got from Me Petronius in French & Latine.

Sunday 28th. I went to church

Monday 29th. Will Home of Gr. sent to me for the 60 lb of an[rent] still due I sent it. and he sent me a disch: to Polwarth house. I went to Polwarth house and dined. Mrs Al: & And came home wt me at night. It has raind flying showers these severall days this night was a high wind

Tuesday 30th. I went to Hutonhall wt the 2 Gentlemen wher we dined. we returned by Blackader wher were Ardoch & his Lady who had been and Cornwell well [sic] they were going to Wedderburn & to see me. we went wt them to Wedderburn & from that the 2 G. & I went to Nisbet wher they stayd all night & I came home. I[t] raind in the morning & the Afternoon was windy W.S.W.

Wednesday 31st. I went over to Nisbet & took Roby wt me & dined yr & went wt Cavers & the 2 G. to Coldstream & visited My Lo: Raith & my Lady who are ther drinking Cornwell well water. we see my Lo: Home & my Lady who come to visite my Lo Raith. the E. of Home has got the Liberty of the Merse upon Bail. We hear no news from abroad because of Contrary winds. ther is a report that the French have taken Dixmude but it is of no moment. I returned home at night. It was windy in the Morning but very calme at night. Mr Ad: Waddell came here in the forenoon but I made my excuse to him that I was going to Nisbet &c so he went to Wedderburn. he got Plauttus Morale Clochenne. I lent Mr Al: Home 2 u. Cortez Conqueste de Mexique. When I came home at Night I found Watheret has Brought me my box wt my books from Edr. and 1 chopin & 2 mutckin Bottles of Syrip of wyld poppy.

Thursday August 1st. I was at home all day

Friday 2nd. Ardoch and his Lady and sone came here in the afternoon wt Sr Jo: Home they went from this to Polwarth house and from that to Stichill

Saturday 3rd. I was at home all day.

Sunday 4th. I went to Church I heard the toune of Namur was surrendered on terms but that the Castle holds still out. And that one M or L. Generall Allemburg a Dane had treacherously sold Dixmude & Disne to the French for 17,000 Louisdors and was gone to Paris

Monday 5th. Dr Abernethy sent me Voyage de p. Avrile & the 2. vol of Mem. de pontis from Nisbet. he came not himselfe because he had been up some pt of the night wt the young Lady Mangertone. I wrote to Mr Al: Home & my Lo: Polwarth about my arriers.

Tuesday 6th. Mr And: Home sent me Justine Graevij. It has been cold and windy and rainy this good while.

Wednesday 7th. I sent my two cows to the market but could not get them sold beasts are very low now I gave my brother David a sample of some bear I have to sell he was wt me last night. I went to Blackader in the mor[n]ing and took Roby wt me Sr John went after dinner to Hutton to Mr Lawry the Ministers Wifes buriall the Lady went to Stichill. Sir John told me that Collonell Oferrell was the other that had betrayed Dinsy or Dixmude.

Thursday 8th. I have now the Gardener and his man and one for Dayes wages laying the conduits in the Garden. Da: Robisone lends me his cart and horses & a man to drive it. The Lady Hiltone and her 2 sons & Shury Mangertone & his Lady Mrs Al: & And. Homes Cavers & Elshy Trotter came here this afternoon. After they were away My Lo: Harcasse & his sone came here.
  Mem. I payd Tho Rutherford his anrent on Wednes. morning

Friday 9th. I was at home all the day.

Saturday 10th. I was also at home at Night Mr And: Home came here having been at Huttonhall he tells me his mother is very ill of a Squinance that morning they sent for my Lord.

Sunday 11th. This day was a collection for severall Glasquo men taken by the Sally men ether going to or coming from ye Madera's

Monday 12th. I went to Polwarthouse my Lady having been ill of a sore throat my Lo: came home yesterday he tells me ther will be nothing done in our arrears till towards Octr. we hear the Fr. K. will not keep the Conditions wt the Regiments taken in Dixmude and Dyvise refusing to restore them for a months pay. Tis thought Offerrell gave up Dynse rather out of Cowardise than treachery he having a considerable Estate in Holland more then the Fr K. could possibly give him for that place. the Castle of Namure holds still out. I borrowed from Mr And. Ryssenins containing acompend [sic] of Turettin. At night when I returned James Car came for my Corp juris Glossatum whc I gave him to Mr And. ther are 5 folio's.

I payd Al: Taite his anrent due at Whit. last he says he must have his money at Mart.

Wednesday 14th. Was sermon at Edrom Mr Dalgleis in Roxburgh lectured Mr Lawry in Hutton and after him Mr Areskin in Chyrnsyde preached.

Thursday 15th. I went to Dunse found Sclaithouse & spoke to him anent that bond he refused to signe for the 1,000 Ms I borrowed from Mr Tho: Aikman I gave him the bond and he promised to give me ane answer on twesday next.

Friday 16th. I receaved from James Jaffrey 36 lb Scots.

Saturday 17th. I went to Church Mr Dysart & Mr Colden preached

Sunday 18th. Being the Communion Mr Moody in Fogo preached in the morning after him Mr Guthry and then the Communion was given. In the Afternoon Mr Dysart preached

Monday 18th.[19th] Mr Borthwick and Mr Colden preached. It has not rained for severall days but it has been gloomy and rainy.

Tuesday 19th.[20th] Mr Ad: Waddell Came here in the morning. he gave me back Barrow of Industrie. I got from James Forsyth 51 lb Scots. ther being a meeting of the Commissioners I went to Dunse. we ordered the cesse to be brought in and Appointed my Brother to be Collector for the 3 terms cesse laid on be act of Parlia. a gave him halfe a months cesse for Collecting it whc is 1,406 lb. 10. 6 halfe of it to come in now and the other halfe at Lammas come a year. out of whc Mr Al: Cockburn is to get as clerk 240 lb and and [sic] Sandy Trotter as officer 60 lb so ther rests 1,106 lb 10. 06. My Lo: Polwarth was preses ther was ther also my Lo: Mersintone Sr John Home Swintone (who is one of the Commissioners knights) &c. We had the pole in Consideration and appointed severall persons to take in lists of the parishes I have got the parish of Hiltone My Lo: Polwarth Sr John Home Swintone and I are to meet at Tho: Mitchells on thursday to Consider of the most easy and affectuall way of getting ane act of the pole and giving it in to the meeting appointed to be on Wednesday come eight days. It has rained much this afternoon and still rains.

Wednesday 21st. I was at home all day and see no body.

Thursday 22nd. I went to Tho. Mitchells and met wt My Lo: Polwarth & Swintone we were a long time on the Outreck for the levies to find out who were deficient. Sr Wm Douglas having in this country Falsyde who is ane Ensigne in his regiment to call for them he was wt us and we find but 2 wanting one by Bemersyde and the other by the toune of Lawder. but ther will still be a difficulty for ther were 2 casts made at that time the first of whc Bemersyde said he obeyd and gave his money in to Sr Wm Scot and by the other that came out afterward he was made a leader &c. we considered likewise the Proclamation for the Pole and made some notes to be advised by the rest of the Commissioners. When I came home I heard my Lo: Arnistone and Sr John Home had been at my house. My Lo: And his Lady came to Blackader on twesdays night. Yesterday I sent my man to the herring the[y] being got for 14sh the thousand this day he came back wtout any because in the morning the[y] were 30sh the 1,000 and waited till the afternoon at whc time none were taken. he was a sote for neglecting the morning opportunity

Friday 23rd. Sr John Home came here about 2 a clock just as I was designing to go to Blackader to waite on my Lo: Arnistone. he had been setting him a peice on his way he being gone to Stevensone wt his Lady Sr John staid till near night.
    The Lady Hiltone having been at Polwarthouse wt her sone in law came home this way

Saturday 24th. Mr Elliot Bailif Homes sone in law and his wife and her sister went this way from Pol: house to Blackader

Sunday 25th. I went to Church It raind heavily in the afternoon

Monday 26th. I was at home all day I see no company

Tuesday 27th. Mr Ad: Waddell came here and staid all day he returned me Allans Catechisme he had of me I find he does not designe to take the oath.

Wednesday 28th. Was a meeting of the Commissioners I went ther wher were my Lo: Pol Lo: Mersintone Sr John Home Swintone Sr Ro: Stuart &c. most part ther enacted themselves to keep the dyets under pain of a Croun if absent and halfe a croun if after the meeting is constitute, because of much bussines we have especially in relation to the pole We considered the instructions to be given to those who are to take up the pole in the different parishes, we had Bemersyde befor us anent his not having put out a man to the levies. his excuse is he contributed wt Sr Wm Scot in the first cast and so cannot now be lyable in the next. the toune of Lauder pretends they are only lyable in 13 Militia men and so should put out but two. the Commissioners say they are lyable in 3 because they are lyable in 18 to the Militia. we put no end to the matter. It raind much this afternoon. we are to met twesday next at 11 a clock on friday

My Lo: Pol: Sr John Home & Baillif Home are to meet on John Homes late Collector his accts.

Thursday 29th. Mr Elliot & his wife and Baillif Home came here in the afternoon I went wt them to Wedderburn. the Laird was not at home being at the Hirshill at the Christening of my Lo: Homes Daughter. they went from that to Dunse. It has been windy all day

Friday 30th. The morning was heavy and rainy the afternoon the wind very high w.s.w.

Saturday 31st. The folks of Betshile brought me down 13 turs[?] of heather for covering the conduits in the garden.

Sunday September 1st. At Church I see Mr Walter Pringle who came from Blackader. he showed us a news letter but ther was not much in it the Castle of Namur still holds out and the French Army is near it the report is that Bouflair is killed wt a splinter of a Bombe.

Monday 2nd. It has raind most of this day wt a wind out of the N.E. Mr Walter Pringle came here in the Afternoon returning to Stichill.

Tuesday 3rd. I went to Dunse to a meeting of the Commissioners My Lo: Pol: Lo Mers. Swintone Sr R. Stewart &c were ther, Sr Jo: Home was at a visitation at Hutton. Swintone brought us the news of the Castle of Namurs being surrendered the Confederats made ane attack at 4 severall places and were repulsed at three but on the attack wher the Brandeburgers were (the English not being able to mentain the place wher they made their attack & joining in wt the Brandeburgers) they made a lodgment and the Lo: Cults commanding a lieutenant of McKys regiment wt 30 Men to passe some palisades and attack a batterie of Guns he performed it wt a great dale of bravery and turned 9 of the enemies Guns upon themselves. The Castle presently beat a parley and agreed to surrender marching out bag & baggage wt 6 Guns &c. ther are many of the Confederats killed and Wounded but we have not yet got the printed acct. We ordered the proclamation of the taking up of the list of the polable persons to be made on Sunday next and the Subcommissioners to have their lists ready agst Wed: come a 14 night being the 18 of this month. We had some work about the Late levy My Lo: Polw. had written to Sr Wm Douglas that we had put out all our men and Ensign Mowat is come back from Sr Wm alleging still their are some wanting &c. We are again to meet on twesday next.

Wednesday 4th. Cuth Brady came here about bussines I am engaged to him in for my Brother wch is not satisfied I promised to Write to my brother about it He tells me that the King has made the Lieute in McKys regimt that passed the palisade a Lieut Coll. & the 30 Men all Capts. I would suppose commissioned officers. He says that Villeroy Had strict orders from the Fr: K. to fight and Boufflers not surrender. Yet they found both impracticable

Thursday 5th. Jos. Home came here this morning after dinner I went to Nisbet wt him and left him ther wt Cavers sones It has raind lesse or more all this week. on saturday Da: Robisone cut doun some oats in the Easter croft. This day he has cut doun the rest and thinks he may have shearing dayly.
Since sundays night the weather has been so cold I have allwise a fire in my chamber. At Nisbet this day they had a fire in the dining room.

Friday 6th. I went in the afternoon and visited Mr Ad: Waddell. I see ther his mother & Ka: Hepburn was ther.
They told me that the Lady Blackader was brought to bed of a sone. I went from that to Blackader I found all well & see the Child & the Lady. she was brought to bed on thursday the 5th instant twixt 3 quarters after eight & nine at night I met as I came home the Lady Stichill Elder going ther. Jos: Home came here at night

Saturday 7th. I went afternoon to Huttonhall Jas. went wt me I came back by Blackader. ther came a very heavy rain wch continues still.

Sunday 8th. It raind all day & ther being no sermon in Edrom our Minister preaching in the meeting house in Berwick I went not abroad.

Monday 9th. It still rains this morning Jos: Home came here about 12 a clock and went after dinner to Purveshall. it is faire since about 11. My Sister Julian Came from Blackader.

Tuesday 10th. ther was a meeting of the Commissioners But because my Lo: Polwarth was not wt us for the following reason we adjourned any bussines we had till wednesday come eight days.

Capt Cockburn Lantones sone wanting out of his seller in Dunse ale Brandy and severall other things and blaming his servants and changing the locks still wanted so his man one Darling wt other 2 young men resolved to sit up in the sellar to see if ther were any body came ther in the night time. on Sunday morning one opened the door and came in whom they presently seased his name is John Crawford a common fellow who had been in Cavers's ground in Nisbet and being found stealing bread in his bakehouse Cavers put him away. His house was searched by the toune Bailiff and a great dale of Cloath found that severall litsters knew to have been theirs and had been stolen out of ther houses. My Lord Polwarth Sheriff being informed of this called ane assize agst this day and his lybell being red to him and he acknowledging his having stolen the Cloaths produced and his having been in Capt Cockburns seller (wch also the 3 Witnesses proved) and owning he had opned the door wt two false kees that were produced and seased on him & whc he said he had made himselfe wt a file of 2 other kees. was found guilty and sentenced to be han[ge]d before sun set. ther was a great dale of work to get up a Gallows and to find a Hangman that of Dunse being dead but at last my Lo: Polw. was content upon Mr Colden the Ministers & severall others ther intercession to repreve him till Wednesday come eight days at 2 a clock. Whether the Sheriff has any priveledge after 3 suns or not I know not so I cannot tell whether he will be hanged then or whether he will need a sentence of the Lo: of the Justiciary. It was pleasant and warme all day.

Wednesday 11th. The tenants are now bussie shearing this day was very pleasant in the afternoon came here my sister Isbell & Cath: Heburn from Blackader.

Thursday 12th. I got a letter from Whytefeild anent my bussines wt my Lord Home wherin he desires me to send for Mr Al: Home for drawing papers betwixt my Lo: & me that he will be here on Saturday or munday as he goes to my Lo: & that Mr Al: & I will be sent for to the Hirshill but tells me the designe of selling Aitone is Laid asyde at this time. I hear that Mr Al: was expected at Billy this week. I went to Hiltone & took up the pole of the people ther I was at Blackader he desired me to dine wt him to morrow having some thoughts to Baptise his sone he expects my Lo: Crosrig this night or tomorrow I got a day or 2 agoe a letter from Meg Home containing her jealousies about the Ninewells papers At English Mauldy and regrating the want of money to bring over the 2 bairns and for paying severall other things. And this night another much to the same purpose and mentioning that it is fitt a bill be given in to the Councill to secure that coffer wher Ninewells's papers and accts are.

Friday 13th. I went in the morning to Whytefield I found him all alone his nieces being gone for Edr. I spoke to him about what he wrote to me. he tells me he finds Sr Pat: Home is not so frank as he expected and therfor the designe now in hand is to settle wt me and if I think fitt to take the managemt of the Estate of Aitone & pay myselfe out of the forend and the rest to Creditors and Count wt my Lo: once a year. but he offers so low that I know not what to say. He promised to be here on munday next and I am to give him a note of what is due me. I came to Blackader and dined. after dinner my Lo: Crosrig came And after that the Childe was Baptised and Called David. Sr Ro: Stuart & his Lady and Da: Home in Ninewells were ther. I returned at night this day was warm and pleasant but it lookt gloomy at night

Saturday 14th. I took a vomit having found I needed it for some time past. this day is foggy and warme wt some rain. In the afternoon [a line has been deleted and the next page torn out] I was troubled wt a pain in my stomach wch affected me so much that in the night I was forced to send for Dr Abernethy. I rested very ill

Sunday 15th. I was a little better in the morning but still ill. the Dr came about 9 a clock all he ordered me was a Clyster of milk.

Monday 16th. I thank God I find my selfe better but not so well as befor. the Dr went away about 10 a clock. I gave him 5 R. Dol. as he went away. Sr Al: Purves came hither and was going to Blackader to speake wt my Lo: Crosrig about the bussines of the Estate of Purves hall, but meeting my Lo: coming hither he returned wt him. Whytefeild came here. I got little time to speak to him because of the others that were here, he went to the Hirshill after dinner. (I forgot that Mr Al: Home came here wt my brother & supt on sundays night. But wanting room he went to Dunse wt my brother). My Lo: Crosrig stayd here and we began the accts of his intromissions wt my estate when I was abroad. Will Purves came here in the afternoon & spoke to My Lo: about selling some Lands to pay debt. My Lo: Caused him grant him a paper not to quarrell any advice he should give him upon the pretence of a pro tutor Wm having no Curators I was a wittnes to it

Tuesday 17th. My Lo: Crosrig went to a presbytery in Dunse. I am not as yet so well as I was. He returned at Night we went thro his discharge ther were some bills and other instructions wanting But I found by my book I had draun such bills.

Wednesday 18th. My Lo: Crosrig went to Dunse ther being a meeting of the Commissioners I durst ventir abroad. Mr Ad: Waddell came here in the morning and stayd till night. My sisters came from Blackader but went to Wedderburn ther being no roome here. James Ridpeth gave me 40 lb. At night my Lo: Came back and Sr John Home wt him. Mr Al: Home came here just befor them and went from this to the Hirshill

Thursday 19th. My Lo: Crosrig and I were on our accts all the morning. My Lo: Polw. his Lady sones and Daughters came here in the afternoon from this to Blackader.

Friday 20th. My Lo: Crosrig & I were still on our accts. Cat Hepburn came here befor dinner & went away after. all this week has been foggy dark weather this day rain wind & a fog from the N.E.

Saturday 21st. My Lo: Crosrig went to Purvishall anent his Nephew Wm Purves's bussines Blackader went likewise I would not goe fearing to be the worse. in the afternoon. the Earl of Home Whytefield & Mr Al: Home came he the the the [sic] E. only sd to me he desired I might goe on in my gift because Annandale was going on in his & desired I might send him the state of my affair wt him & he hoped we should settle. he went to the Harcasse I took my horse & waited on him to Dunssteils. I askt at Whytefield who returned wt me what termes My Lo: was to settle on wt me he sd he was content he & I should be conjunct factors and that I should pay my selfe in the forend but all this time we are not come to any settlmt of the Quota on quh the Whole depends. Mr Al: Home staid wt me & Whytefield went home. This day has been pleasant & warm

Sunday 22nd. I went to Church this day was a thanksgiving for the successe of the Campagne. We had a Collection for a Boat on Tweed for one Laird Beat.
   Will Turnbull was ther and told he heard at Berwick the Venetians had defeat the Turks at sea burnt and taken all ther fleet (whc consisted of 80 sail) except 6. Mr Al: Home went in the morning to Polwarthhouse

Monday 23rd. I went to Blackader to count wt Sr John Home & my Lo: Crosrig. I got out of Sr Johns books ane acct of charge and discharge but it was not it seems all to be laid to my charge. But my Lo: Crosrig states on Sr Johns debt to me. all the money he gave out for me when I was abroad whc breaks the money bearing anrent wch Sr John oued me and will not so much as allow me counting to exhaust the anrents of the summe he oues me. for he says he is not personally lyable only I am to have out of my grand Uncles James means yt summe and that he is not as yet Lucratus having intromitted wt no more nor would pay Jamess debts. We Expect more papers from Edr for further clearing our accts. I wrote at night to Edr to Meg Home to ask for money for defraying of the Expenses of the bill to be presented to the Councill in her Nephews name for securing the papers belonging to Ninewells at English Mauldy from

Mr Alexr Home. he having considerably of Ninewells's money in his hand to Witt the price of his horses &c, I sent in to her the Gift of the E. of Homes Escheat wt 20 Ms Scots to be given to Mr Al: Home to raise a declarator on it. I wrote to Mr Al: Home to raise it and a charge agst the E to enter air. I wrote to him likewise to give Meg Home money for defraying the Charges of the bill befor the Councill & to both to know what day the Commission of Parlia for the old pole has appointed for the officers to whom arriers are due to attend them. This wt And Watheret who is to goe to toune tomorrow.

(Tuesday 24th. I went to Blackader to Clear accts wt My Lo: Crosrig and Bl: my Lo: was still on the same strain of defaulting from the priple summe due by Bl. to me what money he had given out for me. I got some accts out of Blackaders count book of money given out by his factors on my acct but we came to no close their being severall papers my Lo.) [this paragraph has been scored out by the diarist]
This day Wednesday [24th] & Thursday [25th] I was on my Lo: Crosrigs accts. Wm Purves and Jos: Home dined here on Wednes.

Friday 27th. I went to Blackader but when I came ther the papers we expected from Edr were not come. all I did was to show my Lo: Crosrig that severall bills he charged on me as payd out of Blackaders money were allready stated in his discharge given in to me. I returned at night and drew out the pole of the parish of Hiltone, and the pole payable by my tenants in Kimmergh.

Saturday 28th. I went to a meeting of the Commissioners for giving in the list of the polable persons but My Lo: Being gone to Edr ther was litle done we adjourned to Wed: next. My Lo: Crosrig was ther and my Lo: Mersingtone. Crosrig went wt Mersingtone designing for Edr on Munday. The Secretary Johnstone went to Berwick on thursday on his journey for London.

Sunday 29th. I went to Church ther was a great hoarfrost on the ground in the morning it was clear but cold all the day.

Monday 30th. This morning I see that Mr Al: Home Pol[warth]s. sone riding to Huttonhall. I calld him up he sd he thought I would not a been up. he staid a very litle. about 10 a clock came his brother & Geo: Kirtone Mr James Kirtons sone. they were a foot. they dined here & went to Huttonhall. I teinded most of Da: Robisons bear this afternoon. Mr Borthwick past while I was teinding. he had been preaching yesterday at Berwick.

Tuesday October 1st. Yesternight Jos Home came here. This morning Mr Al: Home returned this way from Huttonhall. I wrote yesternight to Swintone to Know if he knew of the time appointed by the Commission for the Officers to attend about their arriers but my man brought me back word he was gone to Edr yestrdays morning. Mr And. Home & Geo Kirktone came back this way in the afternoon. I teinded Jamy Forsyths bear and Rye.

Wednesday 2nd I went to Dunse to a meeting of the Commissioners. ther were only my Lo: Mersingtone Sr Jo: Home Edrom & I. we did nothing but appoint a proclamation that all the books be brought in agst this day eight days and adjourned till then. After I came home Mangertone & Mr A: Home calld here but would not light. These days past have been windy wt some rain.

Thursday 3rd. The Heritors being obliged by the Pole act to give up ther tenants pole according to the Valued rent of the Land they possesse my valued rent stands thus

It should be 02 or 4

Kimmergh payes monthtly of Cesse	014 - 14 - 08
whc at 11 lb 12 sh upon the 100 lb as the rule in	------------------
this shire is makes the Valued rent to be	920 - 16 - 04
	------------------
the Hundred pt of this is	09 - 04 - 02

This divided among my tenants according
to ther possessions makes them as follows.

	lb		
Imp Da: Robisone possessing the Heugh and Kimmergh Mains --------------------	05	11	00
Al: Jaffrey Greenknowe & Kingslaw ----	01	06	04
James Jaffrey possessing Westfield ----	01	17	04
James Forsyth the Mill -----------------	00	09	06
Betshile. Jan: 1698 I find in Caldras book 5lb 13sh 8d [added later]	09	04	02

The Months cesse is ------------------	05	13	08 [or 6]
The Valued rent is ------------------	335	04	06
The Hundred part is ------------------	003	7	02
This upon the reall rent is			
Geo Broun ----------------------	000	17	06
James Redpeth ------------------	000	16	08

John Millar	------------------	000	01	06
Wm Waddell	---------------	000	04	06
Pat: Knox	---------------------	000	08	08
John Knox	---------------------	000	04	06
John Jamisone	------------------	000	01	08
David Young	--------------------	000	01	08
Wm Home	---------------------	000	01	02
Al: Maw	-----------------------	000	01	08
Wm Brack	--------------------	000	11	08

003 11 02

Friday 4th. I sent my man to Kelso writt to Dr Abernethy who sent me some things to Roby to put away the Scab. he sent me pit Ar. 2v. Mem de R & Rays Proverbs he had. I got halfe a pound of Tobacco. Jos: Home went to Ninewells. I teinded the Easter Croft the Bruk of Harrage bewest the road to Midlestots, the Bank head & Inglis's land.

Saturday 5th. I went in the afternoon to see Mr Ad. Waddell & took him Chiminais sermons.

Sunday 6th. I went to Church the wind was very high S.W.

Monday 7th. I teinded some of the out field.

Tuesday 8th. I went after dinner to Polwarth house. My Lord came home on Saturday. He told me of the great debate they have in councill about Bradalbins liberation. the King sent to the Advocat ane order to be presented to the Councill for his Liberation but wt all caused Robert Pringle to Write to him to use it according to law and yt if it was not according to law to remit it to him. Upon this Bradalbin gave in a bill to the Councill craving the Ad. might be ordered to present the K's order. Ther was a great debate about it and proposed that the ad.[sic] Might be examined upon oath on what terms the order was committed to him. the Chancellour and his ptie alledged that could not be done because it was not fitt the Ad. should divulge everything wherein the K. sought his advice. the other pti for B. aledged that the order being come it was B's. by a jus quasity. it was long debated and much urged by the E. of Argile that it should be put to the Vote whether the Advocat should be examined or not. The Chancellour at last told them he could not be present wher such a thing should be voted whether the K. could call for his Ad:'s opinion wtout the Councills taking notice of it or ras [sic] not and removed

from the table and all his ptie wt him. the rest sat still a litle and then went away. likewise they were equal 12 to 12 so the Chancellours vote would have cast the Ballance. My Lo: told me that Meg Home had her petition in for Ninewelles papers at English Mauldy but it was not red. but my Lo: obtained of the Chancellour ane order to Midletone of Balbigny & Wm Strauchan to seal them wt their seals & send them over to the Cts of Councill
Dr Irvins lady came out wt my Lo: Polwarth & Jeriswood & his Lady. the 2 last are now att Mellistane.

Wednesday 9th. Ther being this day a meeting of the Commissioners I went to Dunse My Lo: Mersintone Edrom & Kettleshile were only ther all we did was to appoint a new dyet this day eight days and appoint Edrom to adjust some accts due to the toune of Dunse by the forces. The Councill has assigned the first of Novr for bringing in the Books to the Exequer and appointed the ministers to be poled as Gentlemen. I got a precept some days agoe from Da: Robisione upon Capt Cockburn of 600 lb wch when I sent it to him he accepted only for 400 lb saying things were not fully clear betwixt Da: and him. it was payable this day. I left it wt my Brother Capt Cockburn promising to pay it this day or to morrow. My Brother shewed me severall considerable Errors in the Book of Earlstone & says ther are the same in many others and one of 120 lb valued rent poled only to 13sh 4d wheras it ought to have been 1 lb 4 wch is just the Hundred pt.

Thursday 10th. I teinded in the afternoon the millars oats and from that went to Swintone the Lady Riddle was wt him and a sone of hers Wm & one Ridle of Newhouse. we went out & killd a hare I part wt them in the feilds.

Friday 11th. One of the Issues in my shoulder being very troublesome to me about 6 weeks agoe I let it out wtin this 14 night or 3 weeks I have been troubled wt a shortnesse of Breath wch sometimes follows on such cases. so I sent to Tho: Auchinleck who came here this morning and put in one wher it was. I went after dinner to Blackader and returned at night. the folks ther and here have ended their shearing this night. I see Sr John Have the new acts of Parlia.

Saturday 12th. I gave Robie some of the pouder for the Scab that Dr Abernethy prescrived him but it was too weak and wrought none but he was disordered wt it. I wrote to Dr Abernithy & ordered John Lidgate away wt it to morrow morning.

Sunday 13th. Roby purged a litle but I found him hot all the day I went to Church. When I returned I found Jo: Lidg. come home but he found not the Dr. he was at Sr Wm Elliots who is sadly tormented wt a gravell. he left the letter they saying he was to be back that night or to morrow

Monday 14th. Having some days agoe drawn out the Acct of what is due by the E. of Home to me whc amounts at Mart. next to 26,897 lb 10sh. I went to the Hirshill and gave me me [sic] a coppy of it as he desired me. When I came ther I found I had forgot it was &c.

When I came home I expected to have found Dr Abernethy but ther was no word of him. I am much troubled wt a shornesse of Breath and fits like hectick ones wch I have now been troubled wt this fourtnight. I have written to him this night again and ordered John Lidgate away to morrow.

Tuesday 15th. Mr Adam Waddell came here in the morning and Dr Abernethy just as we were going to dinner. he condescended to stay all night and went over to Nisbet to make a visite and I went out and teinded the bear in the Bank the Buttry buttes and the servants's oats and some stinting left in Harrage. mr Ad: went out wt me and in a litle went home. Dr Abernethy returnd at night and told me to purge Roby wt syrup of pale roses. for my selfe he thought I should purge wt some gentle purgative as tinctura sacra or syrupus Rham, Cath. and drink Cornhill water warme upon it. if I could vomit to doe it wt Oxymil Scylliticum. he prescrived me some Roots & herbs for ane infusion in ale to be taken morning and at 4 a clock wt 2 Spoonfulls of the Chalybeat Syrup. I offered him his fea but would by no means take it. he came this far out of his road to Newcastle. being to goe ther to the fair and see Mr Strauchan his brother in law and his sister. I desired him to buy me a pound of Sarsa if he could get it good.

Wednesday 16th. The Dr went airly away this morning. I went to Dunse to a meeting of the Commissioners. My Lo: Polwarth was long a coming. we did litle only ordered the books not brought in to be brought in & took in some accts of the soldiers due to the toune of Dunse and adjourned to this day eight days. I gave (we hear the K. is returned) in my book of Hiltone the total wherof is 52.-11s.-10d.

Thursday 17th. Yesternight I got a letter to Sr Ro: Stuarts Daughters buriall wt the Lady I went ther about 3 a clock. I ended the teinding this day. At Night Mr Guthry came here from the Synode at Kelso. he tells me they have declaired Mr Kirkwood not capable of being Clerk session and precentor but have not as yet touched whether he should be turned out from being School Master.

Friday 18th. In the morning Cavers and Hiltone called here. Cavers and his Lady having been at Huttonhall all night. he was going fox hunting in Lantone parks among the broom. I promised to follow them. Mr Guthry went home & I followed Cavers. ther were a number of people ther My Lo: Mersintone Swintone Caimly Purvishall &c. they had holld a fox befor I came and were working at the hole. Cavers went from that wt his dogs to Brunslaw. I staed wt Capt Cockburn to get my Grayhound entered so Swintone he Will Turnbull & several others went up toward Dunse commune and killed 2 hares. we came to Sandy Lorans in Duns and got some meat and so home.

Saturday 19th. Yesterday I got a letter from Wedderburn Inviting me to dine wt him and his sone. & his Lady & Sr Pa. Home. The[y] came to the Country on Wednesdays night Sr John Home Cavers & Edrom were ther &c. My Lo: Polwarth was likewise invited but he had a tryst wt Swintone & Mersintone upon deciding a difference betwixt him & Kettleshile in Greenlaw Common. I returned home about 5 a clock.
   Note Counting what the principill summe of the anrent of 5,000 Ms is I find it to be 83,333 Ms 7sh. 6d.
   Heughead was at Wedderburn this day. he tells me Whytefeild is not to Edr as yet
   I remember that some time agoe Whytefeild would fain have had me Engaging In the purchasse of Aitone. the rent is ordinarily comput 5,000 Ms the principill soume of wch is 83,333 Ms: 7s. 6d. I have upon it about 40,000 Ms ther rests 43,333. 7s 6d beside I have a current annuity of 1,800 Ms. but if upon transaction wt the Earl I should give doun and reduce my selfe to 1,000 Ms. yearly this being valued as ordinarly to 7 years purchasse.This makes 7,000 Ms and reduces the summe resting to 36,333.7s.6d. Then considering they will probably be entaild on Land a yearly cesse of six or eight months cesse and the Cesse of Aitone being 370 lb- 6sh monthly I comes in 8 months to 444 Ms 4sh yearly and the reparations of Houses being 200 Ms yearly this will amount to 644 Ms wch is the anrent of about 10,730. ther will remain to be payd in 25,603 Ms 7s-6d but tis not probable that the E. will take in so small a summe nether is it the Custome in buying land to count Cesse & reparations and I am not in a condition to purchasse except these were allowed one in defalcation all the hope would be in moneys coming to 5 in the 100 but that is not sure.

Sunday 20th. I went to Church.

Monday 21st. I went to Polwarthouse Jeriswood and his Lady were ther I hear the King as soon as he came home called a Councill and dissolved the then p[rese]nt parlia and has called one agst the 22nd of Novr next. ther is great work betwixt the Dissenters & the Church of England for the election I heard no other news.

Tuesday 22nd. I went to Harcasse in the afternoon. When I returned I wrote

a letter to Whytefield telling him I had given the E. of Home a note of what is
due me agst Mart. next. that I wisht he would come to this Country befor he
went to Edr to desire to know if my Lord Could advance me any money at the
terme. Complaining that Mr Al: Home had not sent me the diligence agst the
E. of Home and desiring him to write to him by the post; And desiring to know
if ther were any arrestments laid on the rents of the Estate of Aitone and to
keep us frie of Saughten & Beilmouth.

I found a letter from Cavers desiring ane answer of his former letter to me in
June whc I had promised long agoe.

Wednesday 23rd. John Fish of Castlelaw came here this morning & told me
of a debate he had wt one Watsone who pretended to his sate in the Church as
having right to it from James Home of Castlelaws sone. Tho the Heritor of
Castlelaw had allwise been in possession yrof this Wattsonne having pretence
to it as having acquired two acres of Ground formerly belonging to the Estate
of Castlelaw. He desyred I might take my Lo: Polwarths opinion in it.

We did nothing in our meeting of Commissioners My Lo: Polwarth Came
late.

Mr Al: Home was at Dunse. he gave me my summonds upon my gift of
Escheat agst the E. of Home wch I gave presently to Pa: Cockburn to be
Execute. I am very sollicitous about the 4,000 Ms I ought to pay to Friershaw.
Sandy not knowing wher the money is to be had,

I got a return from Whytefield. he writes My L. Home has writt to him that he
has gott my claime as he calls it that he will goe ther on friday but cannot call
here. that on Munday or twesday I shall be sent for that all possible means
shall be used to keep me free of Saughten and Mr Ro. Lawder

Thursday 24th. Yesternight I took halfe a dram of pil. stom of gumiess being
much troubled this month wt a shortnes of breath. It purged me 3 times this
day. Mr Ad: Waddell came here in the morning from Wedderburn. In the
afternoon Mr And Home & Jeriswood came here. I sitt wt them in the Dining
room about 2 hours I think I have got cold by it. Mr Ad: Went home & they
went to Huttonhall.

Friday 25th. Will: Brack came here from Betshile and he told these that were
to goe to the Coals from that would come here on tuesday morning and goe wt
Da: Robisons horse.

I sent John Lidgate to Kelso wt a letter to Dr Abernethy telling him I was still
troubled wt a shortnes of breath. he brought me a note from him telling he
would be here on Munday next. He sent me a pound of Sarsa wch he had
brought from Newcastle. I caused John Buy me some bread ther &c. About
sunset Coldenknows Mr Al: Home & St Ebbs came here. the 2 last went to the
Hirshill. the first staid a while after them & went to Nisbet. I talked wt

Coldenknows & he tells me the E. of Annandale is obliged by act of parlia to pay me the debts of the Hornings upon wch he has taken the Gift of the E. of Homes Escheat. having taken it on my hornings.

Mem. I wrote yesternight to. Cavers that I designed to pay his anrents agst Mart. that for the prple Jos Home and I should Corroborate it assoon as he were served air to his father & that if he did not think that sufficient I desired Candlemes to provide the money. I wrote likewise to Whytefeild that hearing he was at Wedderburn I desired to speake wt him befor he went to the Hirshill. Cavers was gone to the Hunting Whytefeild sd he would satisfy my desire

Saturday 26th. Young Wedderburn Whytefeild & Sr Pa: Homes sone came hither in the morning. Wedderburn and his Bro: in lau went back. Whytefeild stayd and dined wt me. He showed me a rentall of the Estate of Aitone whc comes in money to 970 lb 16: The Oats 174 b. wch at 4 lb the boll comes to 696 lb. the bear meal & malt 364 bolls wch at 5 lb the boll is 1,820-00-00 totall 3,486 lb 16s. in Marks 5,230 as we called it to make even money (tho ther be 2sh 8d over). this 18 years purchasse as Whytfeild says Sr Pa: Home offers is 94,140 Ms and at 20 years purchasse as the E. demands is 104,600 Ms

Sunday 27th. Being indisposed I went not to Church. my Brother came here at night having told my man to desire him.

Monday 28th. I have been these days past still troubled wt this shortnes of Breath. In the Afternoon Dr Abernethy came as he promised and I got from him some directions for my health. part. to make use of pil Bals. prescribed by Mortone & to vomit wt oxymil of Squills & ag. lin. called Mixt. Riv. and a dyet drink. He has bought a good like Bay mare at Newcastle. he tells me the King is come to Notinghame and is to hunt in Shirwood Forest. The Dr Borrowed Solyset from me. At night a dozen of horse came from Betshile to goe to the Coals. I gave them 4sh to bring home the Coals 2pts small a 3d great and the men being six a six pense to drink

Tuesday 29th. The Dr went away this morning I gave him 6 R.D. this day is very pleasant. As we were at dinner the Lady Hiltone came & hir Daughter Shusie & Robert & John & Elshy Trotters Daughter Jane. she staid a litle and went to Nisbet. going to Polwarthhouse & from thence to Langhame wher now her daughtr & Mangertone live. I desired Thuanus of her & she spoke to Tho: Thomsone who has the kee of the closet to give me any I calld for on my note.

The Bedshile [sic] folks brought home the Coals but they would not take a halfe croun I sent.

Da: Robisons folks brought home 20 Loads of Coals Sr John Home came here after the Close of the night and stayd a very litle. he had been at Polwarthhouse. he tells me Joseph Home is gone to Edr this morning.

October 1695

Mem: I got a letter from Cavers last day wherin he says he is content of Ninewells & his Curator and my security for the 3,000 Ms but Im Jealous he has mistaken my meaning for I suppose he expects the curators are to bind for the debt wheras they are only to bind Curatorio nomine.

Wednesday 30th. I was at home all alone.

Thursday 31st. I went and dined at Blackader and went out wt Sr John to see him stake out some ground on the West side of his hous wher he designs ane entry beside the south one. My sister and Mrs Helen were gone to Whitsome.

Friday November 1st. I have been waiting all this week for a call from the E. of Home in order to settle things twixt him and me instead of whc Whytefeild and St Abbes came here this morning. Whytefeild told me he had full commission from the E. to settle wt me but going to Edr on Munday we should meet ther and terminat the bussines. they stayd and dined wt me and went home after dinner. I went and visited Mr Adam Waddell. I got a loan from him of Caves hist. of the fathers that Immediatly succeeded the Apostles. The title is Apostolici.

Saturday 2nd. I got yesterday a line from Mr Al: Cockburn telling me My Lo: Polwarth Expected I should meet him at Dunse this day I went. it was about the additionall excise James Broun having quartered on the Brewars for more than they say they Brewed he oppons the Survey Books whc were not his properly. but he got them from one Emmletone who has the Annexed Excise. we thought we could not get over the survey books and yet found severalls were ready to depon they had not brewed so much. & they sd Ch. Emmeltone being sundry times convinced of the Errors in the Survey books did not Exact the whole, & alledged ther was one of the Surveyers in toune who would acknowledge they had been in a mistake sometimes, this was admitted to the defenders to adduce the Gadgers to prove this. But we observed at last that severall of the survey rolls were vitiat and upon casting up the summe found it greater than the totall written ad longum at the foot by the Surveyers and so thought no faith was to be given them. But it being late we adjourned to Thursday next. James Home Sr John's Brother came ther just as we rose & went home wt his brother.

Sunday 3rd. Ther being no sermon at Edrom and the day threatening rain I went not out.

Monday 4th. Pat: Cockburn brought me the Summonds agst the E. of Home upon his Escheat and the Executions therof agst him & the tenants of Aitone

November 1695

Cap: Home Came here this afternoon My Lo: Polwarth was at Blackader all night and went to give his Vote in the Election of the Parlia Burgesse at Berwick. Sr John Home went wt him.

Tuesday 5th. My Lord Polwarth Came here wt Nelly Home and my sister Tibby from Blackader. My Lo: tells me that Mr Gray Lo: Grays brother & Mr Ogle Mr Luke Ogles sone are chosen. whom he voted for. I find they dont think Sr Francis Blake so good a Country man they stayed a very litle and my sister borrowed a dollar from me. she says she will be at Dunse to morow. Ther has been a very pleasant weather all the month of Octr wch still continues

Wednesday 6th. yesternight I took 2 scruples of pil st oz gummes wch wrought a litle too gently only 3ie. Mr Ad: Waddell came here and went to Harcasse finding me under physick. I sent my 2 cows this day to Dunse fair. both were sold. the litle one but the fattest at 19 lb 15sh . the biggest my brother has got and conditiond. 20 lb for her.

Thursday 7th. I sent my Excuse to the Commissioners and the Survey rolls I got to review.
    I got 55 lb Scots from Al: Jaffrey of his rent Mart next ensuing. He tells me the Millars wrong them about the Moulter wch I must enquire into.

Friday 8th. I was alone all day looking over some papers

Saturday 9th. I went to Blackader & dined Sr John told me he had gott a letter from Meg Home telling she would give over medling in bussines concerning her Brothers children for want of money. Geo: Home the factor for that Estate came ther and told us ther was no money to be had at present from the tenants and that ther was as much due him as in the tenants hands. assoon as I came home I got a letter from Meg by Purvishalls man wherin she writes much to the same purpose she says the late Ladies mother designes to take home the Children to her. and presses to know what money may be expected.
    I got also a note from Cavers for Mr Wyses Adresse for getting trees whc I sent him.
    Mem: yesterday I sent the Gardner to Kelso to Dr Abernethy wt a letter telling him I found the shortnes of breath abated but that I had somewhat more inclination to cough and was hot and sweate when I goe to bed. he sent me a bottle of the Syrup of shel and wrote he would be here mund. or twesday.

Sunday 10th. I went not abroad the day being rough & I indisposed

Monday 11th. I went no wher.

97

November 1695

Tuesday 12th. In the afternoon came Dr Abernethy who had been at Blackader all last night. He stayd wt me allnight. at night came Mr Ninian Home. he Brought me my bond to the Kirk session of Fogo and I receaved from him as the Kirk sessions money mortifyed for the use of a School master 135 lb. and granted bond for 215 lb having retired my former bond. Mem. I payd him the anrent of the 80 lb from Whit to Mart. last.

Wednesday 13th. Dr Abernethy went away in the morning. Mr Ad: Waddell came here he tells me 80 of the sticklers agst the kings interest in the house of Commons are turned out.

Mem: Yesterdnight Dr Abernethy telling me Sr Jo: Home was going for Edr this morning I wrote wt him to Mr Al: Home & sent him the Summonds of Escheat agst the E. of Home and Hays horning agst him & for the other two. I desired him to get one of them from Tho: Pringle the other I want the Execution of it wch Tho: Pringle lost when he got out a Caption on it. So I desired him to take them both out off the Register in Case Tho: could not find his. I wrote likewise to try if Ether it was possible to delay or Get money for Friershaw.

Thursday 14th. In the afternoon I went to Whitsome wt Mr Adam Waddell his mother being not well but finding her up Mr Adam came back wt me

Friday 15th. I cleard wt Kath. Neilsone her fea 8 lb her shoes 1 lb 8s formerly payd. I gave her 7 lb 16s. 8d. and retaind 9sh. 4d as her pole.

I went to Kelso after dinner. I went to Dr Abernethies whom I found in toune I sent my horses to Widow Dicksones I sent for Mr Trotter who being wt old Lintone I desired they might meet me at Widow Dicksons wher Dr Abernethy & I went. we staid a litle wt them. Lintone told us his sone James had written home yt he thought his Collonel would be Broke being one of those who signed the Capitulation at Dixmude. tho we heard he had refused it. we sat a litle & I went and supped wt D. Ab & then returned to My chamber.

Saturday 16th. I sent for James Bichet and desired him to send for the money I owe him on tuesday next. I went to Dr Abernethies. from that wt him & Mr Trotter to[o] & see Cavers's son's whom we found playing in the Church yard. from that to Mr Kirkwoods who is full of his plea wt the Minister from that I visited Elshy Trotters wife & from that went to Tho: Ingliss & got some things at yt Drs order. Mr Trotter & I dind wt the Dr. I gave Mr Trotter Mrs Scot letters of Horning agst my sist Isb. wt her discharge & my bond and desired him that discharge be drawn to me by Pat Adamsons Childrens curators. about 2 a clock I took horse & came home from Kelso to Ednam I rode in 23 minuts. from that to Ecles in 33. from that to Mersintone in 24. from that to Tho: Michels in 29. from that home in about as much. The Weather is

98

November 1695

very warm for the season of the year

Sunday 17th. Yesternight ther arose a high wind s.w. It continues this day. I went to church. Coming home Cavers told me yt pres. Stair was ill of a strangury and twas thought would never come abroad again. that twas thought the Advocat would succeed him and Sr James Ogilby him. The My Lo: Presmennen was dead and talkt that Commissary Scougall would succeed him. That the Register Tarbet was ill of a rupture.

Monday 18th. This day is clear but frosty some wind w.n.w. I payd James Denholme Wm Trotters sone in law and factor (Wm being in Tinmouth) 16 lb. 13sh. 4d. as halfe a years anrent of 1,000 Ms due at Mart. last retention allowed his discharge being written befor he came here is for 20 lb but I have marked he has receaved no more then as above.

Tuesday 19th. James Bichet & Al: Taite came here and I payd them the bond of 172 lb wt anrent since Whit. I got up my bond and agreement betwixt my father & And Haitly. And a back bond of And Haitlys to Wm Taite & Elizabeth Shoniswood his wife. They tell me ther is also a backbond be And: Haitly to Mar: Shoniswood tho And: Assigns Margs summe to Geo: Home his nephew & sone to Peter Home of Harcasse Or rather I suppose that And having intrusted Geo: wt these papers Geo: filled up his oun name in Margs. right wch I acct as as much lost money. These that should have got it having got nothing.

Wednesday 20th. I went to Dunse ther being a meeting of the Commissioners. I got a letter from Capt Home that had come out wt his Brother Sr Johns Horses. twas from Mr Al: Home. he writes that Tho: Pringle denies his having the horning I wrote to him of and that he must take them all of the Register. As also that the Adjudication Tho: Iles wants the Execution whc cannot be or he has lost it. I must strive to get the date of it and get another. That Friarshaw must have his money at this terme that he thinks he may get 2,000 Ms of it if I can possibly get the other 2. I spoke to my brother to see if he could get any to borrow. We had a meeting of the Commissioners we caused order that all they lyable in pole should pay it at the respective Collectors houses. I see a proclamation about the old pole that all they lyable to pay it should produce their discharges to the subcollectors appointed by Sr Robert Dicksone of Sornbeg who has now taken it and that they who had not payd should pay in to the sds subcollectors martimes now past or 30 days after under the double & after that under the Quadruple. Cap: Home tells me that a Councill of War has been held upon Allemberg and the rest of the Officers who surrendered Dixmud & Danse. that Allemburg is sentenced to be beheaded. Offerill to perptuall imprisonment and the rest off the Colonells broke. Cap: Home came home wt me and Elshy Trotter for whom I had sent the Gray nag yesterday wt Al: Tait to Kelso

Thursday 21st. Cap: Cockburn came from Dunse wt his 2 Greyhounds. we went out and Killd one hare the 2d we lost the dogs but by blood on the dogs we supposed she was killd we came in and dined here. after dinner Capts Home & Cockburn went to Wedderburn. I receaved from Al: Jaffrey 40 lb Scots.

Friday 22nd. I was at home all day it being some rain. Mr Trotter was wt me.

Saturday 23rd. Mr Trotter went to Nisbet & dined Thomas Rutherford came to me in the afternoon he told me that his sone had a ewe that for 3 years had 3 lambs yearly. he says that about Tofts and Lambden burn it is ordinary that when he was tenant ther he had but 40 ews one year & that 11 of them had 2 lambs a peice. that the cows will have sometimes 2 calves & mares 2 foals. that of the ews is ordinarie in [blank] in Flanders wher they will not keep a ewe that has not 4 lambs. Mr Trotter came back at night. Da: Robisone was going to Berwick this morning and his stond horse died by the way they alleage his bull has wounded him.

Sunday 24th. I went to Church & Mr Trotter wt me the day eight days & I believe a day or 2 befor ther is but on sermon

Monday 25th. I went to Betshile and counted wt the tenants and receaved some money according to acct I came to Polwarthouse at night. Mr Trotter was wt me. It raind on us all the way from Betshile to Polwarthouse.

Tuesday 26th. I stayd dinner at Polwarthouse my Lord shewed me ane extract of Sclatehouses accts of Bells Estate wherin he makes Bell his debtor in 1,800 lb. stating 50 Ms for his factor fea during the time Ninewells was in the Country and 100 Ms since wt a great dale of incident charges. After dinner Capt Home & Capt Cockburn & my brother came ther. I came away met Cavers coming from the hunting & came by Nisbet mil wher Mr Trotter had gone in the morning to meet Broomhouse but could not perswade him to come away. I gave my Lo: Polwarth ane acct of what is treating betwixt the E. of Home & me. he seems to incline much that I should take Aitone and sell Betshile.

Wednesday 27th. I went to Dunse to a meeting of the Commissioners But ther being a commission from the Councill to try Crawford again we did not meet only adjourned till this day eight days. In the Commission were My L. P[olwarth]. the Sheriff deput who is James Home of the Flas. Blackader

Swintone & Sr Rot. Stuart or any 3 of them My L. the deput and Sr Ro: St
were ther. the panall adhered to his former confession and the wittneses to ther
former depositions. he was sentenced to die this day eight days. I spoke to
James Home of Flas of some money I heard the Lady Greenknow had and
offered my Brother Cautioner or if that did not satisfy my L.P. also he being
allready bound in the bond due to Friarshaw. I returned at night and Mr Trotter
wt me. I caused John Hanna get some stuff from my Brother for a frock to
Robbie.

Frank Home Wedderburns sone being to goe to Edr tomorrow I wrote to Mr
Al: Home to secure the 2,000 Ms he wrote to me of. To get from Whytefield
the rentall of Aitone to see if on the Adjudication ther is any mark of the day
that a new execution may be got for I spoke to Pa: Cockburn and he is so
carelesse as not to keep a book for the dates of his Executions.

Thursday 28th. I went wt Mr Trotter & dined at Nisbet. I spoke to Cavers
and told him that my rents not coming in as I expected I could not pay his
interest so punctually as I designed but that about Christmas he should be paid
he sd I might take my oun time. I designe to cause Da: Robisone pay him he
telling me he will have about 60 lb st agst that time. I returned at night.

Friday 29th. I wrote to Dr Abernethy and sent Jo: Lidgate to Kelso. Mr
Trotter went airly away this morning having borrowed a beast from Overhall.
Ro: Robinsone engaged me a cow from Da: Forsyth in Swintone at 31 lb 5sh.
she is dear but they say is a good one & new Calved and he promises she will
give 3 pints of milk at a male [sic]. Robin tells me also I may get the bear I
have in the loft sold wch is about 6 bolls so I have ordered him to Give his
brother a sample of it who is going to Berwick tomorrow. At night the Cow
was brought & I paed the money. Jo: Lidgate Brought me a letter from Dr Ab:
and some things I had ordered him.

Saturday 30th. I receaved from James Jaffrey 27 lb Scots in pt of his
Lammas rent. A stack of Bear of 15sh was cast in wch speaks to six bolls. I
was no wher yesterday nor this day the weather continues still warme for the
season fresh weather & cloudy

Sunday December 1st. At Church I heard the Vicount Stair dyed on munday
of a strangury or as some say ane Ulcer in his bladder. he was 77 years old.
That same morning was Fountain the dauncing Master found dead in his bed,
And about that time what day I know not Mr Wm Lauder My Lo. Pittmeddens
father died taking his pype after dinner. Dr Abernethy was at Church having
been at Nisbet all night. he goes for Edr next morning. when I came home I got
a return from Mr Al: Home of the letter I wrote to him wt Frank Home he tells
me Friershaw is content to take 2,000 Ms any time this week or the beginning

of the next and suspend the rest till Candlemis. he says no more being in hast. I wrote to him wt Dr Abernethy telling hehoved [sic] to try to get the money at Edr for I could not possibly get it in the Country (he having desired me to bring in what money I can) and that I designed God willing to be in toune friday next or tuesday come eight days.

Monday 2nd. I spoke to Rot. Robisone about my bear he tells me his brother was offer 11sh 6d st for it but being English money he would not take it and Scotch is ill to be had ther. I went to Blackader and dined I played 2 games at Chesse wt Cap: Home the first we ended equal I having the K. & a bishop wt whc I could not give mate the second I win

Tuesday 3rd. I went to the Hirshill & dined wt the E. of Home I spoke to him for a rentall of the Estate of Aitone for lybelling agst the tenants wch he says Whytefield hes and Mr Al: Home may get from him. I desired to Borrow from him Taylers Ductor dubitantium. he called for it from Mr Geo: Waddell who sd it was At Whitsome. Mr Geo: Being lately come from Edr told me the Cobs were ordered to passe by weight and that ther was some regulation about the Clipt 14sh peices but did not tell me what. Mr Geo: says he heard that in Fyfe ther has been young pyets & young larks this season and severall birds laying. I spoke to my Lord anent Blackburns insisting agst me for the anrents of the bond granted to Martine but got litle satisfaction as to the paymt only my Lo: would fain have it allowed out of the teinds of Ryslaw. I returned home after dinner having supt litle I felt so hungry & faint a bed that I was forced to call for something.

Wednesday 4th. I continue still faint all this day. Yet went to Dunse to a meeting of the Commmissioners but all was done was to adjourn to that Day eight days. the poor fellow John Crawford who was condemned this day eight days was execute this day. James Home of Flas Sheriff deput told me I might get 2,000 Ms from the Lady Greenknow upon Polwarths bond and mine. I caused draw the bond by Al: Andersone and my Lo: and I signed it & I granted my Lo; a bond of releif. I gave my Brother the bond who is to goe about it on saturday I receaved from my Brother 5 lb & I think 12 shillings. st of the 5 lb 18sh & 2d st. Capt Cockburn oued me. At night Robie playing himselfe in the Kitchin fell off a chest upon the Ground & cut himselfe very ill just above his right eyebrow. I writt a note to Mr Auchenleck to goe to him tomorrow to come & look to it for fear ther be a mark. I sent this morning to Mr Ad: Waddell for Taylers Ductor dubtantium and got it. I receaved a letter from my sister Isabell desiring me to send horses for her tomorrow

Thursday 5th. Mr Auchinleck came and dressed Robies brow. I sent for my sisters. This day is boistrous the Wind n.e. when they came they told me Sr Jo:

Home was come home to return to Edr agst munday

Friday 6th. This is the first winter day we have had this season the Wind blows hard from n.e. and it has snowd and haild this day. Tho: Rutherford was at me telling Ad: Turnbull would take Greenknow and Kingslaw so that I may get more for it than it pays. Robies brow was drest this day and Mattered much. I got a letter fro my Lo: Pol. about my Brother anent some sodgers quarting on him &c.

Saturday 7th. This day is boystrous from the same airths. Cat: Heburn came from Wedderburn here in the morning and told the E. of Home was ther and was coming here in the after noon. he came then and stayd a litle we spoke litle of bussines only he desired me to meet wt Whytefeild at Edr and be Frank for now all he had to doe wt were upon him. At night my brother came and brought me the 2,000 Ms from the Lady Greenknow.

Sunday 8th. Sr Jo: Home came here in the morning and I went to Fogo Church wt him he and his brother went to Stichel going to Edr next day.

Monday 9th. Will. Brack Pat: Knox & James Redpeth came here from whom I got some money according to their acct My Brother went to Dunse this morning. Dr Abernethy came here being returned from Edr he told me of the great debate is in the Colledge of Physitians about a preses they [sic]. Drs devided and Chose every side one. It is Jacobite and Williamite. The animosities were so great that Dr Abernethy would not vote tho he was sent for Expresse by Stevensone to be on his syde. Nota I forgot to insert in Frid that I wrote to the Mr of Polwarth & enclosed one to Sandy Home desiring him to get me 50 pears from Wyse 30 apples I think 12 plums 4 Apricoks 4 peaches. It to buy me a bushell of Accorns a quarter of a pound of lime tree seed 2 ounces of pitch tree seed and ane ounce of asparagus and if he could conveniently to get me my dyall from Whitehead.

Tuesday 10th. I gave my sisters 16 lb Scots a peice & Mar: for the house about 7 lb & John Murdo as per acct. 12 lb. I gave my sister Isabell a precept of 50 lb Scots on Ja: Jaffrey she had receaved as she says from David Robin 5 lb 14sh from my selfe befor 2 lb 18 now 16 lb and this precept. I likewise Gave my sister Julian a precept on Geo: Broun In Betshile for fourty eight punds Scots. and gave her 1 lb 4sh of copper money over the 16 lb she got befor. I took my horses about 8 a clock I brought Da: Robisone wt me to Betshile to view the houses that timber may be gotten and wt a wright in Greenlaw one James Nisbet. I got 6 lb 12sh from Ja: Jamisone. I came from that and dined at Ginglekirk and from that I came to toune about 7 a clock. I lodge in Mrs Heburns. I went and visited my Lo: Crosrig wher Mr Tho: Skeen gave us ane acct of a Councill of the Scotch Councellours held befor the King anent bussines that passed in this parlia wher the Secretary Stair is accusing Johnstone of severall things. &c. We hear the parla of England is mightily incensed agst the act in the Scotch parlia for the E. India trade. the E. of Rochester made a harangue of the Losse Eng. would suffer by it and having our act in his hand tore it the D. of Leeds sd that Scotland was a wiser people than Eng. and if this continued would be a richer. Johnstone is much challanged for thes acts passing here. I went afterwards to Sr Jo: Homes chamber and visited him Sandy Home whom I had sent to I found in my chamber he says a thousand lb he expects to morrow for paying Friarshaw. Meg Home came afterwards and we talkt much about Ninewells's bussines. I ordered my horses home next morning and causd buy a pair of shoes to Robie.

Wednesday 11th. Mr John Craig told me ther was a protestation up agst me at Blackburns instance Sr John Home came and told me his bussines had been debate wt John Doul and that he is to inform agst tuesday next. Drs St Clair & Dundas came here Meg Home & her Brother Cap: Car. The 2 Drs particularly St Clair are much incensed agst Abernethy who by his coming to toun hes disobliged many of his freinds and the other ptie is also angry because they Counted on him & he was non liquet. I dined in my Lo: Crosrigs after I went to my aunt Ninewells's and from thence to my Chamber. Sandy Home came to me (he fell doun 7 steps as he came here and has hurt himself) & told me he expected to a 1,000 lb upon my bond to morrow. I gave the Coat I brought from London wt me to Mr Somervail to have a searge lining put in it the other being too thick.

Thursday 12th. I went not out not having got my cloaths and And Watheret not being come wt my trunk. Whytefeild came and sat besyde me we trysted to meet tomorrow at 4 a clock about my bussines wt the E. of Home. The Countesse Douger had this day a plea agst him he is obliged to pay her yearly 3,000 Ms free of all burden & in case 1 term run in two she is to return to her former right of infeftmt from her husband of 5,000 Ms wch the E. obliges himself to pay in case of the irritancy incurd it seems he did not pay punctually and she pursues him for the Irritancy. the Lo: have given her 500 Ms of Expenses and discerned the E. to pay her betwixt end January what is due under the pain of Incurring the Irritancy and if he fail 30 days after each terme he incurs the Irritancy. my Lady thought to have Got him subjected to the Irritancy at this time & in all time coming considering her husband had no power to grant such right. she ought not to complain for if this E. had challanged it at first and not confirmed her right she would have been in ane ill taking but he did it upon Chancellour Perths & Sr Geo. Lockharts threats . Whytefeild likewise tells me My Lo: Polwarth is content of a submission to two or mo[r]e of the Los: of Session in differences betwixt him and the E. of

Home. Mr Al: Home promises to get me 1,000 lb tomorrow on my bond.

Friday 13th. And Watheret Brought me in the trunk clock bag I writt wt him to Da: Robisone to get me 2,000 Ms & to pay Cavers 1,197 Ms and in case he could not make up the first betwixt Christmasse & Candlemis to borrow it and to take my brothers help. I wrote to my brother to cause collect the pole of Hiltone and to secure the 100 lb st he told me Cap. Cockburn would have at Christmas. To Call for Al: Jaffrey and raise his rent to 560 Ms and Ja:s to 740 as formerly or at lest to 726 Ms.8.10 as it paid [before his father Entered - deleted] when Da: Robisone and his mother had it. but not to conclude anything wt a new tenant In case they should refuse till I were advertised. for Hector Turnbull has been speaking both to Da: Robisone & my brother about Als: roome tho they have told me nothing of it but others have. Mr Al: Home promises again the 1,000 lb on my bond. Whytefield and I met at night about my bussines wt the E. of Home but he made so mean offers that we did nothing. I told him that the bygons were 40,000 Ms (besides what was given out upon Cautionry for my Lo: and his mother whc we did not speak of other persons being concerned) that of this I could not abate any thing but that I would commune upon what I should quitt of my annuity in time coming. All his profer was 20,000 Ms in consideration of bygons & 900 Ms of annuity in time to come. Earnslaw & Mr Al: Home was wt us We trysted again agst Munday at 2 a clock at Mr Al: Homes Chamber. Earnslaw was telling us Dalmeny was going to London having gaind a plea ther and thinking to transact Mortgages on his Ladies Estate for 2,000 lb st & therby to make of it ane Estate of 1,500 lb st a year that he himselfe had some thoughts of going wt him upon a particular whc he told us not.

Saturday 14th. I dind in McKenzeis wt Sr John Home and Mr Walter Pringle. Mr Al: Home says these people to whom Friershaws money is to be payd are not at leasure this day. I came to my chamber a litle after dinner since I came to toun it has been allwise frost yesterday it snoud some and this day is very cold. Dr Dundas came and sate beside me a litle & Jos: Home. I lookt over some papers after they went away.

Sunday 15th. I went to Church in the afternon at night Sr Jo: Home came and supt wt me.

Monday 16th. I went and visited my Lo: & Lady Polwarth. I sent Mr Jo: Craig my suspension agst Broun of Blackburn. I met in the afternoon wt Whytefield about my bussines wt the E. of Home. we could come to no conclusion or rather broke up he offered me only 23,000 Ms for bygons and 900 Ms of annuity or 30,000 Ms in the whole but this last only wt provision he could sell the Estate. I came at night and sat wt Meg Home Sr John Home &

Parvishall came ther.

Tuesday 17th. Yesternight as I went to bed I took a colique whc troubled me all the night. in the morning I purged and after yt got some ease but I was surprised to find that wherever I itched (for I itched much) & had cratched that when I lookt on my thighs & arms I found them all as if I had been burnt wt nettles I think I remember to have been so once befor. I went no wher out only I went up stairs to my aunts & staid litle and playd 2 games at Chesse wt her sone C. Car we parted equall.

Wednesday 18th. I went not out in the morning. in the after noon I went to the street and Mr Al: Home Chamber. Mrs Mar: Home bought me 2 Stone of Irish butter whc I sent out wt the Whitsome carier. I payd Mr Sturten the Dalmahoys anrent to Mart.

Thursday 19th. I dined in my Lo: Crosrigs. I payd to Mr John: Wilby factor to Friershaw and John Craik of Stuartone to whom Friershaw has assigned my bond In pt of the price of Stuartone whc he has bought from Friershaw 333 lb 6.8 of priple and Mr Al: Home has payd him. 1,000 Ms in all 2,000 Ms Mr Al: Has borrowed this from Mr Rot Innes to whom Mr Al: & I are to give bond and Mr Al: is to give me a bond of releive of the same and it is to be in pt of paymt of what he oues me. Yesternight Young Wedderburn visited me. he says he is going to Extract a decreet of Reduction & improbation agst his vassalls Blackader being beside & holding Dykethead of him promised to look to it and see that none of our friends particulary Ninewells should be lezed by it

Friday 20th. Hearing the Mr of Polwarth was come yesternight to toune I went I visited him this morning he Came in coach wt Sr Richard Newtone and severall others to Durham but the snow was so deep ther the coach could come no further. we have seen litle snow here but they say ther has been much in the Merse it was from the South E. Sr Tho: Liviston was in another Coach in company wt them he came this day.

Saturday 21st. Mr John Craig brought me my processe agst the Marquis of Douglas whc has been called and I find the Clerks of the Marquis's Decreit are ordaind to produce the Executions; and my Summonds of Declarator of Escheat against the E. of Home. Nota yesterday I went wt Swintone to the bank office to see the books that bussinesse looks very well and as if it would be profitable. I dined wtin this day after dinner I went to my Lord Crosrigs from that my Lo: Going to a subcommitty of ye Generall assembly (wch sat down on twesday my Lo: Carmichell is Commisssionary) I went and visited the Lady Jeriswood from thence I came to my aunt Ninewells's and from that to my Chamber. Capt Home Came & after him Cap Ker. we plaid at Chesse I

win one game of H. and K. win one of me and they 2 plaid 2 games & parted
equall. These 2 days it has been pleasant enough winter weather it is windy
this day s:w.

Sunday 22nd. I went to Church Morning and afternoon to the Tolboth
Church

Monday 23rd. I payd Gil: Somervail 60 lb Scots of what I oue him.
Yesterday and this day has been & is boistrously windy from S.W. I dined in
my Lo: Polwarths after dinner the Master of Polwarth & I went & found Huegh
Broun Clerk to the Committee of Parlia for the arriers he told us we might give
in our Claims time enough yet. I sat wt the Mr of Polwarth sometime in his
chamber and from that Came home.

Tuesday 24th. I gave Mr Al: Home my summonds of Adj. agst the E. of
Home yesternight to raise me a Charge to entir air in Speciall agst the E. for
adjudging the Estate of Home. he says he is upon it this day. I dined in my
Chamber wt Sr Jo: Home & Mr Trotter. I went after dinner to the bank and
ther meeting wt Swintone he & I came to the Coffee house and from that I
went to the Councill. the E. of Braealdban has got a remission but it is not as
yet past the seals but he being set at liberty came to councill wher the
Chancellour refused to suffer him to sitt. his remission repons him to all his
places but the remission not having past the seals & he pressing to sitt & the
Chancellour refusing ther was nothing done & the Councill adjourned. I visited
Whytefeld & got a rentall of Aiton fro him but it is not full.

Wednesday 25th. I got a letter from Dr Abernethy dated 13th ins. but the
carrier told me they came not away last week because of the illnesse of the
weather & travelling he sent me also a triple dose of Bals. pills. I wrote to him
about his brethren & told him I had sent out the Acts of the Generall assembly
wt my horses to be left for him at Nisbet. I got likewise a letter from Da:
Robisone wt ane acct of What he had receaved from my tenants since August
1694 wt all alledging he does not think at Clearing he will be ouing so much as
I say after Cavers is payd & desires a precept on himselfe may be sent to him.
I wrote to him & told him he would find himselfe grossly mistaken and that the
more I should canvasse his accts the more he would be found in my debt. I
wrote to Cavers and sent him a precept on Da: Robisone of 798 lb Scots due at
Mart. last. the Mr of Polwarth Sr Richard Newtone Mr Al: Home & Geo
Kirtone came to my chamber. after they went away I got my selfe drest & went
& dined wt My Lo: Polwarth. my Lady has been ill of Rhumatik pains. Ther is
Great noise here in toune about ane adresse of the house of Commons to the
King agst our African & India act wherby they alledge that our Commodities
being free of Custome for 21 years we will be able to undersell the English &

so ruine their trade & desires the K. may provide some remedie to it. his answer was that he had been ill served in Scotland but that he hoped ways might be found to prevent any inconveniences. or something to yt purpose. The Advocat went this day for London

Thursday 26th. The E. of Bradalbane came and took his place at the table The Justice Clerk opposed it much but they suffered him to take it upon his perill. they say that had he been sentenced for treason & got a remission he ought to have been reopened by ane expresse order from the K. but being only accused it was not necessary. Others alleage that he being committed by the K. (for the parlia did it wt the Commissioners consent) he doing this removed hin from all the charges he had under him they being only durante bene placito and his pleasure being by this signified he could not come to the Councill till the K. declaired his mind about it. I dined in My Chamber Mr Al: Home dined wt me .

Friday 27th. Ther is a great noise in toune that one of the Secretaries are turned out and my Lo: Rosse in his place. others say they are both out but ther is no certainty both pties are at present affraid tho they say Stair would be content to goe out provided the other went off also. The Commons have made ane adresse to the K. about they losse England is like to sustain by the Scotch African and Indian trade alleaging that the trade ther being free to the Scotch & the traders paying no custome for 21 years they will under sell the Engl. and steal in their commodities upon them. the Ks answer was that he was ill used in Scotland but that he hoped some remedy would be found out for these inconveniences. We are here very angry the English should meddle wt us as if we depended on them. Mr Johnstons trouble is all from this and they say the Lo: Stair foments it. I dined wt Mr Al: Home. I went to the Bank wher the books are fast filling up.

Saturday 28th. I went out to Mr Al: Home to get the Charge to enter air agst the E. of Home but it is not ready. I went from that to Sr Jo: Homes Chamber. Ther is no sure acct of the Secretaries as yet.

Sunday 29th. I went to the Tolbooth Church in the Morning. I heard Mr Linnen preach he insisted upon the sins of the Land particularly Covenant breaking Bloodguiltinesse & persecution. The day was very cold and frosty when I came to my Chamber I found my selfe very cold so as I could not be warm wt the fire and a little after I purged some mucus mixt wt blood I continued so till night that I went up to my aunts to sup but could eat none. I came to my chamber and felt so unwell that I sent for Dr St clair he judged it a fitt of ane ague but I took nothing

Monday 30th. I rested ill all night being cold and feverish but swate a litle in the morning and was pretty well. but my loosenesse continues but the mucus is not mixt so much wt Blood. We hear no certainty of our secretaries Johnstons freinds have heard from him they say & he says he is in no danger. The Duke of Queensberry the Es. of Murray & Bradalban & viscount of Tarbet took journey for London this day

My Brother who it seems the Commissioners have (as he says at Mr Alexr Cockburns instigation) discharged to receave the pole till he find Caution (wch he has not yet done) has been in toune since twesd. or Wed. last week he went out wt Cap. Home and left the bond wt me wch is not signed as yet. This day and yesterday the frost is strong.

Tuesday 31st. I did not sleep well this last night and the noise of the house disturbed me in the morning. Dr Nisbet sent me his discharge wt his man & reading it I found he had allowed too litle retentention whc would have brought him under usury. I sent it back wt his man to be helped. all the thanks I got from him was that when his man took him the money ther being some old 14sh. 6d peices in it he would take none of them tho they were so good that I past them at the bank. I thought shame to contend wt him & sent him other money.

I signed a bond of a thousand lb Scots wch Mr Alexr Home got me and wch Mr John Wilky got for Friershaw. the money it is from Mr Rot Innes writer to the signet but he says the money is not his but Al: Innes's who lives in Cathnesse. I went this afternoon to the bank and signed for 6,000 lb having payd 600 lb as the Use is being the 10th pt.

As I came out My Lo: Polwarth spoke to me about his being Cautioner for my Brother. I find my Lo: is jealous of his ill management and asked me if he had got his portion. I told him he had he said if he had knoun so much he would not have been so forward as he had been. Wtout a greater tryall I find my Brother has suffered a party to ly on him a great while wtout ethir giving a list of deficients or acquainting the Commissioners therwith whc looks very ill. I have writtten to him this night acquainting wt what past and telling him his only way is to bring in his accts hither as soon as possible & clear what he has payd out on the acct of John Homes falling short & what he has receats for since and My Lo: Polwarths letter appointing him to pay what John Home Came short.

Dr St clair came at night and told me the Councill had done nothing in the Drs. Bussinesse

I got a letter from Dr Abernethy but got no time to answer it. I went at night and visited my Lo: Crosrig but he was bussie Sr John Home came here a very litle.

1696

Wednesday January 1st. 1696. I went out in the morning to Mr Al: Homes Chamber & called for the Charge to Enter air agst the E. of Home but it was not ready. I dined in my Chamber and went to visit My Lady Polwarth who has been ill of a Rhumatisme and is not well as yet. I went at night and visit Pa: Johnstone (now a Bailiff) and his wife.

Thursday 2nd. I got a lettter from Pat: Cockburn Mes[senger] in Dunse wt ane Execution of the Summones of adjudication agst the E of Home. I got a letter from Da: Robisone and And Watheret brought me a furlet of meal. Da: writes he will be ready to clear accts &c. he tells me Robie is well.

I payd Balgair the Lady Tarsappys anrent due at Candlemis 1695, he having only a discharge to that time. I likewise counted wt Mr Michil Lumisden for the anrent of Cath. Chartreses money and found (as I had reckonded befor) that I was due 3 years at Mart. last I payd him 2 of the 3.

I got from Mr Al: Home the speciall Charge to enter air agst the E. of Home and sent it out to Pa: Cockburn as also the letters of Horning upon my decreit for my annuity to Charge the E. of Home for two years annuity past at Martimis last for whc he has not been charged.

Friday 3rd. Mr Tho: Aikman came to me this morning and told me he hand [sic] found a hand for the money I got from him In June last wch (not geting Bell & Sclatehouses subscription as I promised) I offered him when I came first to toun but he said he could not take it till Candlemis. he would have taken it now & so I would have been free of a months interest but I told him that since he had not taken it when I came to toun I had now disposed of it but if he could take 400 lb of it he might have it. but I promised to try if I could make it 500 lb. I spoke of it to Mr Al: Home but he has no money. he sent to me at 12 a clock but I sent him word I could give no further than 400 lb.

I went to the Mr of Polwarths Chamber Mr McDougall his old quarter Mr was not wt him. Mr McDouill asserts ther is 12 Months pay due to the troupe and says he got not above 16 bolls of meal & 8 bolls of oats from the Commissers while we were at Innerlocky for whc they state 108 lb 08[6?]sh d st [sic] I got up from Mr Al: Home 3 hornings. I appointed him to extract out of the Register of hornings on of 2 sheets. & 2 of one each sheet is a dollar and he gave Geo: Robisons man a dollar & the Registers dues is 2 lb. I went after dinner & visited the Lady Hiltone and from that came to Mr Al: Homes chamber and got the Horning Hay agst the E. of Home

Mem. I formerly got from him the Letters of Escheat. I gave him the Execution to fill up whc I got in from P.C. I went from that to Geo: Robisons who lent me a sermon preached at the D. of Luxemburghs funerall by a Jesuite Pere de la rue. I came from that to My aunts from that to my Chamber whc I was forced to quitt being full of smoke so went to Dr St clairs. the E. wind whc blows makes it smoke unlesse a window be open. Mr Th: Aikman sent to me again and I sent him word I could spair no more the 400 lb.

Saturday 4th. I went to Mr Al: Homes chamber but he has not got my Execution ready. from that I went to the Mr of Polwarths Chamber. I dined wt Sr John Home in my chamber. Mr Tho: Aikman drew a precept on me payable to one Mr Tho: Elliss a sone of Southsydes wtout his receate I payd the money whc was 400 lb. I went at night to my Lo: Crosrigs. the assembly rose this day & is to meet the the [sic] 2d or third of January 1697. The have transported about 22 Mrs to the north and declaired as many transportable in case of a call of this number our minister Mr Guthry is one. this transportability is a new terme and thing In the Church so far as I can be informed. they have likewise suspended one Mr Hepburn who it seems has had undecent expressions agst the Assembly saying the Episcopall Clergy had laid on the Capestone in taking the test and now this Clergy had laid it on in taking the Oath of Alleageance and assurance or something to this purpose. he is a conventicle preacher for I hear not yt he is settled in any Churrch.

Mr Al: Home tells me that Mr Robert Innes has filld up his oun name in the bond I signed on tweBday last.

Sunday 5th. I went to Church in the afternoon.

Monday 6th. I got from Mr Alexr Home a summonds agst Wedderburn for buying the teinds of Kimmergh.

Tuesday 7th. I heard that Secretary Stair has demitted his place but it is not knoun who is to succeed him. I met wt Earnslaw who told me that the money wherwt the Countesse of Home is paid was borrowed 4,000 Ms from Wm Hendersone of Todrig who had it in Scatsbusses hand and Scatsbusse having sold some lands (wherof the E. of Home is superior called Mersitone) to the Chancellour the E. has sold likewise the superiority for 1,000 lb and about 1,000 lb was sent in by my Lord. My Lord Polwarth sent for me [Sr J Home - above] in the Morning. he tells me the morning I found them together in the parlia Closse My Lo: very kindly offered still to be bound for my Brother for the Pole. Sr Jo: Home said that he had allwise resolved to be bound for him but that he was Hectored to it and that had hindered him but that now the bussinesse being not entire he thought it would look like a young man if he should engage &c yet he would further think on it. My Lo: Polw. sd he behooved to send out to morrow for ther was but agst Wed: come eight days alloued for Bringing in the Pole. I met likewise wt young Wedderburn he told me he heard I was going to buy my teinds I told him I was. he desired I might not doe it. I told him I found it a troublesome thing to have them to pay to another and the law allowing me I was resolved to doe it. he sd it might occasion differences betwixt us. I told him I should be sorry to be the occasion of any but that I hoped no body would take Exceptions agst what I did wherin I was so clearly warranted by law and that I was sure he would doe as much if he were in my place & that if differences should arise I thought I would be in a condition to defend my selfe. After dinner my Lo: Crosrig came to my Chamber I went wt him to visite My Lady Polwarth. At night I signed the bond of Cautionry my Brother left wt me and sent it to My Lo: Polwarth. these 2 or 3 days have been very warme for the season the W.s.w.

Wednesday 8th. I went to the Mr of Polwarths Chamber he told me that ther was no demission in Stairs case but that the K. told him he had no further service for him. That then he desired the K. to give him ane approbation & remission which the K. refused telling him if he had done ill he should goe home & answer for it. the Matter of Glencoe sticks in the K's mind & I suppose that Stair must discover who put him on it to procure so severe letters from the King & to write severer himselfe. His freinds who pretend a demission make the story litle better they alledge that the last day of Johnstons waiting he brought some papers to be signed by the K. who sd to him bring ym to me tomorrow. Sr sd he that is the first day of the other secretaries waiting However says the K. doe you bring these pages & I shall signe them. Stair was present & heard all wherby he Understood the K's mind toward him & went & demitted next morning.

I got a note from my Lo: Polwarth wt ane act of Councill enclosed wherby the Collectors are obliged to find Caution for Collecting the pole so I caused draw a bond & signed it for my Brother & sent it to my Lo: Polwarth as he desyred.

Mr Al: Home raised me a summonds for buying ye teinds of Betshile agst the E. of Home & my Lo: Polwarth both pretending the right.

Thursday 9th. In the morning Pat: Cockburn came to me about some diligences I have to employ him in. I trysted him to Mr Al: Homes chamber but he having taken a fitt of the Gravell came not abroad this day so I delayed till to morrow. I went and visited Mr Al: Home then I went to the Session house wher I found Sr John Home had win his plea agst John Doul. I dined in my Chamber Sr John Home came and dined wt me after dinner I went to my Lo: Polwarths lodging and spoke to him about my giving in a bill to the Lords to get my annuity since my decreit. he desired me to write some thing on it as a mem. and gave him. I came after to my aunts and then to my chamber wher Dr Dundas. Sr Jo: H. & Meg H. came and staid wt me. the Dr left a narrative of a house haunted by a Spirit in House of And Mckee in Ring Croft of

Stocking in the parish of Rerrick in the Stuartrie of Kirkudbright put out by the Minister of the parish Mr Al: Telfair and attested by severall persons eye & Ear wittnesses of its throing stones setting the house on fire bating people speaking whisling & from Feb. to May last. wch I read. I went after & visited Whytefeild.

Friday 10th. I gave Pat Cockburn Mess. orders to Charge the E. of Home for the 2 last years annuity, and to denounce afterward and to arrest in the tennants of Aitone & Gordons hands and others his tenants. I have raised a summonds of sale of my teinds of Kimmergh and Betshile but I fear my not being infeft hinder it yet. I have given Pat: Cockburn agst Wedderburn &. the E. of Home. I dined wt Sr John Home Cavers & Mr Walter Pringle in Rosses. I mett after dinner wt Earnslaw Mr Al: Home & Will Home of St Ebbes at Mr Al:'s Chamber. After I came to my Chamber. Meg. Home Came at night & told me yt Lady Ravilstone died about 6 a clock at night. she had stong impressions of it above 8 or 10 weeks agoe and sd allwise she would die of a fever in January tho she was in Good health when she sd it, this all about her know & Dr Dundas lookt on it as Melancholy however it had this Good effect that she set her selfe carefully about the things that Concerned her soul.

Saturday 11th. Going out in the morning I met wt Wm Somervail who is carying on a sale of Scot and Brounfeilds lands wch they have of yr wifes on wch Ninewells has a debt due to him & ane infeftmt he desires the Creditors may Join to Cary on yt sale. I after met wt Cavers & Mr Wedderburn who were going to Scougalls the painters Cavers sat to his picture for the first time. Robies nurse and her husband came to see me in the morning.
[four lines deleted]
I went in the afternoon & visited Will Elliot & his wife. I went to my Lo: Crosrigs and borrowed from him a sight of Baxters Christian directory.

Sunday 12th. I went to the Tolbooth Church fore and afternoon after sermons I went to my Lo: Polwarths. I see the flying post but ther was litle news in it. a long acct of the seige of Ceuta in Africa defended by the Spaniards & attacked by the Moores who have beseiged it a year and made litle progresse by the Moorish Emperor has ordered his generall to ly befor it till he take it tho he should ly all his life. Ther is a promotion of Cardinalls at Rome. I came home & supt in my Chamber

Monday 13th. I went abroad in the morning and met wt the Mr of Polwarth. I see blind Will Home who is solliciting the magistrats to allow him something for their having broken his tack he had of the toun of the Calender wt Pauls Work &c. I dined wt Sr Jo: Home Swintone Capt Home & Cap. Cockburn in Rosses. Capt Cockburn offered me a sh. st for my clipt fourten pence 1/2s. My

Lord Polwarth sent me a horning agst the E. of Home that had been produced some years agoe in a forthcoming at my instance agst the E. of Home befor the sheriff but ther was nothing done. This my Lo: Pol.s Birth day and Polwarth fair day & St Mungos day. they say holy St Mungo never left the weather as he found it. But hither to it is the same very warme for winter weather & a high S.W. wind. The Lady Ravlestones corps was transported from her house to the High Church at 5 this afternoon. Sr Jo: Home came here at night. he goes out to morrow [having gained his plea - deleted] being assoilzed from Jo: Douls plea agst him.

Tuesday 14th. Sr Jo: Home came here in the morning being just going to his horse. Mr John Craig brought me a Scroll of my decreet agst Wedderburn. I gave him my summonds of adjudication agst the E. of Home. I dined wt my Lo: Polwarth after dinner I went wt the Master to Sr John Karkaldy of Granges buriall (he was Earnslaw Cusen German) In him is ended that family wch they say was ane ancient one. At night Cavers came to my Chamber & sat some time then Meg Home.

Wednesday 15th. I went out in the forenoon and spoke to Mr Al: Home to get me letters of open doors agst the E. of Home. I dined in my Chamber. I went not abroad in the afternoon the Lady Ravlestone being to be buried & not having Black cloaths at lest in order. I consulted Mr Walter Pringle in my Bussines agst the Marquis of Douglas. And in my Gift of Escheat agst the E. of Home and spoke to him of my Bussines agst Broun of Blackburn. I gave him a guiney & ane halfe. I left wt him the Marquis of Douglass processe and the gift of Escheat and 3 Extracts of Hornings & the summonds of Declarator. I wrote to David Robisone wt Cavers who goes home tomorrow to send me my horses & wt money he has agst Mund. next

Thursday 16th. I went to Mr Al: Homes Chamber & spoke to him again about letts of open doors. I went to the Master of Polwarth and he told me that the E. of Murray the Marquis of Athols sone was secretary. I was told that the plea of the airs of line was come in agst the E.of Home. It has been a terrible s.w. wind all this night wch still continues. Elshy Trotter dined wt me in my Chamber. I hear this day the plea at the Instance of the airs of line is come in agst the E. of Home his folks would have me to take it up as being Concerned but not being Called. I see not any prejudice a decreet at their instance can doe to me. Gave Mr Al: Home the extracts of 3 hornings to raise me letters of open doors agst the E. of Home. I got them from Mr Walter Pringle in the Afternoon

Friday 17th. I spoke to my Lo: Crosrig who had promised to speak to my Lo: Whytelaw to know if my Grandfathers seasine & my speciall service of air to him was sufficient for a title to buy teinds. he says it is not and that I must produce my own seasine. I dined wt my Lo: Crosrig. After dinner I met wt Coldenknows we talkt of the bussines of the airs of line agst [Aitone - deleted] the E. of Home. I sate wt the Mr of Polw. in Ch: Jack's and from that home Mr Al: Home & Whytefeild came to my Chamber and sate wt me. And after that Meg Home I find if the Lands of Bigger be sold she has a mind to have the money for her portion but promises to give in the anrent yearly to her Nephew.

Saturday 18th. Mrs Home Al: Home of Murrays the K's taylers relict was wt me this morning. she is very earnest to have the money her husband and I stand engaged in to Helen Douglas Whytefeilds Neice payd. I went out and sat in the Coffee house and after went wt Whytefeild to see St Ebbes who is unwell. And then returned to my Chamber.

Sunday 19th. I went fore & afternoon to the Old Church. and supt at home.

Monday 20th. I dined wt the Mr of Polwarth Mangertone & Elshy Trotter in the Ship. I went to my Lo: Polws. after dinner and told him the best way for us to Get paymt from the E. of H: would be to procure him his Liberty that he might be subject to captions my Lo: sd he would think on it. At night Jo: Lidgate came in wt my horses he brought me a letter from my Brother wherin he writes that Al: & Ja: Jaffreys have been at him for settling for the Land. & that Adam Turnbull has ben at him about Als. rooms. that Hector Turnbull in Earnslaw would take all Da: Robisone possesses Da: Robisone sent me in a bag 71 lb 16s 6d as I have counted it but writes only 71 lb 8s 6d wherof 36 lb from James Jaffrey 19 lb 8s 6d from James Ridpeth. & 14 lb from Will: Waddell so ther is 8sh over whc belongs to some of them.

Tuesday 21st. I was in the morning in the Coffee house Swintone told me ther were letters come from London from our partners in the bank & that by ther advice they are going to print the Undertakers names. those are capable of being Governours wt *** or 3 stars those that are capable of being deputy governours wt 2 & those of Managers wt one. I was rather of the opinion they should print the Summes for whc each subscribes wt their names and by that everyone would know what everyone has subscribed for. We have also 2 letters published about our African trade. Jeriswood was ther and engaged me to dine wt him. At 5 a clock I met wt Whytefeild Carubber Earnslaw and Mr Al: Home about my Lo: Homes affair wch It seems they would fain settle upon ther oun termes but I still adhere to bygons and beside I cannot see what firm security my Lord can give me in the Condition he now is in. We did nothing but only talked on the matter, and adjourned till next morning at ten a clock.

Wednesday 22nd. I met wt them but Earnslaw was not ther. Carubber proposed I might take security out of the Estate of Aitone for 30,000 Ms, this proposition I lookt on worse than that made be Whytefeild of 30,000 of present money but that was in case the Estate should be sold and certanely it is I still adhere to the 40,000 that is due me & told them that tho I should be put in possession yet It would not be a peaceable one because my Lord Crosrig was going on in eld. so we fell to speak of treating wt my Lord Crosrig whc I told them behooved necessarily to be. they desired me to speak to him so we parted wtout doing anything. I dined wt Sandy Home after dinner I went and told my Lord Crosrig he sd he did not see what right my Lo: Home could now give that could be valid and that he would not give any deduction upon any such temporall possession be he was content to hear what they would say but could not meet wt them this day. I told Whytefeild this and I think they may meet tomorrow.

Thursday 23th. I dined in my Chamber and after dinner went to my Lo Crosrigs wher Whytefeild came also. we went to Arnots and met wt Caruber & Mr Al: Home. The Conclusion of halfe ane hours discourse was that [my Lo: Cros - deleted] they offered my Lo: Crosrig possession of the Interest of 12,000 Ms out of the Estate of Aitone. My Lord desired first to know how this should be secured from Incumbrances befor he would tell them that he would either accept or not accept of their offer tho he assured them they had no ground from this to think he would accept therof. This Whytefeild promised to doe and my Lo: went to the house. I staid a litle but we did nothing. It has snowd much this day & it freezes I went at night to my Lo: Crosrigs and he told me that tho the [proposition - deleted] security they would propose should please he would not accept of the summe they had offered.

Friday 24th. Ther is much snow fallen this day but it being from the West It will not be so great in the Merse as when it comes from ye s.e. it is not so great here as wt us. the news this day are yt Tarbet having demitted his place in the Kings hands (as some say not douting but the K. would continue him) the immediatly took him at his word and bestowed it on the E. of Selkirk the late duke of Hamiltons second sone and some say also that the E. of Arran is coming in favour and is to be Chancellour Thesauror or Capt. of the K's Guard here. They talk also that My Lo Whytelaw is to be president. All this is imputed to be the Effect of Lord Geo: Hamiltons marying Mrs Villiers &c. I dined wt my Lo: Polwarth and went not abroad after I returned to my Chamber at 3 a clock

Saturday 25th. It is a great frost this day. My Lo: Crosrig & I thought to have got in writt the way my Lo Home designs to secure My Lo: & me upon the Estate of Aitone but the paper is not ready. my Lo: sat in my Chamber a pretty while wt Whytefeild & Mr Al: Home. I went nowher after dinner. Elshy Trotter dined wt me.

Sunday 26th. I went to the Old Church. ther was a mad man came into the Church and made some disturbance but he went out befor the Sermon begun. I went to Mr Al: Homes betwixt sermons but he was dining abroad. my Chamber smoakt so I could not stay in it the wind s.e. It snowed much. I went to the Trone Ch. in the afternoon from that I went home wt Mrs Julian Home and from thence to the Mr of Polwarts and thence home.

Monday 27th. I see in my Lo: Crosrigs hands some proposalls of security by my Lo: Home wt My Lo: & me in case we came to settle. on the quota my Lo: was writing some notes on them. I gave Mr Al: Home a horning agst the E. of Home to get me letters of open doors agst the E. of Home Meg Home came to me this night and told me that Ja Galbreth had been wt her & told that he feared Mr Jo: Bon's was disposing of anything he had to his wife (My Lo: Fesdo's sister as his procuring) & his children in all probability to evite paymt to Ninewells in case he should fall short of his accts of his intromission wt Newtones Estate to whc he was factor for the Late Ninewells & for whom I stand Cautioner. Mr Al: Home came here at night and was very earnest I should settle wt my Lo: Home It has been a great thaw this day & the Wind s.w.

Tuesday 28th. Mr Al: Home told me Ja: Nicolsone would not take in a bill of open doors wtout ane execution from a Messenger declaring he had searcht all the grounds of the Lands and could not find anything to poind. I dined wt my Lo: Polwarth. I was wt my Lo: Crosrig and askt him if he had made observations on the Overtures given in to him by Whytefeild he sd he had not had time but that he though[t] he would give up wt the E. I went to the Coffee house to see the news. in the votes of the [Eng p - deleted] House of Commons I see the have declared it a high Misdemeanor to take oaths by virtue of a forreigne power and have ordered all the Scotch men concerned in the Scotch E. India Comp to be Empeached for Misdemeanour. It has been clear and thaw all the day but windy.s.w.

Wednesday 29th. I got a letter from Sr Jo: Home desiring to know what was done about the bank Da: Robisone came hither this morning being cited in as a wittnes for prov the price of Corn in the sale of the teinds of Eccleshiels at My Lo: Polwarths instance agst the E. of Home [blank] he brought me in [a coppy - deleted] the Executions of my summonds agst the the [sic] E. of Home & Wedderburn for the buying of the teinds of Kimmergh & Betshile. After dinner I signed a bond Conjunct principill wt my Lo: Polwarth & Mr Al: Home of 2,000 Ms to Caimbs another Conjunct principill wt My Lo: Polwarth & Hiltone. & the Lady Hiltone his Curatrix for 1,000 Ms the 1st is to pay a debt to Friershaw in whc I was not bound the 2nd to James Broun Adv. in wch I was bound. I got a bond of releif

117

from my Lo: for both. I visited the Lady Jeriswood Earnslaw came to my Chamber & told me his case anent his engagemts for Bughtrig.

Thursday 30th. Mr Al: Home found me out my precept of Clare constat granted by the late E. of Home by a late act of parlia. I may be yet infeft upon it so I have ordered him to draw me a seasine to be sent out on Wed. next wt the Carier. and I resolve to get my selfe infeft by a notar in the Country. In the afternoon ther was a meeting of some Concerned in the bank My Lo: Polw. my Lo: Crosrig Halcraig. Rankillar Anstruther were ther & Wintone & severall others & Sr Pat. Akinhead. ther were severall debates for clearing the matter whither they who [were befor - deleted] are Banquiers by profession should be trusted as managers it was thought fit that some of them should be in but not the major pt. whether the patentees have done right to order the votes to be put into the box wtout the names it was approved. Whether salaries were to be given to the Governour Dep. Gov. and Managers it was answered that would be better considered when a Scheme of the Bussines should be brought us from London by Mr Holland whom all agree should be Governour. I payd Mrs Hebburn 52sh st for 52 nights. I have been in her house from Decr 10th to January 30th Inclusive.

Friday 31st. I came from Edr about 8 a clock. Da: Robisone was wt me I bated at Gifford hall & stayed about ane hour & from thence by the Ridstanerig. I came home about 6. I ordered Ro: Knox to goe to Berwick for provisions &c.

Saturday February 1st. James Jaffrey payd me 20 lb 2sh of his Lammas rent and Al: Jaffrey payd me 9 lb. in full paymt of his Mart. rent. They spoke to me about their rooms. I bid them come to me on munday.

Sunday 2nd. I went to abroad the morning was pleasant enough and Clear the afternoon became rough and Cloudy wt a n.w.wind.

Monday 3rd. James Jaffrey payd me 32 lb. 7sh. I agreed wt him for 710 Ms for the Westfeild wt 24 cariages and 12 Cain fouls halfe hens halfe capons but the odde ten Ms he only referred to my will.
I settled likewise wt Al: Jaffrey for Kings law & Greenknow for 550 Ms. I supose I might have gotten more for Hector Turnbull (Adam Turnbulls Brother who married Beetty Watsons Daughter) was here and would have taken it for Adam.
Sr John Home & Sr Jo: Pringle came here in the afternoon and stay about ane hour
I wrott to Mr Al: Home to know if my Lo: Crosrig had made any

progress wt the E. of Homes doers. to try if Sandy Belshesse can secure me 2,000 Ms (for Friershaw) of whc he was speaking to me. to send me a seasine of Betshile draun out ready to be signed by a notar (because they are very ignorant in this Country) that I may infeft my selfe in Betshile. To try if my Lo: Homes doers will consent to suffer my Declarator of Escheat to be enrolled in the next weeks roll.

I wrote a letter to the Gentlemen patentees of the Bank desiring them to receave enclosed my six votes for Governour & deputy Governour I put this letter open in one to my Lo: Crosrig desiring him to put in a ticket wt the names of such as he should think fittest and [Close - deleted] seal it and send it to the patentees. I wrote also to Mr John Craig a letter enclosed in my Lo Crosrigs desiring to know if my suspens agst Blackburn be in the roll this week and that I might get a terme to prove by Tho: Calderwoods oath who filld up Blackburns name in the bond that it was condescended that at the signing of the bond of Corrobaration to Mr Ro: Lawder The Bygone anrents should be allowed to my Lo: Home principill debtor out of the teinds of Ryselaw.

Tuesday 4th. David Robisone & I were treating about the mains and Heugh His tack being out at Whitsonday but we are not settled. After dinner I went to Blackader and visited Sr John & his Lady. Geo: Home factor for Ninewells came ther & had his accts since the late Ninewells's & his last Counting. we gave him the letters of supplement to cite Aymouth Linthill & David Home agst the 19th of this month befor the Commissaries of Edr to see inventaris given up. I returned home at night Yesterday and this day have been both very pleasant this day it has been a keen frost. I lent Da: Robisone systema Agriculturae.

Wednesday 5th. Da: Robisone came here this morning we settled for the Redheugh as it payd befor 620 Ms and he gives me 1,480 Ms for the Mains wch is 80 Ms more than he payd I wrote to my Brother to get me ane answer about 2,000 Ms he told me he thought would be got to borrow. Cavers & Dr Abernethy came over here in the afternoon. Ther fell much snow this morning from N.E.

Thursday 6th. I drew a minute of a tack wt Da: Robisone for the Mains for 1,480 Ms yearly & the personage teinds drawn & 2 horse grasse & 2 cows grasse reservd to my selfe wt the peice meadow at the foot of the garden. & for the Redhaugh for 620 Ms and the 36 Coal Cariages & 36 Cain fouls halfe hens halfe Capons. The Wind from E. has been very high wt rain till night the Waters will not ride.

Friday 7th. I sent Jo: Lidgate to Kelso to bring me Bread and some pil. Bals. It was windy and some rain from N.E

Saturday 8th. I went to Blackader. And Watheret Brought me no ans from
Mr Al: Home. I got a letter from Mr J. Craig telling me my susp. agst
Blackburn was not as yet in the roll and that my Declarator agst the E. of
Home was not yet enrolled. Sr Jo. Had a line from my Lo: Crosrig telling he
had put Mr Holland for Governour & Swintone for deputy Governour in our
letters to the Bank. Sr John Home read me a letter from Ro: Pringle Under
secretary wherin he says that tis thought all the English concerned in the
Scotch E. India Company will submitt themselves to the parlia and quitt their
interest in the Company. My Lo: Crosrig writes that Secretary Johnstone is
also turnd out of his place whc is upon the East India bussines to please the
Eng. parlia. that Argile Andandale & Sr Geo. Maxwell of Pollock are Lo:s of
the treasury I returned at night.

Sunday 9th. I went no wher abroad

Monday 10th. This day has been pretty pleasant but windy S.W. I wrote to
Bell telling him that since he had refused to signe the bond wherin I was to be
Cautioner for him for the money he oues me I hoped he knew of a better way
of payment and desired he might Communicat it to me otherwise he would
oblige me to proceed in Diligence agst him wch I had no inclination to doe. He
wrote to me a world of Excuses for his not having done it. that he knew not
what answer to return me about paymt at this time being under my Lo:
Polwarths tuition and he hoped I would not use any legall diligence agst him.

Tuesday 11th. It is a very high wind this morning. I sent for Da: Robisone to
tell him I designed for Edr to morrow and to see what money he can get me all
he has is 6 or 7 lb st. James Redpath payd me 30 lb 6sh as by his acct.
  Mem. My Brother came here yesterday & told me Rot: Rutherford
Edgerstones brother had money in Charles Lauders hand in Lauder and I might
get what I pleased of it. I desired my Brother to goe ther this day and settle wt
them about the security to witt I and he or if they pleased My Lo: P. & I.
  The Millar of Betshiel mill payd me 8 lb James Forsyth [blank] Da: Robisone
60 lb. I gave him 19 lb in Copper of whc he gave Marg. Foord 6 lb and is to
get the rest Changed for silver. I likewise Receaved fro him four receates of
Mr Al: Homes of 20 lb st being 5 each.

Wednesday 12th. I got some money from James Jaffrey wch Clears his
Lammas rent 1695 last past I gave Da Robisone 6 lb Scots wch makes 19 lb
Scots he has of me to Change. I came from Home about 8 a clock and came to
Betshile. I got some money from Wm Waddell, Wm Brack and John
Jamesone. I came from that to Lauder wher my Brother was he having spoke to
him to get me 3,000 Ms. they had sent away for Robert Rutherford Edgertones

Brother who lives at Whytebank. he came and brought the money & Ch: Lauder drew a bond by My Lo: Polwarth & me wch I signed and Gave to Mr Rutherford who is to sent it in to Mr David Halyburtone writer to see My Lo: Polwarth signe it. I receaved the money and Brought it a long wt me. It was past four befor I came from Lauder. I road on till I came to Cranstone about 8 wher I lodged in one John Iruins a servant of my Lo: Oxfords. I never was in Cranstone befor. it is a very pleasant place & my Lo: Oxford has 2 very good houses ther. for at first the halfe only belonged to his father the other to Philliphaugh but they falling a pleaing Oxford forced the other to sell him his interest wheron ther was a house. I[t] was boistrously windy all this day till night that it fell calme. The wind S.W

Thursday 13th. I came to toun about 11 a clock and Lodge in Ro: Cambells I went and dined wt my Lo: Polwarth. After dinner I went to Mr Al: Homes Chamber and from that I got Sr Jo: Home who came in this morning he came to my house a litle after I came away but they did not tell him I was to halt at Betshile he came on a peice upon the supposition but fancying he had forgot some papers he went home again and dined and was at Tranent all night. We hear all the Scotch places or officers are in danger. The Chancellour some say is to be turnd out and that place turnd to a commission. Some say that things goe not so well in the parlia of England as was expected and that the Cause why Mr Johnstone is turnd out is that Annandale and the Advocat lay the blame of the E.India acts passing on him. We hear that Sr Geo: Rook is recalld from the Straits the Thoulon Squadron being so strong that he will not be able to resist them and it seems we are not in a condition to reenforce him at present. Ther are some English men come hither from London for Carying on the E. India Trade not wtstanding of the parlias opposing it.

Friday 14th. I went to my aunt Ninewelles to Sr Jo: Home & Meg for Inventaring Ninewelle's movables. Sr Jo: Home had a list of debts due to him by his tenants we went and gave it to Sandy Home. I dined in Rosses wt Sr Jo: Home after dinner we mett wt Swintone and wt him Mr Patersone the great projector for trade we sat in a coffee house wt them a litle and from that we went to the bank meeting to hear the Governour and deputy governour declaired who were Mr Holland and Mr Wm Areskin my Lo: Cardros's brother. ther was a letter produced from Mr Holland being ane answer to one writt to him desiring him to come hither to set the bank on a right foot he writes that if we will allow him 6 per cent out of the profit or 10 per cent out of the profit after ther shall incresse 12 per cent to the undertakers. he will come hither after some discourse the bussines was committed to prepare their opinion agst Tuesday the Company is to meet. I was at night wt Mr Al: Home & Earnslaw & Sr John Home & St Ebbes Sr John being of the Committee Left us and went to it: Earnslaw St Ebbs and I went to Grahams I drunk some Mum wch is very good this year.

Saturday 15th. I payd Friershaw 2,000 Ms wch rested of my bond of 4,000 Ms I got up the bond to his father but not the bond of Corrobation to himselfe wch it seems by one Craik of Stuartone to whom Friershaw had assigned the debt and it is not got out of the Register as yet but I am to get it on Munday. I dined wt Mr Al: Home went in the afternoon to my Lo: Crosrigs and wt him to my aunts and returned wt him ther were Sr Jo: Home & Halyburtone who was seeking up from Purveshall a disposition be Sr Wm Purves to him of salvage apprysing whc was among Sr Wms papers &c. I supped wt my Lord Crosrig

Sunday 16th. I went to the Tron Church Befor and afternoon and supt in my Chamber and Meg Home coming sometime befor I keept her to sup wt me

Monday 17th. We hear the Advocat is now a great man at Court many things are talkt that a litle time will try. I dined wt Geo: Robisone in his chamber. I went to Mr Tho: Aikman to give him his money but had left the receate and so could not clear wt him. I went at night to My Lo: Polwarths and found him wtin I spoke to him anent the bond of 3,000 Ms I signed at Lauder to Ro: Rutherford. he told me one had been at him wt it this morning but he was going out. I expected it would have been sent to Mr David Halyburtone in wch case he promised to have brought it to me that I might have gone wt him to my Lo: Polwarth so I can not imagine who brought it. I went from thence to my Chamber. Yesterday died John Stuart the Lady Kettlestons sone a boy of about 10 years of age. I got a letter from Hiltone to his buriall this morning at 9 a clock but could not get out so soon. Anne Pringle a sister of Sr Jo: Pringles died also yesterday she has been long under a Rheumatisme which turned in end to a decay.

Tuesday 18th. I went and gave in my list of the Managers of the bank here and in London. the list of those in England I got from Sr John Swintone but ther has been a ptie that has concerted here that will cary it. others have acted at Randome. I dined wt Mr Al Home. I was most part after dinner till ten at night at the meeting of the bank. Wher we had Hollands offer considered about ether 6 of the Hundred of profit or 10 of the Hundred of profit after we shall have 12 per cent of profitt and all expenses defrayd. The report of the Committy whc was apointed last day was to prefer the last wch all agreed to. But In respect that in such cases (as in the Case of the Orphans bank it is wt Mr Patersone) these projectors use to oblige themselves not to enter into any other society or bank prejudiceall to that of whc they are managers It was proposed that he should be obliged not to enter into any such society or bank in prejudice of ours it was answered that he had allready a Stock in the Royall bank at London and that he would never be induced to quitt that it was answered that what he was allready engaged in we would not desire him to quitt but that for the future he should not doe it. Mr Rober Blackwood said also that his being engaged in it would be no prejudice but rather a profitt to our bank because he would be able to convince any other bank of the advantage of the passing of our bank bills. At length it was resolved that the letter writt to him wch was draun by some ther p[rese]nt accepting of his proposall should conclud wt a reference to [words crossed out and diff to read]

Wednesday 19th. I went to see the Scrutiny for the Managers wch begun yesternight it was not closed till afternoon and is to be sent up to London first post I dined wt my Lo: Polw:. I caused Gideon Elliot to put in ane issue in my left Shoulder whc has been out some time.

Thursday 20th. Mr Tho Aikman sent me a precept of 400 Ms wt Mr Elliis wch I payd. I dined wt Mr Al: Home after dinner Sr Jo: Home and I signed three doubles of Inventarys of Ninewellss & Movables & the rentall of his Estate to be given in to the Commissaries wherof we are to have one and 2 are to ly beside the Commissaries for the nearest of Kin on the father & mothers syde. I went afterward to a French painters one Eude who had been at Blackader taking the Ladies picture & Jonies & Robies and was finishing them here but he was sick. I went afterward wt him to Scots the Joiners he was to bespeak a case for his clock but made no bargain.
Nota. yesterday I was wt my Lo: Pol: in P. Steels Swintone brought Mr Patersone the Great projector in trade to us. he seems to understand the theory of it thorely. It I forgot that My Lo; told me that the trees I had writt for to London were come wt his to Newcastle and from that to Polwarth house or Kelso I writt to Peter Broun to send to John Lidgate to cause him take them home and desired Peter would cause sett them in some good light peice of Ground by way of Nursery till I could dispose of them.

Friday 21st. I went in the morning to the house. I talkt wt Sr Pa: Home about the E. of Homes affairs sometime. I met wt Tolquhon who told me the Laird of Drum Iruin was dead and left his Lady wt Child. I came home & dined in my Chamber I met wt My Lo: Polwarth who told me that one from Rot: Rutherford had brought the bond to him of 3,000 Ms whc I signed at Lauder and that he had signed it yesterday. At night when I came to my chamber I drew a bond of releife and went to my Los: Lodging & gave it him he was alleadging the King would not name a president of session at this time he told also he heard that the Chancellour and his family & friends were resolved to put in 20,000 lbs st to the E. India trade. Davie Burnet was telling me the French King had discharged any of his ships to medle wt the Scotch ships.

Saturday 22nd. I visited my Aunt Ninewells in the morning who continues very ill. I went to Leith wt Mr Al: Home & Will. Home and dined. these dayes past have been very dry but somewhat windy the way is very dry at present.

Nota yesterday I met wt Blackwood & gave him my decreet agst Wedderburn. he promised he and I should meet on munday.

At Lieth we see the weavers of the Linen manufactory work damask table linnen.

Sunday 23rd. I went in the forenoon to the French Church in the aft noon to the Tron Ch. and supt at home. the day was boisterously windy

Monday 24th. I met wt Blackwood who sd he had not yet persued my decreit. I dined wt my Lo: Crosrig I hear some talk that ther is a fear of ane invasion from France and that upon that acct severall regimts are to be sent from England to our borders and 2 to come from Ireland the Jacobite party would fain persuade us that the designe of sending them is to break our E. India trade but that cannot be designed.

Tuesday 25th. I met wt Blackwood this day again and he sd he had not as yet considered my decreit. I dined wt my Lord Polwarth. at night I was wt Mr Al: Home & Earnslaw who had been last night wt Mr Patersone the projector who promises us great things in our E and W. India trade. I took Dr Stevensones advice in my health it now being a season fitt for purging.

Wednesday 26th. I dined wt George Robisone in his chamber. In the afternoon was a meeting of the Bank and the Directors declaired as follows.
   [several lines blank]
I met wt Blackwoods agent Mr Olifant Condees sone and Mr Jo: Menizies. they seem not to see a reasone why the Marquis should not enter me But we could not find Blackwood.

The Books of the Indian and Affrican Company wer opened this day and much thronged to they say ther would be 70,000 lb st signed for befor night.

I got yesterday a letter from my Brother wt a denunciation agst the E of Home whc I gave in wt the Horning to Geo: Robisone this day to be registrat tho the Horning be allready registrat yet he says it must be registrat over again. I was in Grahams wt Earnslaw & Mr Al: Home at night.

I got up from Wm Home Messenger the 2 summonds of sale of the teinds of Kimmergh and Betshile wt the Executions and payd him for them.

Thursday 27th. I went to the Indian Company room wher many subscribers of all sorts come very fast in. Afternoon I returned thither and signed for 500 lb st and gave the ordinary bond for the 4th pt payable agst the 1st of June. Whytefeild went also wt me & signed for as much. we got a receate from the overseers that we had granted such a bond.

I met wt Blackwood but he has not as yet considered my decreit. I got a letter from Da: Robisone that my house would bear a thack and devitt roof and that the gardner wanted a spade. I wrote to my Brother to get the thack from Lantone (having spoke to him for as much wheat strae as would doe the turn) & to Da: Robisone to send people to draw it and to Buy a spade to the Gardner

Friday 28th. I went to my aunt Ninewells's and caused set on the lock on the Cabinet wch I had caused take off when at Ninewells in summer last I brok up to seek Jo. Johnstons seasin. I likewise took out and gave mr John Dicksone two Charters of the Lands of Hornden & Paxton be Geo: Ogilby of Dunlugas to Dav: Home of Ninewells in Octr 1576. and this Wedderburns precept of Clare Constat to the late Ninewells of all his lands holdin of Him in 1675 and his seasin in 1676 to be produced in a reduction and improbation at Blebos instance agst Ninewells. I dined in my aunts. after dinner we caused also give in a bill representing that ther was a certification Contra non producta agst the late Ninewells and desiring it might be stoped in respect this Ninewells was not called. I was at night wt Earnslaw & Mr Al: Home When I came to my Chamber I got a letter from Sr Jo; Home desiring to know how the Indian trade went on and some directions about getting him a case for his clock. I writt to him what I know of the one & that I should try what I could doe in the Case.

Saturday 29th. As I went to the street this morning I heard ther were two expresses come which gave ane acct of a designe to assasinat the King. They say the Duke of Berwick and severall others are come from France and designed to have Murdered at his return from hunting whither he used to goe ill attended but providence ordered it so that he did not goe when they expected it [and so- deleted] the King on friday was informed of the designe (We hear not what way) and saturday put him selfe in a hunting garb but all of a sudden quitt the designe and at night caused make a search and severall of the conspirators were apprehended ther are proclamations issued to apprehend the rest. The French had draun 30,000 Men to Dunkirk and Calis wher K. James was to come to be Embarked assoon as the blow was given The councill met this day and has ordered the Country to be in a posture of defence and Sr Wm Sharp and Sr Wm Bruce are secured. I dined in my chamber and was wt Caruber Mr Al: Home &c Carruber had a letter from John Spotiswood by the expresse wt this acct. Jeriswood's sone died yesterday & was buried this day. The weather is pleasant for the season but Cold.

Sunday March 1st. I went to the French Church in the morning and to the Tron ch. in the afternoo. I suppd wt Mr Al: Home

Monday 2nd. Ther was emitted a proclamation for apprehending all the horses & armes of suspected persons. I dined wt Swintone Saltone Stichill and

Mr Smith one of those come from England on our Indian trade. ther is litle more news this day

Tuesday 3rd. I met wt Blackwood from whom I can not get back my decreit agst Wedderburn. I dined in my Chamber I visited my Lo: Crosrig in the afternoon My Lo: Home was brought in prisoner yesterday and is in the Castle.

Wednesday 4th. Yesterday came ane Expresse. signifying the French fleet from Dunkirk is at sea. we are in a very ill posture of defence the Country ill armd and many ill inclind. I hear not what methods the Councill has taken for securing the Defence and peace of the Country. I dined wt my Lo: Polwarth. these days past have been cold the wind Northerly and it has snowed much this morning.
I receaved a letter from Da: Robisone that he would send me money next week and that in a week he should have my house thatcht. I wrote to him to try among my tenants if he or any of them would be concerned in the E. India trade. I wrote the same to my brother. I wrote what news we have here to Sr John Home and gave him acct that Scot would not make his clock case under 40sh in answer to a letter of Sr Jos. to me to try if Scot would make it for 20sh.

Thursday 5th. I went in the morning and gave Heugh Broun Clerk to the Committy for the Old pole the acct of my arrears and Ninewelles's I dined wt Geo: Robisone Earnslaw And Wm Sim I mett wt Dr Stirlin sone to Geo: Stirlin apothecury and agreed wt him for 300 Ms for the Bond of 132 lb and bygone anrents he has of mine to his father. the anrents extend to 200 lb the rea[son] why I askt any defalkation and got it was that I gave bond for ane acct wtout having deduced any thing from it wheras in apothecaries accts if we pay marks for pounds t'is enough very oft too much. I went to the Coffee house wher I see the news letter. ther are many ships in Calais & Dunkirk for ane invasion on Britain But Russell is at sea. severalls of the Conspirators are taken And England is in a good posture to receave the Ennemie.

Friday 6th. Sr Jo: Home came to my chamber this morning Having come to toune yesternight. I went up a litle after and met him on the street and went to the house wher they keep the India books. he signed for 600 lb st. I dined wt him and Mr Smith and talkt upon the trade of the E. and W. Indies ther came ane expresse last night bearing the D. of Berwick was set to sea from Dunkirk wt 4 or 5,000 Men for Scotland. the Councill has emitted a proclamation for the halfe of the Militia of Merse the Lothians, Selkirk Peebles Fyfe and Kinrosse and the fencible men of Wigtone, Kirkudbright, Aire Lanark Dumbartone & Renfrew. Sr John Home is appointed Collonell Sr Rot Stuart Lieutenant Collonell and Capt Cockburn Major and the Commissioners of the Shire are to Choose the Captains and to meet on Munday next. I got a letter from Sandy Home at London wherin he mentions on writt befor whc I never receaved he says he has sent my trees and seeds wt my Lord Polwarths. It snowed this day the wind is still north.

Saturday 7th. This day came out a proclamation for the Heritors that have qualified themselves or will doe it to come out on thursday next at their respective rendevous'es. ther are none calld out but the Heritors of the same shires of wch the Militia and fencible men are called for. I am nominat to the Heritors of Berwickshire. I dined wt Sr Jo: Home Swintone & Mr Smyth. I visited my Lady Polwarth afternoon but found not my Lord and afterward meeting him on the street he trysted me at night but when I went ther I met him going to the E. of Annandale & Lord Yester who are arrived this night from London. I came to my Chamber. Meg Home came and sat wt me a while I went wt her and visited her niece and Nephew.

Sunday 8th. I was not abroad being indisposed in the morning and the day cold I went at night and supped wt my Lo: Polwarth. We got the account by this post of the designe of the Invasion. That some time in feb. the Fr. K. held a council at Marly wher it was resolved to invade England and Scotland at the same time and to cut off the K. that whc moved them to it was that ther being a detachment of the fleet to be sent to reinforce Rook in the Straits the French would be Stronger than the English in these seas the English were in great security. and the Scotch & English like to divide about the E India trade. wherupon it was resolved that the 2 Kingdoms should be invaded. this was communicated to K. James who having receaved 100,000 lb st in Gold from K. Louis set out for Calais. the D. of Berwick had been sent to England and concerted matters wt his freinds ther he returned and gave ane acct of his negotiation. At Calais severall Battalions & Squadrons were Embarqued and had not providence ordered the winds contrary they had landed in England befor any such designe was smelt but the Contrary winds obliged them to debarque about the same time their plot was discovered in England

Monday 9th. This day we have ane Expresse that Wirtemberg is landed in England wt [blank] men from Flanders. We hear that Admirall Russell is 60 ships strong and that he has the French shut up in Calais & Dunkirk so that we hope the present Danger is over.
I payd Dr Stirlin 300 Ms this morning and retired my bond. And Mr Tho: Aikman 20 lb 1sh 4d and got up my bond. I dined in Geo: Robisons Chamber wt him and Dalmeny and got up my horning I had given him to registrat agst the E.of Home for whc he would take nothing. I was sometime wt Whytefield and Mr Al: Home & St Ebbs. I went afterward to My Lo: Polwarths and found the Master who is come in this day. Ther has been much snow this day and yesterday so it is deep travelling the Wind N. and somewhat easterly.

Tuesday 10th. I went to My Lo: Crosrig he having desired to speak wt me befor I went out of toun. it was to cause my man appear for him on Thursday on Fogo Muire. I went to Sr Tho: Livistone to know what we should doe after our meeting on the Muire the Councills order being to keep them together well for 10 days till further order. he sd he was not well acquaint wt these things but that he should remember it at the meeting of the Councill. I came to my chamber and payd all due Rot Cambell preceeding this day and got his discharge I hired horses to Ginglekirk having writt (by Sr John Home who went home yesterday moring [sic]) to David Robison to cause my horses meet me ther Mr Alexr Home Polwarths sone & I came away after 9. the day was very pleasant but a keen frost. after we past Dalkeith all the way was covered wt snow and the Nearer home the more snow. at Ginglekirk I found my horses and sent back the hirers. we were very late and Hyndsyde Moore very deep it was about 8 when we came to Greenlaw. I Crossed the water ther and took Fogo Moor but went wrong and fell in on Rowistone we called at a house ther and with difficulty enough got a fellow to show us the road. they are generally affraid of being pressed to be soldiers. It was past ten befor I got home.

Wednesday 11th. I wrote to Tho. Maughlane in Berwick who had been Polwarths Trumpeter to the Militia to come out to me tomorrow. I sent to the Doucoat and got 12. pair of pigeons. Tho: M. came out at night. About 6 a clock Sr John Home & Mr And: Home my Lo: P's sone came from a meeting of the Commissioners they told me they had delayd the Rendevous of the Militia till tuesday because advertisements could not goe sooner. But had no power to order the meeting of the heritors yet Sr Jo: Resolved he would goe to Fogo Moore tomorrow this day has been very cold wt snow and hail and wind n.e.

Thursday 12th. I receaved 32 lb 5s as per acct from James Jaffrey. Sr John Home came about 12 a clock and we went to Fogo Moore wher we met wt my Lo: Polwarth whom we did not expect but he told us that the councillors were gone to all the places of Rendevous. ther were very few Heritors so we dissipated and appointed all to be ther on twesd. whc will be intimat by proclamation on sunday. the day was Clear but Cold frost w.n.e. Sr Jo: Home came home wt me and I found Mr Ad: Waddell who staid wt me all night

Friday 13th. Mr Ad: Went over to Wedderburn this morning this day was pleasant in the morning but fell rough at night.

Tuesday 17th. Sat. sund & Mund. have been so ill allwise snow and boistrous winds from s.e. that I went no wher abroad.
This day being appointed for Rendevous of the Heritors and Militia Sr Jo:

Home and Sr Ro: Stuart came this way and I went wt them to Fogo Moore. It snow all the day from S.E ther were about 68 heritors one and other but most ill mounted and ill armed. I took a list of them many who had not taken the oaths were ther but we made no distinction. The foot came pretty well out but had no arms. My Lo: Polwarth Came ther and after we had taken the lists. He intimat the Councills orders to dismis till further order whc we did. He has also orders to take ane oath of all that have not taken the oaths what horses and arms they have had since the first of January and what way they are disposed of. Sr Jo: Home Sr Ro: Stuart & I came to Charterhall to Kettleshiles house young Kettleshile has been ill of the Gravell and past a stone. he had a letter from Berwick the news were that the French that should have land here and in England are commanded to ther Garisons. that Russell is returned to the Douns. that Sr Cloudsly Shovell is still wt a strong Squadron on the Coast of France. That the E. of Athlone has burnt a French Magazine at Givel of provision for 3 months for 100,000 Men. that he is upon the Meuse upon some further designe. that severalls of the Conspirators are still apprehended. That Ferguson is taken and is accused to have written severall seditious lybells. I lent Sr Jo: Home the first Volume of La Croises Geographie.

Wednesday 18th. I sent home Tho: Mauglane whom I had sent for on Munday I gave him 29sh Scots It has snowed much this last night ther has not been such a load of snow on the ground this winter.

Thursday 19th. I went no wher abroad the weather continuing still very cold and the wind n.e. and still snowing

Friday 20th. Mr Adam Waddell came here in the afternoon and stayd all night. he tells me that Charnock King and Keys are condemned upon the plot of assasinating the King. The Evidence are Capt Geo: Porter one Bertram a preist and [biank]. I have been troubled all day wt a grippings I Sent John Lidgate to Kelso for some Bread Beef and some p. Bals. This day is still very cold. Mr Adam told me the Councill had appointed Sund next for a fast whc I had not heard of. he had some difficulties about the Lords day whc was a day of thanksgiving's being converted to a day of Humiliation.

Saturday 21st. I sent Jo: Murdo home wt Mr Adam. he brought me 6 bottles of his ale mine being done and that in the toune new. I sent up the first 2 volumes of the turkish spy to my sister she having written for them. The Wind has been somewhat high this day & more northerly.

Sunday 22nd. The weather being still rough & I indisposed in my health I went not abroad this day.

Monday 23rd. This day was somewhat pleasanter than these past but still frost.

Tuesday 24th. Ther being ane order of the Commissioners for listing the young unmaried fencible men I went to Edrom thinking all the Heritors would be ther but I found the methode was that they had taken up the pole in the Respective parishes were the same whc took up the list of ye fencible men. I went from that to Blackader Sr John was at Hutton taking up the list of the fencible men yr when he came home he told me I should have been at Hiltone but I told him I had got no advertisement. I sent my man from that to tell them to attend next morning. this day was clear but frost

Wednesday 25th. I went to Hiltone and took up the list of the young unmaried fencible men wherof ther was but one in all the parish. I dined at Blackader and returned at night by Mr Adam Waddells house but he was at John Trotter in Aytons buriall. When I was at Hiltone I visited Mr Da: Douglas he showed me ane Bible of Tindales first Edition but all torn. he told me it was very faulty but that he set out another Edition much more correct &c. the wind was cold s.e

Thursday 26th. I went to Dunse ther being a meeting of the Commissioners. we got in from the parishes most of the lists of the fencible men but in regard [it - deleted] was informed many were listed that were not fencible it was ordered that the commissioners of 2, 3, or 4 parishes as they lay should meet together and review the parishes again that none that could reasonably be refused should be listed. My Lord Polwarth had the news letters and the last speaches of Charnock King and Keys who were execute for designing to assasinat the K. the first two acknowledge the designe but affirme they know nothing of K. James or the Fr. K.s knowing anything of it Keys says nothing to it at all. They say that the Fr. K. is highly offended it should be thought he had any hand in it but the Venetian Ambassadors (as says the letter) who are on ther way from Venice to England say the Fr. Ambassador sd to them at parting they would not find the Prince of Orange in England. And tis sd that the Duke of Orleans using all the argumts he could to bring the D of Savoy off from the Confederacy used this as one that the prince of Orange would not be long in a condition to help him and in another he writes to him the prince of Orange was at the last Extremity.
Fodder is extremely Scarse and dear at present.

Friday 27th. I sent Jo: Murdo to Whitsome wt a Note to Mr Ad: Waddell to buy me some hay from John Johnstone a tenant ther. he agreed for 48 lb Scots, Mr Ad. came here (going to Polwarth to a buriall of a Child of Mr Geo. Holywell) and told me he had made the bargain whc is cheap enough at present but at another time I would not a given above 20 lb for it as I could guesse when I saw it. The morning was very rough wind n.e. and some snow it felt calmer in the afternoon. I sent John Lidgate to Polwarth house for the trees I had written to Mr Home for and wch are come home wt my Lords by sea to Newcastle and by Land from thence. I got them home wt some seeds. As follows.

pears

10	of La Marquise marked	1	4	Amadot	8
8	Burrees -	2	2	Russelet de Rhyne	9
6	Rosheus -	3			___
4	Brown Monsieur Jean.	4			50
4	White Mr Jean	5	Apples		
6	Autumne Bergamot	6	5	Golden pippins	10
6	St Germains	7	5	Golden Rennets	11
			5	pear Mains	12
			5	Golden Russet	13
			5	Golden Munday	14
			5	Nonpareillis	15
					___
					30

Apricots 2 Large 1 Early. 1. Orange but they are all miscaried tho payd for
Peaches 2 Early Newintone Mar 19 2. Burdine M.20. My Lo Polwarth not having heard of them keept one of the last and sent me a pasle violet in its place
Stampol The plums. 2 Orleans M. 21 2 Bleu primordin. M. 22
2 Quinces other M. 23
Wall plums 2 Blew perdrigon M. 24 2 la Royal M.25. 2 Chesson M. 26
Ther wants likewise one Golden Rennet Tho they pretend all the pears and apples are dwarf yet Peter says all the apples are on free Stocks and all the pears on pear stocks except the Burrees & the St Germains wch are on Quince Stocks and so the only true dwarfs but they are all Grafted low and this makes them call them dwarfs.
Not having proper places ready for them I have set them in nursery in the easter quarter in rows at 2 foots distance from North to South beginning at the west syde first the La Marquis. being 10.2. the Burree. 8.3d Russelet de Rhyne. 2.4. pears Roshea 6./5. Broun Mr Jean. 4/.6 Whyte Mr Jean. 4/7 Autumne Bergamot. 6/8 St Germain.6./9th Amadot 4/ the first of each Kink has the figure or number cut on a peice stick
the Apples follow on according as they are above set doun
The plums stand are at the south end of the pears & apples from E to W. 1st the 2 orleans/ 2ly the 2 Queen Mother 3d the Bleu premorden.

March 1696

The peaches and wall plums are on the Wall.

[nearly a page blank]

I gave Peter Broun a dollar. Ther was 8 bolls of oats taken to the Mill this day to be dryd and made into meal.

I called for Geo Archer who tells me ther is 18 bolls of bear and 35 bolls of oats this year of teind

Sunday 29th. I went to Church. ther Sr Jo: Home told me he had a letter from my Lo: Crosrig who tells him ther is 208,000 lb st signed for the E. India trade. that ther has been a meeting of those concerned and they have appointed Wednesday next for 20 to be chosen for managers in Conjunction wt those that are nominat Managers or patenties by the act of parlia. That Mr Holland is also come to set the Bank a going. I receaved also a letter from Mrs Marg: Home to provide her 200 Ms agst whitsonday Dr Dundas having signed for her for 50 lb st. in the Indian Company. And. Watheret being to goe for Edr tomorrow I writt to my Lo: Crosrig and in his letter enclosed one for the Patenties of the Indian Trade and desired him to enclose a list of them he should think fittest. I wrote also to Mrs Mar: I should strive to provide her money and she having writt for money for boording the 2 litle ones in the Country I told her I should speak to Geo: Home about it. I wrote also to Mr Al: Home. to let me know if any bussines required my being at Edr.

Monday 30th. I went to Blackader and from that wt Sr Jo: Home to Chirnsyde to review the fencible men for Casting lots for the levies and from that we went to Hutton. I dined at Blackader & returned home at night.

Tuesday 31st. I went to Edrom for reviewing the fencible men ther and returned straight. sund: and mund. were pleasant but the wind south East as it uses to be at this time of the year this day the wind is west and the day very soft.

Wednesday April 1st. I went to Dunse ther being a meeting of the Commisioners for the outreik of the 40 Men appointed by act of parlia. the Shire generally had been taken up by the parishes wt a designe to divide the whole fencible men into 40 districts but this day we fell upon the militia methode and appointed every precinct wher ther are 20 Militia men to put out a man some gentlemens interest was cast together others not My Lo: Polwarth and Sr Jo: Home wrought at it all day and we are to meet to morrow. Ther came in a party of 12 men wt a Capt and Lieutenant of My Lord Lindsays regiment to receave the men. The snow melting in Lammermoore makes the waters great Blackader was very great when I came home

April 1696

Thursday 2nd. Mr Adam Waddell and his Brother Geo; Came here in the morning Mr Ad: told me he had been yesterday at Aitone at the Buriall of Mr Geo: Wilsone at the revolution Minister of Westruther and likewise at the buriall of Will Home of St Ebbes Wife who both died at [blank] were buried at Aitone. He likewise told me that Sr Wm [blank] and Sir John Freind were condemned upon the present invasion and Execute munday last that one Harris had offerred a fuller discovery of the plot and invasion and delated 1,400 persons. That King James is still said to be at Calais. Our commissioners meeting this day I went to Dunse. it was 4 a clock befor the Cast begun yesterday was ended and it makes up but 38 of the fourty the militia roll not being full 800 Men. My Lo: Pol: took upon him to draw the proclamations &c so we adjourned till twesday agst wch time all are appointed to bring in their men. we must try for Vagabonds for making up the other 2 men.

Saturday 5th. I was no wher from home frid: was a pleasant day Dr Abernethy came here about 5 a clock at night and stayd a litle and went over to Nisbet being next morning to give a vomit to Mrs Christian Car. Sat.it was rainy.

Sunday 6th. I went to Church

Monday 7th. Being to goe to Hutton to see the people cast lots ther to goe out I took my men on this and Betshile ground to Blackader to Cast lots wt his men from yt I went to Hutton. Ladykirk being no cast in wt the Huttoners who had agreed wt a man to goe out for him and the people of Hornden the Huttoners agreed wt him for the same man and Ladykirk having given me his bond to produce a sufficient man they did not lot. I came back and dined at Blackader. On Tuesd: befor he & I coming from Hutton met ane Idle fellow who we sent and apprehended he conterfeited himselfe lame but was not Sr Jo: has caused cloath him and designs to put him out for a man. But the fellow counterfits the mad man

[The remaining pages, almost forty, of the notebook have been torn out. The next diary begins Monday 20th Sept. 1697.]

16 Dec 1695
to wash 2 shirt 3 h. sh 3 pair sleeves 1 wig cap. 2 l crav 2 p Crav. 1 nap

24 Decr 1 wig Cap 2 Caps for N.caps. 2 Mutch. Cr. 2 N. grav. 2 Halfe sh. 1 night shirt, 1 snuff nap. 3 p sleeves
Jan: 6 1 shir 1 halfe shirt, 3 snuff napk. 2 Muz Cravats 1 laced Cra. 1 night Crav. 4 p. of sleeves. 1 litle Cap. 1 N. Cap.

20 July 1696 Given to wash. 3 h. shirts 2 Night shirts 5 pair of sleeves 3 Muzlan Cravats. 2 Night cravats 3 napkins. 1 Laced Cravat. 1 Cap 1 Night Holland Cap.

mault	03	00	00
hopps and Quichin: 00 10 00			
Caldron	00	02	00
Coals	00	12	00
pains	00	06	00
	04:	10:	00
4 gallons of ale at 2sh the pinte	03	04	0
8 gallans at 8d the pint	2	02	8
	5	06	08
	00	16	08

A Table of anrents for small summes at 6 per Cent

lb	s	d			
5	00	00	0	06	00
2	10	00	0	03	00
1	05	00	0	01	06
0	12	06	0	00	09
0	6	03	0	00	04 1/2
0	3	1 1/2	0	00	02 1/4
0	01	6 3/4	0	00	01 3/4

0 00 9

A table by Marks Scots

M		
05 or		
lb s d		
03 6 08	0 04 00	

2 M & ane halfe or	
lb s d	
01 13 04	0 02 00

1 M- and a quarter or	
lb	
0 16 8d	0 01 00
0 08 4	0 00 06
0 04 2	0 00 03
0 02 1	0 00 01 1/2
0 01 0 1/2	0 00 00 3/4
0 00 6 1/4	0 00 00

Nota 7 pennies & the 5th pt of a pennie is the anrent of ten sh.

	List of my Debts	lb s d
Thursd. 20 Feb. 1696:		
	Imp: to William Trotter	0666 13 04
	It to Sr James Oswald of Fingaltone	4266 13 04
payd.	To And: Halyburtone Exer to James Robisone	0933 06 08
	To John Waughup of Edmistone sometime one of the Los: of session sr Jo: Home & I oue Equally betwixt us 1,000 Ms Inde	0333 06 08
	To Mr Geo: Meldrum Minister in the Tron church	0666 13 04
	To Baylif Young	1333 06 08
	To my sister Iasabell	3666 13 04
	To my sister Julian	3333 06 08
	To Wm Clerk Brother to Pennycook	0800 00 00
	To Catharin Chartres Daughter to Mr Laurence Chartres	1000 00 00
	To Whytefeild	1666 13 04
of this payd Lb sh d 133 6 8	To Tho: Dalmahoy sone to Robert Dalmahoy	4000 00 00
	To Mr James Dalrymple of Killoch	2000 00 00
	To Dr Nisbet	1333 06 08
	To Cavers exer to My Lo: Jedburgh	2000 00 00
	To Carmichael of Bonintone	2000 00 00
p 100lb	To Thomas Rutherford in Dunsetiels	0200 00 00
	To Heugh Galloway Taylers Exers	0066 13 04
	To the Kirk session of Fogo	0215 00 00
payd	To George Stirlin Chirurgeon	0132 00 00

	To the Lady Tarsappy	0666 13 04
	To William Home of Greenlaw Castle	3000 00 00
	To Alexr Hendersone sone to Wm H. of Todrig	0564 00 00
	To Helen Douglas neice to Whytfeild	0333 06 08
	To Walter Burn writer in Edr	0666 13 04
	To Mrs [blank] Gladstons	0666 13 04
	To Mr Donald Robisone	0400 00 00
[deleted]	(To Sr Jo: Clerk of Pennycook	1333 06 08)
	To Carmichael of Bonintone for Bygon anrents	0550 00 00
	To Gilbert Somervail Taylor	[blank]
	To David Falconer of Newtone	0666 13 04
	To Borthwick of Pilmer	0400 00 00
	To Wm Grive in Dunse	0152 00 00
payd	To Mrs Margaret Home	0333 06 08

To Sr Wm Baird (this was borrowed to pay
Tolqhon (by Polwarth Ninewells & me) and
it should be equally among us tho: till we should
count Ninewelles got my bond of releif)   0666 13 04
To the Lady Greenknow   1333 06 08
To Rot Rutherford Brother to Edgertone   2000 00 00
To Gideon Elliot Chirurgeon Apothecary   0166 13 04
May 8th 1696 in place of Sr Jo: Clerks money I
borrowed from the Bank wt whc I payd the sd Sr John   1320 00 00
It Sr Jo: Home having borrowed from the bank 7000 Ms
I got from him 50lb st of it   0600 00 00

[written at the side] Total 44349:6:09 13070 Ms
                  166:13:4

44516:06:8 13236 13 4

Mem: My Lo: Crosrig & I   sr Geo for the   ) *partially obliterated*
7000 Ms &c they for me for the 2000 Ms   )

Fri 21 st   Note of Debts that are not cleared
Feb 1696

                To the Marquess of Douglas for the nonentry duty
This is done   of the Lands of Kimmerg I have a gift of them
away I being   including the year 1673 and they say it is a tenlb
now en   Land so ther will now be due about lb 0220 00s 00d
aprd vassall   It ther are some accts of Cesse and some rests
to the King   of his portion betwixt my brother & me but I
                have likewise a Charge on him for some intromission
                wt my rents and for staying wt me 2
                or 3 years. Nota this is over payd above 30lb ster.
                beside my Cautionry for him for his intromissions wt Cesse and
                pole money

Tho [sic] teinds of Kimmergh wt Wedderburn are
not cleared.
The Teinds of Betshile wt ether the E. of Home
or my Lo: Polwarth are not cleared. of them I have
got a discharge from the E. of Home of Crop 1696 & preceeding.

Fri 21   Note of Debts due to me
Feb 1696 Imp: by the E. of Home of principill anrent at Mart   lb
         last 1695 about 40,500 Ms Inde   27,000 00 00
         By My Lord Polwarth   [blank]
         By My Lo: Crosrig   ]blank]
         By Mr Al: Home   [blank]
         By Halyburtone a ticket to my father of   00029 00 00
         By Bill   [this column is
         By Al: Trotter of East end of Fogo   blank from
         By David Robisone of his accts   now on]
         By Sr: Jo: Home upon acct of my fathers
         expenses in the plea of Redheugh wt
         Edingtone of Baburtone
         It I have his fathers bond of 5000 Ms but
         my Lo: Crosrig says it is more than Exhausted
         but I cannot get from him the acct how
         it is so
         It I have payd out for the Earl of Home to Tolqhon. Watsone
         of Saughtone Mr Ro: Lawder for the diligence upon the gift of
         Escheat
         It my arrears during my service in the army
         of wch I think I am like to get but very bad paymt.

A Lists of my debts continued
March 97 Sr Jo: Swintone Balif Home & I borrowed from
Th: 25   Mr Wm Law professor of philosophie In   lb s d
          the Colledge of Edr for the Chancellours use & mine   1333 06 08

Th: Having Counted wt Mrs Mar: Home on
1st Ap   the bond of 500 Ms I was due her and
          what I had payd her and her giving me
          in 51 lb scots I retired my bond of 500 Ms
          and granted her one for wt anrent   266 13 04
          from Whit next

Fri: 2   Borrowed upon my oun bond from Jeriswood
Ap.   wt anrent from the date payable at Mart.   1200 00 00

137

May 25   from the Kirk Session of Fogo wt anrent fro
         Whit 1697   0100 00 00

Mem: I have put the former summe and this
in one and having retired my bonds and
payd the anrent of the first bond to Whitsonday
I have granted one (wt anrent from that time)
for 315 lb.

1698   Whytefeild and I having use for money
January to pay the African Comp. Borrowed for [sic]
Mund:3d Wedderburn of Blacknesse and Dallas of St Martines
         tutors to Mr And Balfours children   746 lb Scots
         whc we divide betwixt us Inde to each   0373 00 00

lb s d Mem It bears anrent from the date and
3273 0 0 is payable at Whit. next.

          List of Debts I stand Engaged in for several persons

          Imp for Sr Jo: Home of Blackader to   lb   s   d
          Mr Tho: Aikman   1000 00 00
          It to Wm Clerk brother to Pennicuok   1000 00 00
          It to Mrs Anne Dundas & she having been
          marid to Sr Jo: Foulis the debt is his   [blank]

          For My Lord Chancellour   [blank]
          To Mr Wm Aikman
          To [blank] Scot

          For Com: Home
          To Sr Pa. Home advocat   0666 13 04
          To Robert Hamiltone Mert.   0333 06 08
          To [blank] Heburn Late Minister of the West Kirk
          assigned to Sr Jo: Clerk of Pennicook   0533 06 08
          To Mr Ro: Innis Writer to the signet   1000 00 00

ane inventer containing the names and designationis
of the lands belonging to the Laird of Kimmerghame and ane account
of the movabls as well airship movable as other subscrived be Jean
Countes Donager of home Charles Yom brother German to the Earle of
home John home of Zenwick Esigh Jonson of hiltonn and patrick cockburn
of berthwick Curators of the said Laird of Kimmergham at altonn the
twentie seventh day of april on thousand six hunder and Eightie yeirs

Impirmis the lands of Kimmerghome comprehending the Mains of Kimmergham
with the Maner house and yard the roome cald Mellspots and that Room cald
weesfald the Room cald Kinglaw the Roome cald Greenknow item the half
of the west mille of Kimmerghame item the lands of Leidheugh item the lands
of betsheill Comprehending the Mains of betsheill and thirtie Eight akerer and
three quarter in the toun of betsheill item the Room cald whitknows item the Room
cald weetfnt item the mill of betsheill

the accoint of the movables

Imprimis of oxen twentie Eight item of byn Stin kyn and ane bull four calues
item of young stots thirtie five item of quayes thirtein of old shap of Ewes and wadder
three hundred fourtie and five of hoges and hinder thirtie three item of Rideing
horses two item of work horses and meirs eleven item of stages five item of thresh
en oats Kmu six bolls three furlitt item of threshen beir fifteen boles two
furlitt item of threshen pies thirtem boles item of wheat in the stake fourtie
five thrave item of beir in the stakes four hunder thirtie nin thrave item of —
pies in the stak three hunder fiften nin thrave item of oats in the stak on thou
sand three hunder and fourtain item of timber work for the laboring seven pair
of wain wheills and cart wheill new and old new and old item two wain bodies a stain
Carte bodie and ane cuip bodie two taings six harrowes and one break lakmgtein
four plough with there furniter item tuelu tres and tomtu Eight baills
item of houshold furniter in silver tuikker a silver salt and a bozen of Silver
spoons item of linen sheu new and old Knuten pair item of straken sheet new
and old and harden thirtie six pair item of bornk two table clothis and bozen
of servat and three tuells item of linen six table clothes four Dozen and ane
half of servats si straken fiu table clothis and four tuells item linen of lime
for two of me pair of cantams and seventem Coadwares of linen item of —
blankeis twentie nin pair item four gran table clothis two Zlakes ane sued —
covering five comen coverings a timen covering four sue it conteins two —
sute of old cantams Eight fether beds Ztin fether bolsters and nm Coades
item sie bedpeids peids and three us betsheill three folding beds item sie cheise
four trunkes fiu tabls and twentie two old sheirs and stools item ane a cairon
a Zlasken salt seven pands and thirtem barralles three pats on pan four craggs
four peuder stonpes three chamber pots fiftem peider of plats which is the
owholl invitor in so far as it is comd to our knowledge

Ch Home   Jos Jentbon   Jane Douglas
Jo Home   Pa Cokburn   P Hume

TRANSCRIPTS OF INVENTORY

In April 1680 an inventory of the lands, moveables and heirship moveables belonging to George Home the Laird of Kimmerghame was drawn up and signed by his curators because George was still a minor.

Two copies of this interesting inventory have survived, one a document deposited in the Lauder Commissariat (CC15/6/73), and the other among the Marchmont papers (GD158/434). Both documents are signed by the five Curators, and they are similar but not identical. The Lauder copy contains some words which do not appear in the Marchmont copy, a silver saltffoute becomes a silver salt and muck Taings become taings, and there are differences in spelling.

Probably the Marchmont document was copied from the document deposited at Lauder, but as it is in a particularly clear and legible hand it has been reproduced as an illustration (*opposite*), though transcriptions of both documents are given in this appendix

GD158/434
Ane inventar containing the names and Designations of the lands belonging to the laird of kimmergham and ane account of the movabls as weell airship movable as others subscrived be Jean Countes Douager of home Charles Hom brother German to the Earle of home John home of Ninweels Joseph Jonson of hiltoun and patrick cockburn of borthwick Curators of the said laird of Kimergham at aitoun the tuentie seventh day of aprill on thousand six hunder and Eightie yeirs

Imprimis the lands of kimmerghame comprehending the Mains of Kimmergham with the Maner house and yard the roome caled Midlstots and that Room caled Westfeild the Room caled Kingslaw the Roome caled Greenknow, item the half of the west miln of kimmerghame item the lands of Reidheugh. item the lands of betsheill comprehending the Mains of betsheill and thirtie eight akeres and three quarter in the toun of betsheill, item the Room calid whitknowes item the Room called Weetfut item the mill of betsheill

the account of the movables

Imprimis of oxen tuentie Eight item of kyn Nin kyn and ane bull four calves item of young stots thirtie five item of quayes thirtein of old sheep of Eues and wader[s]
three hunderd fourtie and five of hoges ane hunder thirtie three item of Riding horses tuo item of work horses and meirs Eleven item of stages five item of thresh en oats Nintie six bolles three furlits item of threshen beir Fiftein boles tuo furlits item of threshen pies thirtein boles item of wheat in the stake fourtie five thrave item of beir in the stakes four hunder thirtie nin thraves item of pies in the stak three hunder fiftie nin thrave item of oats in the stak on tho usand three hunder and fourtain item of timber work for the laboring Siven pair

141

of wain whiells and cart wheell new and old new and old [sic] item tuo wain bodies a
staind
carrt bodie and ane cup bodie tuo taings six harrowes and ane break laking teith
four plough with there furniter item tuelv trees and fourtie eight Daills
item of houshold furniter an silver tanker a silver salt and a Dozen of Silver
Spoones item of linen sheet new and old Nintein pair item of Straken Sheet new
and old and harden thirtie six pair item of Dornik fiv tabl clothie tuo Dozen
of servat and three tuilts item of linnen six table Clothes four Dozen and ane
half of servats of straken fiv table clothes and four tuelts item linen of linen [sic]
for tuo paire pair of courtains and seventein coadwares of linen item of
blankits tuentie nin pair item four green table Clothes tuo Mates ane sued
covering five comen coverings a timin covering four sut of courtens tuo
sute of old courtains Eight fether beds nin fether bolsters and nin Coades
item three bedsteeds steeds and three at betsheill three folding beds item six cheistes
four trunkes fiv tabls and tuentie tuo old sheirs and stoblis [?] item ane a caldron
a Masken fatt seven stands and thirteen barralls three pats on pan four coags
four pouder stoupes three chamber potes fiftein pedder plats which is the
whole invitor in so far as it is comd to our knowledge

CC15/6/73
ane inventor containinge the names & designationis of the Land belonging to the Laird
of Kymmerghame & ane accompte of the moveabls alse weill airship moveables as
uthurs subscrived be Jeane Countesse Dowager of Home Mr Charles Home brother-
germane to the Earle of Home Johne Home of Nynwells Joseph Johnstone of Hiltoune
& Patrick Cockburne of borthwick Curators to the said Laird of Kymmerghame At
Aytoune the twentie seventh day of Aprill Ane thousand Sex hundreth and fourscore
yearis

Imprimis the Lands of Kymmergham comprehendinge the mains of Kymmerghame
with the manour house & yeard The rowme called Midleshots that rowme called
westfield, the rowme called Kingslaw & the rowme called greeneknow Item the halfe
of the west mylne of Kymmerghame Item the Lands of Redheugh Item the Lands of
Bedsheill comprehendinge the mains of bedsheill thertie eight aikers & three qrters of
Land in the towne of bedsheill, The rowme called whitknows Item the rowme called
Weilffoote Item the mylne of bedsheill

The accompt of the moveables

Imprimis of oxen twentie eight Item of kyne nyne and ane bull Item four calves
Item of younge stots thertie fyve Item of younge queis thertene
Item of old sheepe being ews and wader Thre hundreth & fourtie five Item
of hogs Ane hundreth & thertie thre Item of Ryding horses two Item of work
horses & mars eleven Item fyve stags Item of threshine oats Nyntie Sex bolls
& three firrlots Item of threshine beare fyftene bolls two furlots Item of peis
thirtene bolls Item of wheat in stak fourtie fyve thraves Item of beire in
the staks four hunder thirtie nyne thraves Item of peis in the stak thre
hunder fyftie nyne thraves Item of oats in the stak Ane thousand thre

142

hunder and fourtene thraves Item of tymber work for labouringe seaven
paire of waine & carte wheells yrof ther is ane paire unshod Item two waine bodies ane
stene carte bodie & ane cup bodie Item tuo muck taings sex
iron harrowes & ane braik laking teeth Item four pleugs wt theire
furnitur Item twelve trees & fourtie eight doulls Item of housold furnitur
ane silver tanker ane silver saltffoute & ane dissone of silver spons Item
of lynnyne sheets nyne paire new & old Item of straikine sheets new &
old and harden thertie sex paire Item of darnik table cloaths fyve
tuo dissene of servits & thre toulls Item of lynnyne sex table cloathes
four dissone & ane halfe of servits Item of straikine fyve table cloaths & four toulls
Item lynnyne of lynnine for two paire of courtains & seaventene
lynnyne codwaires Item of blankits twentie nyne paires Item four greene
table cloaths two mats ane sewd coverings fyve comon coveringes ane
temmine covering four suite of courtains & two suite of old courtains
eight fether beds nyne fether bolsters & nyne cods Item thrie bedsteeds
at Kymmerghame & thre at bedsheell Item thre folding beds sex chists
four trunks fyve tables twentie two old chares & st--s[?] Item ane
caldrone ane maskine fate seaven stands therdtene barrels thre pats ane pan
four collets four pewter stoups thre chamber pots & fyftene pewter plats which is the
full inventer so far as it is cumd to our knowledge.

INDEX

This is an index to the diary, not to the introduction.

144

and see Ker.

Cardross, David Erskine, 4th Lord, 75, 121.

Carmichael, John (later Earl of Hyndford), 106.

Carmichael of Bonintone, 135-6.

Carstairs, Rev William,
chaplain to William II, 58.

Carubber, James Hay, W.S., of, 35, 45, 47, 74, 115-6, 125.

Casal, 47.

Castlehill, Edinburgh, 45, 47-8, 71.

Castlehill, Sir John Lockhart, Lord (of Session), 22.

Castle Hume, Ireland, 46.

Castlelaw estate, 94.

Castlelaws house, 14.

Catalonia, 12, 74.

Cavers, John Carre of, and West Nisbet, 11, 14-5, 17, 21, 23, 25, 39, 54, 56, 67, 79, 80, 92-8, 100-1, 105, 107, 113-4, 119, 135.

Cavers, Lady, 54, 92.

Carre, James, son of Cavers, 84, 98.

Carre, Thomas, son of Cavers, 84, 98.

Cesford, Thomas, former stabler and landlord, Edinburgh, 34.

Cesnock (Sir George Campbell), brother of, 44.

Ceuta, 113.

Chancellor, Lord, *see* Tweeddale.

Channelkirk, 18, 21, 41, 48, 69, 76, 103, 128.

Charles I, 76.

Charles II, 53.

Charnock, Robert, 129-30.

Charterhall house (Trotter of Kettlesheil), 129.

Chartres, Catherine, 110, 135.

Chartres, Laurence, 135.

Chatto, laird of (? Ker), 11.

Chirnside, 38-9, 41, 52, 69, 132.

Claverhouse, John Graham of, 1st Viscount Dundee, 48.

Clerk, Sir John, of Penicuik, 1st Bt., 1, 135-6, 138.

Clerk, William, 37, 135, 138.

Cliftone, "Young", Robert Pringle of, 17.

Club, the, 65.

Cockburn, Mr Alexander, Duns, 38, 52, 56, 69, 81, 96, 109.

Cockburn, Mrs Alexander, Duns, 69.

Cockburn, Sir Archibald, of Langton (Lantone), 85.

Cockburn, Captain, son of Sir Archibald, of Langton, 18, 24, 31, 56, 64, 85, 91, 93,

100, 102, 105, 113, 126.

Cockburn, Isabell (Aunt Borthwick), 8.

Cockburn, Patrick, of Borthwick, 22.

Cockburn, Patrick, messenger, Duns, 6. 11, 29, 53, 94, 96, 101, 110, 112-3.

Cockburn, Samuel, 74.

Cockburn, Sophia, 38.

Cockburnspath, 1, 31.

Cochran, Sir John, of Ochiltree, 23, 52.

Coffee house, the, Edinburgh, 47, 107, 115, 117, 126.

Colbrandspeth *see* Cockburnspath.

Colden, Rev Alexander, M.A., Minister of Duns. 85.

Coldenknows, James Daes of, 2, 20, 34, 94-5, 115.

Coldenknows, white apple of, 77.

Coldingham, 2.

Coldstream, 16, 79.

Collenden, -, 58.

Collogne, Bishop of, 2.

Colstone (Colstoun), ? Sir George Broun of, 66.

Company of Scotland trading to Africa and the Indies, 35, 107, 115, 121, 123-5, 127, 132.

Comptone, "young" Mr (? Anthony), Berwick, 22, 24-6, 28, 77.

Comry, Dr, 10.

Comry, Mrs, 27.

Confederats, 3, 11, 47, 83-4, 130.

Cornhill well water, 79, 92.

Cornwell *see* Cornhill.

Craig, Mr John, lawyer, Edinburgh, 18, 104-6, 114, 119-20.

Craik, John, of Stuartone, 106, 122.

Cranstone, 121.

Craw, James, 4.

Crawford, John, 85, 100-2.

Crawford, William Lindsay, 18th earl of, 71.

Crossrig, Lord, *see* Home, Sir David, Lord Crossrig.

Crossrig, Lady, 72.

Crummie, -, in Dunsteils, 57.

Cults, Lord, 83.

Cunningham, Captain, 33.

Cunningham, Mr, 34.

Cunningham, Sir William, 34.

Cunninghams, the Mrs, 44.

Daes, Mr James, *see* Coldenknows.

Daick, -, Edinburgh, 38, 44-8.

Dalgleish, Rev John, Minister of Roxburgh, 81.

146

Germany, 46.
Gifford hall, 118.
Giles, John, 38, 41.
Ginglekirk *see* Channelkirk.
Givel, 129.
Gladstons, Mrs, 136.
Glasgow, Archbishop of, 70.
Glasgow men, 80.
Glencoe, "the Matter of", 70, 72, 74-5, 112.
Glenorchy, John Campbell, Lord (later 2nd
    Earl of Breadalbane), 74.
Gordon, tenants of, 113.
Gordon, Mr Thomas, 22.
Gosford, Sir Peter Wedderburn of 18.
Graden house, 52.
Graham, Mr, shipmaker, 56, 58, 63, 71.
Graham's, Edinburgh tavern, 43, 72, 121, 124.
Grange park, the, Edinburgh, 97.
Gray, Ralph, M.P. for Berwick, 97.
Gray, Robert, tenant in Kimmerghame, 4.
Greenknowe, on Kimmerghame estate, 12, 26,
    51, 63, 89, 103, 118.
Greenknow, Lady (? Pringle), 101-3, 136.
Greenlaw, 7, 52, 103, 128.
Greenlaw Castle, 27.
Greenlaw Church, 52.
Greenlaw Commom, 93.
Greenloan, the, 79.
Gregory, James, Professor of Mathematics,
    University of Edinburgh, 48.
Grieve, William, in Duns, 6, 13, 136.
Guthrie, Rev Adam, Minister of Edrom, 14-5,
    24, 27, 48, 52, 54, 63, 69, 81, 84, 92, 111.

Hadden, laird of (Murray), 64.
Haddington, 31, 77.
Haddington, Thomas Hamilton, 8th Earl of,
    25.
Hague, the, 3.
Haitly, Andrew, 99.
Haitly, John, 12.
Halcraig, Sir John Hamilton, Lord (of Session),
    34, 118.
Halket, Sir Charles, of Pitfirrane, 18.
Hall, James, 11.
Hall, Sir John, of Dunglass, 1.
Halyburtone, Andrew, 2, 44, 53, 61, 64, 135,
    137.
Halyburtone, David, W.S., 121-2.
Halyburtone, laird of (Home), 3, 122.
Hamilton, Lord George, 116.
Hamilton, Lt. Col. James, 74.

Hamilton, Robert, merchant, 138.
Handysyde's, William, tavern, Kelso, 61.
Hanna, John, 101.
Harcarse house, 4, 11, 24, 87, 93, 97.
Harcarse, Sir Roger Hog, Lord (of Session), 2,
    9, 24-6, 55, 63, 66-7, 77, 80.
Harcarse, Lady, 26, 55.
Harcarse, Lord, son of, 2, 25, 54, 66, 77, 80.
Harrage, *see* Bruck of.
Harris, -, 133.
Hartrig, 78.
Hatton house, 47.
Hatton (Halton), John Maitland, Lord (of
    Session, later 5th Earl of Lauderdale), 34,
    46-7.
Havre de Grace, 23.
Hawick, 48.
Hay, - , 98, 110.
Henderson, Alexander, 136.
Henderson, James, W.S., 47.
Henderson, William, of Todrig, 111, 136.
Hepburn, Katherine, 8, 84-5, 87, 103.
Hepburn, (? Rev Patrick) late minister of the
    West Kirk (St Cuthbert's) Edinburgh, 138.
Hepburn, Mrs, landlady, Edinburgh, 35, 69,
    103, 118.
Herdlaw, 6, 10.
Heriots wark yards, Edinburgh, 47.
Hervistone, Lady, 73.
Heugh, the, 89, 119.
Heugh, house of the, 41.
Heughead, *see* Home, Alexander of.
High Church, Edinburgh, 114.
Hill, Lt.Col., 49.
Hilton, parish of, 82, 88, 92, 105.
Hilton house, 85, 130.
Hilton, Lady, (Marie Douglas) widow of Joseph
    Johnstone who died 1683, 32-4, 53-4, 62-3,
    76, 80, 82, 95, 110, 117.
Hirsel, the (Earl of Home's house), 13, 50, 52,
    55, 61, 66-7, 78, 83, 85-7, 92, 94-5, 102.
Hog, Barbara, daughter of Lord Harcarse, 55.
Holburn, Cornet, 24.
Holland, 3, 71, 81.
Holland, John, governor of the Bank of
    Scotland, 118, 120-3, 132.
Holywell, Mr George, 130.
Home, 16
Home, Estate of, 33, 36-7, 42, 44, 46-7.
Home, Alexander, 4th Earl of, 33, 37.
Home, Alexander (son of L. Crossrig), 72.
Home, Alexander (son of L. Polwarth), 88, 128.

(widow of James, 3rd Earl), 2, 5, 13, 15-6, 25, 35, 40, 45-6, 104.

Home, -, Lady Wedderburn, wife of George, of Wedderburn, 93.

Home, Margaret, daughter of James, of Falsyde, 26.

Home, Margaret, Lady Ninewells elder (the diarist's "Aunt Ninewells"), 18-21, 31-3, 36, 38-9, 42-4, 46, 48, 69, 72, 76, 104, 106, 111-2, 121-3, 125.

Home, Margaret (Meg), sister of John Home of Ninewells, 18, 21, 31, 32, 35, 37, 39, 44, 48, 57, 59, 62-3, 67-71, 76, 78, 85, 87-8, 91, 97, 104, 106, 112-5, 117, 121-2, 127, 132, 136.

Home, Marie, daughter of John Home of Ninewells, 78, 127.

Home, Marie, 2nd wife of John Home of Ninewells, 36, 39, 41-4, 69, 97.

Home, Michael, son of John Home of Ninewells, 78, 127.

Home, Mrs Alexander, 72, 79, 80.

Home, Mrs, widow of Alexander, of Murrays, the King's tailor, 115.

Home, Mrs, wife of Will, of St Abbs, 133.

Home, Mrs William, Betshile, 50.

Home, Ninian, 98.

Home, Patrick, brother of the laird of Bell, 23.

Home, Sir Patrick, 1st Lord Polwarth (later Earl of Marchmont and Lord Chancellor), 1-2, 4-5, 7-9, 18-23, 25, 28-40, 42-8, 53, 56-60, 64, 70-4, 80-5, 87-8, 90-4, 96-7, 100-5, 107, 109, 111-8, 120-4, 126-33, 138.

Home, Patrick, Master of Polwarth, 57-8, 73, 103, 106-7, 110-5, 117, 127.

Home, Robert, 48.

Home, Robert ("a son of Erlies"), 65.

Home, Robert, of Kimmerghame (the diarist's father), 8, 9, 99.

Home, Robert ("Robbie", son of the diarist), 13-4, 19, 22, 28, 31, 35, 41, 57, 65, 79, 80, 90-1, 101-4, 110, 113.

Home, Robert (Robie), son of Sir John, of Blackadder, 123.

Home, Sir John, 2nd Bt. of Blackadder, 1-4, 6-9, 12, 14-6, 20-1, 24, 26-7, 29-31, 35-41, 43-9, 54, 56-7, 59-63, 65, 67-70, 72, 74-83, 85, 87-9, 91, 93, 95-100, 102-9, 111-4, 117-23, 125-30, 132-3, 135-8.

Home, Sir John, of Castle Hume, Ireland (formerly of N.Berwick), 46, 74.

Home, Sir John, of Huttonhall, 29.

Home, Sir Patrick, of Lumsden, advocate, 34, 44, 48, 51, 68, 86, 93, 95, 123, 138.

Home, sisters of Sir John of Blackadder, 16, 35, 39, 123.

Home, Shury, of Manderston (Mangerstone), 80, 89, 115.

Home, Sophia, Lady Hilton (grandaunt of George Home), 38.

Home, Will, of St Abbs ("blind Will Home"), 50, 52-4, 78, 94, 96, 113, 115, 121, 127, 133.

Home, William, messenger, 124.

Home, William, tenant in Betshile, 49-51, 53, 90.

Home, William, of Greenlaw Castle, 27, 54, 56, 79, 136.

Home, William, of Linthill, 43, 68, 119.

Home, -, of Eccles, 22.

Hood's, Philip, ?tavern Eyemouth, 68.

Hoptone, Charles Hope, laird of (later 1st Earl of Hopetoun), 66.

Horndean, 125, 133.

Hungary, 51.

Hutton, 68, 80, 83, 130, 132-3.

Huttonhall, (house of the Johnstones of Hilton), 29, 77, 79, 80, 84, 88, 92, 94.

Hyndsyde moor, 128.

Hyslesyde, laird of, 74.

Inglismaddie, Angus, 43, 70-1, 85, 87, 91.

Inglis's land (Kimmerghame estate), 90.

Ingliss, Thomas, Kelso, 98.

Innerlocky, 110.

Innes, Alexander, Caithness, 109.

Innes, Robert, W.S., 106, 109, 111.

Innis, laird of, 58.

Iles, Thomas, 99.

Ireland, 74, 124.

Iruin, John, Cranston, 121.

Irvine, Alexander, 12th laird of Drum, 123.

Irvine, Dr, (? Christopher, surgeon), 46, 74.

Irvine, Mrs, wife of Dr Irvine, 46, 74, 91.

Italy, 58.

Jack, Rev, William, Minister of Kelso, 98.

Jack's, Charles, ? Edinburgh tavern, 115.

Jacksone, Mr George or Joseph, merchant, London, 25-6.

Jacobite (party), 103, 124.

Jaffrey (Jeffrey), Alexander, tenant at Kimmerghame, 5, 21, 25, 27-8, 60, 63, 69, 75, 77, 89, 97, 100, 105, 115, 118.

153

Midletone of Balbigny, 91.
Millar, John, tenant at Betshile, 69, 90.
Mitchel, Thomas, tavern keeper,
    Berwickshire, 82, 98.
Mines, Royal, in Scotland, 50.
Montmorency, son of Duke of
    Luxembourg, 27-8.
Moncreif, Sir Thomas, Clerk of the
    Exchequer, 47, 73.
Moody. Rev Mr, Minister of Fogo, 56, 81.
Moore, -, 44.
Moores, 113.
Morisone, the Lady "at Graden", 52.
Morisson, -, 2.
Mortone, -,? Dr, 95.
Mossman, George, bookseller, printer and
    stationer, Edinburgh, 19, 71-2, 75.
Mossman, George, 33, 45.
Mowat, Ensign, 84.
Murdo, John, the diarist's servant, 2-6, 10-
    2, 14-8, 21-4, 29, 57, 62, 65, 78-9, 103,
    129-30.
Murray, John, son of Duke of Atholl, later
    1st Earl of Tullibardine, 109, 114.
Musselburgh (Musslebrough), 31.

Namur, 74-5, 78, 80-1, 83.
Nasmith, Anne, 38.
Nasmith James, 38.
Neilsone, Katherine, servant at
    Kimmerghame house, 64-5, 98.
Newbaith, John Baird, Lord (of Session),
    18.
Newcastle, 7, 64-5, 92, 94-5, 123, 131.
Newtone's estate, 117.
Newtone, Sir Richard, 106-7.
Newtoune, 13.
Nicolsone estate, 1.
Nicolsone, Rev Alexander, late minister of
    Preston, 64.
Nicolsone, James, 117.
Nidery, trees from, 50.
Ninewells see Home, John of.
Ninewells, Aunt see Home, Margaret, Lady
    Ninewells elder.
Ninewells estate, 41, 119, 123.
Ninewells house, 41, 62-3, 90, 125.
Nisbet (West) house, home of Carre of
    Cavers, 1, 5-6, 11, 14, 21, 24, 26-7, 50,
    54, 59, 61-2, 67, 69, 77, 79, 80, 84-5,
    92, 94-5, 100-1, 107, 133.
Nisbet mill, 100.

Nisbet, Dr James, surgeon in Edinburgh, 21-2,
    109, 135.
Nisbet, James, wright in Greenlaw, 103.
North Berwick, 47.
Norvell, Robert, (brother of Boghall), 43.
Nottingham, 95.

Oferrell, Colonel, 80-1, 99.
Ogilvy, George, of Dunlugas, 125.
Ogilvy (Ogilby), Sir James, later 1st Viscount
    Seafield, 60, 99.
Ogle, Rev Luke, 97.
Ogle, Samuel, 97.
Old Church, Edinburgh, 115, 117.
Olifant, Mr, 124.
Orleans, Duke of, 130.
Ormstone, Mrs, 61.
Orphans Bank, London, 122.
Oswald, Sir James, of Fingaltone, 70-1, 135.
Overhal, ? laird of, 101.
Oxfurd, Robert Makgill, 2nd Viscount, 99.

Paris, 80.
Parliament Close, Edinburgh, 48, 73, 111.
Paterson, Mr Robert, 72.
Paterson, William, "the great projector for
    trade", 121-4.
Pathhead, Berwickshire, 31, 41.
Paton, -, 33-4.
Paxton, charter of (1576), 125.
Peebleshire, militia of, 126.
Peel, lands of, 8.
Persia, Sophie of, 56.
Perth, James Drummond, 4th Earl of, Lord
    Chancellor, 104.
Philiphaugh, laird of, 121.
Physic Garden, Edinburgh, 2, 18.
Physicians, College of, Edinburgh, 103, 109.
Pitfirrane, 18-9.
Plandergaist, Lady (Home), 65.
Poland, King of, 54.
Pollock, -, 45.
Polwarth, 130.
Polwarth fair, 114.
Polwarth house, 3-4, 7, 11, 16, 24, 53-4, 57-9,
    69, 79-82, 87, 90, 93, 95, 100, 123, 131.
Polwarth, Lady, see Home, Grisell.
Polwarth, Lord, see Home, Sir Patrick.
Polwarth, Master of, see Home, Patrick.
Polwarth's miller, 12.
Porter, Captain George, 129.
Portland, William Bentinck, 1st Earl of, 52.

154

Russell, Edward, Admiral, later Earl of Orford, 13, 17, 23, 126-7, 129.

Rutherford, Baillie, Dunbar, 40.

Rutherford, Robert, brother of Andrew, laird of Edgerstone, 49, 120, 122-3, 136.

Rutherford, Thomas, elder, 5, 12, 23-4, 26, 51-2, 63, 68, 77, 80, 100, 103.

Rutherford, Thomas, younger, 23-4.

Rutherford, Thomas, in Dunsetiels, 135.

Ruthven, Sir Frank, 49.

Ruthven, Sir William, 49, 52.

Ryselaw, 12, 42, 102, 119.

St Beé, 40.

St Mungo, 114.

Salisbury, Bishop of, (Rev. Gilbert Burnet), 62.

Sally men, 81.

Saltoun, Andrew Fletcher of, 125.

Sandersone, - , 51.

Sandilands, Rev Robert, minister of Swinton, 25.

Saughton, laird of, 94, 137.

Savoy, Duke of, 130.

Scales, John, 70.

Scarborough, 14, 16.

Scarborough Wells, 17.

Scatsbusse, laird of, 111.

Sclatehouse, in Ayton, 64, 68.

Sclatehouse, see Home, Alexander, of.

Scot, Mr, 72.

Scot, Mrs (formerly Mrs. Patrick Adamson), 64-5, 98.

Scot, Sir William, 82-3.

Scot, -, merchant, Kelso, 17.

Scot, -, "the joiner" (? William Scott, cabinet maker, Edinburgh), 123, 126.

Scot, -, 113.

Scotland, 28, 51, 108, 127.

Scotland, manufacture of paper in, 50, 53.

Scots coinage, 64, 66, 76, 102.

Scougall, Commissary, 99.

Scougall, John, portrait painter, 113.

Seatone, Sir Walter (? of Abercorn, advocate and Commissary Clerk of Edinburgh), 21.

Selkirk, Charles Douglas, 2nd Earl of, (Lord Clerk Register), 116.

Selkirk, militia of, 126.

Session House, Court of, Edinburgh, 112.

Sharp, Sir William, 125.

Sheens (Sciennes), the, Edinburgh, 72.

Sherwood Forest, 95.

Ship, the, Edinburgh tavern, 47, 115.

Shoniswood, Elizabeth, 99.

Shoniswood, Margaret, 99.

Shovell, Sir Cloudisley, English Admiral, 129.

Shrewsbury, Charles Talbot, Duke of, 62.

Sinclair (St Clair), Sir John, of Longformacus, 7, 43.

Sinclair (St Clair), Dr Mathew, Edinburgh, 23, 104, 108-9, 111.

Sinclair, Mrs, wife of Dr Sinclair, 23.

Sinclair (St Clair), Sir Robert, 6, 10.

Sinclair, Robert, son of Sir John, 43.

Smirna fleet, 12.

Sim, William, 126.

Simsone, David, 64.

Skeen, Mr Thomas, 103.

Smith, Mr, 126-7.

Smollet, Commisary, 77.

Smollet, James, 77.

Softla, 11.

Somervail, Gilbert, tailor, Edinburgh, 32, 104, 107.

Somervail, Rev John, (? Thomas) minister in Teviotdale (? Cavers), 58-9.

Somervail, William, 113.

Southsyde, Ellis of, 111.

Spain, Queen of, 54.

Spaniards, the, 12, 74, 113.

Spot, Murray of, 66.

Spotiswood, John, 125.

Stair, James Dalrymple, 1st Viscount Stair, 101.

Stair, Sir John Dalrymple, Master of, (Secretary of State), 34, 58, 65, 68, 74, 99, 104, 108, 111-2.

Stanefauld burn, 63.

Steel's, Patrick, Edinburgh tavern, 39, 47, 72, 123.

Stevensone house, 82.

Stevenson, Dr Archibald (later Sir Archibald), 19, 36, 38, 67, 103, 124.

Stevensone, "young" 31, 34.

Stewart, Sir James, King's Advocate, 34, 37, 74, 76, 90, 99, 108, 121-2.

Stichell see Pringle, Sir John.

Stichell house, 1, 15, 26-7, 63-4, 66, 80, 83, 103.

Stirlin, Mr, 39.

Stirlin, Dr, 126-7.

Stirlin, George, apothecary, 126.

Stobs, Elliot of, 72.

Stow, Mr, Berwick, 25.

156

Strassburgh, 1.
Strauchan, Mr, Newcastle, 92.
Strauchan, William, 91.
Stuart, John, Lady Kettleston's son, 122.
Stuart, Lady, wife of Sir Robert, 27, 86.
Stuart, Sir Robert, of Allanbank, 9, 14, 25, 27, 49, 53, 69, 82, 86, 92, 101, 126, 129.
Stuart, -, 20.
Stuart, -, 43.
Stuartone, 106.
Sturton, Mr, 106.
Sutherland, James, Keeper of the Edinburgh Physic Garden, Professor of Botany, University of Edinburgh, 10.
Swedish ships, 17.
Swinton, 101.
Swinton fair, 66.
Swinton house, 9, 91.
Swinton, Sir John, of Swinton, 6, 7, 9, 18, 24-5, 47-8, 54-6, 66, 81-2, 88, 91, 93, 101, 106-7, 113, 115, 120-2, 125, 137.
Swinton, Lady, 24, 48.
Symsone, David, 66.

Taite, Alexander, 12, 81, 99, 100.
Tarbat, George Mackenzie, 1st Viscount, Lord Clerk Register, 34, 65, 99, 109, 116.
Tarsappie, Lady, 19, 110.
Telfair, Rev Alexander, Minister of Rerrick, 113.
Teutonic Order, Great Master of, 2.
Teviotdale people, 59.
Thom's, Will, Edinburgh tavern, 33, 36, 70.
Thomsone Thomas, 95.
Thoulon, 23, 121.
Tinmouth, 99.
Tofts, 100.
Tolbooth Church, Edinburgh, 18, 70-2, 75, 107-8, 113.
Tollemache, Thomas, General, 11, 14, 17.
Tolquhon, laird of, 123, 136-7.
Tory, James, 54.
Tranent, 121.
Trevor, Sir John, Speaker of the English House of Commons, 52.
Tron Church, Edinburgh, 33, 36, 38-9, 44-7, 117, 122, 124-5.
Trotter, Alexander, East end of Fogo, 137.
Trotter, Elshy, 9, 61, 76-8, 80, 95, 98-101, 107, 114-6.
Trotter, Jane, Elshy Trotter's daughter, 95.
Trotter, John, in Ayton, 130.

Trotter, Mrs Elshy , 98.
Trotter, Sandy, Officer for collecting the Cesse, 81.
Trotter, William, 5, 26, 65, 99.
Turnbull, Adam, in Ryselaw, 12, 103, 115, 118.
Turnbull, Hector, in Earnslaw, 105, 115, 118.
Turnbull, Will, 52, 64, 68, 87, 93.
Turks, 11, 87.
Turner, Agnes, 15.
Turner, Margaret, housekeeper at Kimmerghame, 3, 10, 15, 25-6, 50, 64-5.
Tweed, river, 87.
Tweeddale, John Hay, 2nd Earl and 1st Marquess of, 56, 59, 60, 90-1, 107, 111, 121, 123.

Umferstone, George, miller, Betshile mill, 3-5, 9, 15.
Umferstone, Robin, 5.

Vaillant, -, bookseller, London, 26, 60-1.
Vaitch, William, factor to Sir John Sinclair, 7.
Vaudemont, Prince, 78-9.
Venetians, 87, 130.
Vesuvius, 58.
Vienna, 46.
Villeroy, 79, 84.
Villiers, Mrs, 116.
Vogry, ?-, McClurg of, 22.

Waddell, Rev Adam, minister of Whitsome, 3, 10-2, 16, 24-7, 50, 58-9, 61-3, 69, 77, 79, 81-2, 84, 86, 90, 92, 94, 96-8, 102, 128, 130, 133.
Waddell, Alison, 24.
Waddell, Mr Andrew, brother of Adam, 12.
Waddell, Dr, 10.
Waddell, Mr George, at the Hirsel, brother of Adam, 2, 13, 27, 55, 65, 102, 133.
Waddell, Mrs, wife of Dr., 10.
Waddell, Mrs, at Whitsome, mother of Adam, 84, 98.
Waddell, William, in Betshile, 18, 50-1, 90, 115, 120.
Waddell, -, 10.
Wait, -, in Keilshill, 57.
Watheret, Andrew, ? carrier, Kimmerghame, 2, 3, 5, 10, 12, 29, 52-4, 59, 60, 62, 67, 74, 79, 88, 104-5, 110, 120, 132.
Watheret, Mrs Andrew, 3.
Watson, -, of Saughton, 94, 137.

Watson, Beety, 118.

Waughton,, ?-, Hepburn of, 36.

Wedderburn house, 1, 8, 50, 61, 66, 79, 83, 86, 93-4, 100, 103, 128.

Wedderburn water, 27.

Wedderburn, see Home, George, of.

Wedderburn, Young, see Home, George, younger of,

Wedderburn, Lady, see Home,-, Lady Wedderburn.

Wedderburn of Blackness, 138.

Wedderburn, Mr, 113.

Weelfit, 6, 7, 10, 15.

Weelfit, house of 5.

Weild, John, late, factor of Ayton estate, 78.

Westfield, 12, 26, 51, 89, 118.

West Kirk, (St Cuthbert's), Edinburgh, 138.

Westone, Mr, nurseryman, London, 26.

Westruther, 133.

White, James, 31.

Whiteadder bridge, 1, 4, 14, 53-4.

Whitehead, -, London, 103.

Whiteknowes, 41, 48, 50-1.

Whitelaw, Sir Wiliam Hamilton, Lord (of Session), 114, 116.

Whitslaid, 17.

Whitslaid, - Don, of, 17.

Whitsome house, 12, 96, 98, 102, 130.

Whitsome carrier, 106.

Whytebank, 121.

Whytfeild, see Home, George, of.

Wigtonshire, fencible men of. 126.

Wilky, Mr John, factor to Douglas of Friershaw, 106, 109.

William II, King, 3, 31, 32, 34, 58, 62-3, 65, 70, 74-5, 79, 84, 90, 92-3, 95, 104, 107-8, 112, 116, 123, 125, 127, 129-30.

Williamite (party), 103.

Winram, James, 48, 53.

Winram, Lt. Col., 39.

Wilson, Rev. George, minister of Westruther, 133.

Winter, Robert, 10.

Winton, 10.

Winton, George Seton, 4th Earl of, 10, 118.

Wirtemberg, -, 127.

Wisha, - of, 18.

Wishart, -, 74.

Wood, Rev Andrew, Bishop of Caithness, formerly minister of Spott and Dunbar, 31.

Wood, -, excise man, Lauder, 69.

Woods bowling green, Edinburgh, 70.

Worcester, Bishop of, 62.

Wylies, Edinburgh, 22.

Wyse, Mr, nurseryman, London, 26, 97, 103.

Yester, Lord (son of Marquis of Tweeddale), 60, 63, 127.

Yeul, Mrs (widow Yeul), 33-4, 45.

Young, Bailie, Edinburgh, 66-7, 71.

Young, David, tenant at Betshile, 48, 55, 90.

Ypre, 70.